ANGELS
101

Also by Doreen Virtue, Ph.D.

All of the above are available at your local bookstore, or may be ordered by visiting:
Hay House USA: **www.hayhouse.com®**; Hay House Australia: **www.hayhouse.com.au**;
Hay House UK: **www.hayhouse.co.uk**; Hay House South Africa: **www.hayhouse.co.za**;
Hay House India: **www.hayhouse.co.in**

Doreen's Website: **www.AngelTherapy.com**

ANGELS 101

101

An Introduction to
Connecting, Working, and Healing
with the Angels

DOREEN VIRTUE, PH.D.

HAY HOUSE, INC.

Carlsbad, California · New York City
London · Sydney · Johannesburg
Vancouver · Hong Kong · New Delhi

Published and distributed in the United States by: Hay House, Inc.: www.hayhouse.com • *Published and distributed in Australia by:* Hay House Australia Pty. Ltd.: www.hayhouse.com.au • *Published and distributed in the United Kingdom by:* Hay House UK, Ltd.: www.hayhouse.co.uk • *Published and distributed in the Republic of South Africa by:* Hay House SA (Pty), Ltd.: www.hayhouse.co.za • *Distributed in Canada by:* Raincoast: www.raincoast.com • *Published in India by:* Hay House Publishers India: www.hayhouse.co.in

Editorial supervision: Jill Kramer • *Design:* Charles McStravick

Library of Congress Cataloging-in-Publication Data

Virtue, Doreen.
  Angels 101 : an introduction to connecting, working, and healing with the angels / Doreen Virtue.
     p. cm.
  ISBN-13: 978-1-4019-0759-4 (hardcover)
  ISBN-10: 1-4019-0759-8 (hardcover)
  1. Angels--Miscellanea. I. Title: Angels one hundred one. II. Title: Angels one hundred and one. III. Title.
  BF1623.A53V56 2006
  202'.15--dc22
                                        2005024856

ISBN 13: 978-1-4019-0759-4
ISBN 10: 1-4019-0759-8

11 10 09 08   7 6 5 4
1st printing, June 2006
4th printing, April 2008

Printed in China

CONTENTS

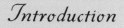

WHO
ARE THE
ANGELS?

$\mathcal{Y}$ou have guardian angels with you right now. These angels are pure beings of Divine light who are entirely trustworthy and who want to help you with every area of your life. The word *angel* means "messenger of God." Angels carry messages between the Creator and the created, like Heavenly postal carriers.

Angels love everyone unconditionally. They look past the surface and see the godliness within us all. They focus only on our Divinity and potential, and not on our "faults." So angels aren't judgmental, and they only bring love into our lives. You're safe with the angels, and you can totally trust them.

It doesn't matter whether you're a believer or a skeptic, because the angels believe in *you*. They see your inner light, they know your true talents, and they understand that you have an important life mission. They want to help you with *everything*.

Surveys show that the majority of American adults (between 72 and 85 percent, depending upon the survey) believe in angels, and 32 percent say that they've encountered an angel. So you could conclude that it's normal to believe in angels.

You don't need to have special training, be saintlike, or engage in religious work to commune with the angels. They help everyone who calls upon them, no matter what. The angels' assistance is free of charge, always available, and there are no "catches" involved.

Every day my office receives dozens of letters from people who've had angel experiences, such as hearing a life-saving warning, experiencing Divine intervention, feeling an angel's presence, or seeing an angelic apparition. The letter writers come from every walk of life and various religious and spiritual backgrounds, including agnostics and skeptics. Each person reports that they know their experience was real, and that they really did connect with their angels.

Those who regularly contact their angels report great improvements in their lives. They feel happier, more peaceful and confident, and less afraid of death or the future. They know that they're not alone, because they have trustworthy guardians watching over them.

I feel the same way. In 1995, an angel saved my life during a close brush with death. Since that day, I've been teaching about angels through my books and international workshops. I feel happier and more fulfilled than ever. It's very meaningful and touching to watch people's lives heal and improve after they begin working with angels.

Prior to my life-changing angel experience, I was a practicing psychotherapist specializing in treating eating disorders and addictions. Like most therapists, my intention was to help my clients live healthier, more meaningful lives. I've discovered that the quickest and most efficient route to happiness is through connecting with the angels.

The angels' love for us is pure. They help us hear, touch, see, and understand God in our everyday lives. So whether you need help with your health, career, love life, family, or any other area, the angels can help you. There's nothing too small or big for them to handle. They joyfully work on your behalf the moment you ask.

A Note about Religion

Although many religions speak of angels, they don't belong to any particular sect. They're truly nondenominational. Angels work with any religious or spiritual path, so you don't need to change your views or beliefs to work with angels.

The traditional idea of angels comes from the monotheistic religions of Judaism, Christianity, and Islam. *Monotheism* means a belief in one God. This faith was founded by the patriarch

Abraham who shaped Judaism, which was followed by Christianity, and then the Islamic faith. All three religions have traditions of angels providing messages and protection to their leaders and followers. In monotheism, the angel is the messenger between God and humans.

Polytheistic (meaning "many gods") religions have deities who are angelic in every way except that they don't have wings. Their deities are shared by everyone, as opposed to personal ones such as guardian angels. *Pantheistic* religions believe that God is everywhere, including within nature. These spiritual paths usually work with traditional winged angels and archangels, in addition to goddesses, elementals (another name for the nature angels), and other deities.

The point is that angels are universal archetypes, extending to ancient and modern faiths. Even though some religions may use a term other than *angel,* we're all discussing the same phenomenon of benevolent and trustworthy spiritual helpers.

Many people with fundamental Christian backgrounds call upon angels in the name of

God and Jesus. Those of the Hindu faith invoke angels, along with Ganesha, Sarasvati, and other deities central to their belief system. The same is true for other religions. The angels will work with any deities or beliefs that feel comfortable to you. After all, they're here to engender peace. You never have to be afraid that the angels would ever ask you to do anything that would make you feel afraid.

In addition, you needn't worry about being "tricked" by a lower spirit, as the angels' characteristics of love and light can't be faked, since they're gifts that come directly from God. When you meet anyone in the physical or spirit world, you can instantly feel if they're trustworthy, happy, and so on. That's why you'll recognize the angels' "calling cards," which consist of pure, Divine love. In other words, you have nothing to worry about when you connect with your angels.

I've found that those who work with angels develop a closer relationship with God, as these individuals heal fears and guilt that they may have absorbed from religious teachings.

It's interesting to me how many wars have occurred in the name of God and religion throughout Earth's history. Yet, no one ever fights about angels. It's the one part of spirituality we can all agree on. . . . everyone loves angels.

Understanding the Law of Free Will

God gave you and everyone else free will, which means that you can make your own decisions and act according to your personal beliefs. God won't interfere with your free will, and neither will the angels.

Although God and the angels already know what you need, they can't intervene without your permission. For this reason, you'll need to ask your angels to give you their assistance.

The angels will help you with anything and everything. As I mentioned before, there's nothing too big or small for them to handle. You needn't worry about bothering the angels, as they're unlimited beings who can help everyone simultaneously. Please don't think that you're pulling your angels away from more pressing matters. There's nothing more important to your angels than helping you.

Angels have unlimited time, energy, and resources. It's their sacred honor to help you in whatever way brings you peace. You can ask for their help as often as you like, without any fear of wearing them out. They love it when you call upon them!

There are many ways to ask your angels for help:

- **Say It:** Speak your request aloud, either directly to the angels or to God (the results are the same since God and the angels are one).

- **Think It:** Mentally ask your angels for help. The angels hear your thoughts with unconditional love.

- **Write It:** Pour your heart out to your angels in a letter.

- **Visualize It:** Hold a mental visual image of angels surrounding yourself, your loved ones, your vehicle, or the situation in question.

- **Affirm It:** Say an affirmation of gratitude, thanking the angels for resolving the issue.

The words you use are unimportant, because the angels respond to the "prayer of your heart," which is composed of your true feelings, desires, and questions. Angels merely need you to ask because of free will. So, it's not important *how* you ask, only *that* you ask.

Please note: All of the stories in this book are true, and the actual names of the people involved have been included unless indicated by an asterisk (*), which signifies that the person has requested anonymity.

Chapter One

THE ANGELIC REALM

There are countless numbers of angels who want to help you, me, and everyone live in peace. Just as people hold different specialties, so do the angels. Here is a brief guide to the various types of Heavenly beings who would love to help you:

Guardian Angels

The angels stationed permanently by your side are called *guardian angels*. These are non-human celestial entities sent directly from the Creator. They're not our deceased loved ones, who—while they can definitely act like angels—are called *spirit guides.* Our departed friends and family members, like all people living or deceased, have egos. Although they may be well-meaning, their guidance isn't as pure and trustworthy as that of guardian angels, who are with us from the moment we're born until our physical death.

No matter what we do in life, our angels will never leave us. Guardian angels are protectors and guides, ensuring that we stay safe, happy, healthy, and fulfill our life mission. Yet, we must act as a team with our guardian angels to fulfill these intentions. That means asking for help from them and then receiving the help they give you.

Speaking as a lifelong clairvoyant, I've never seen anyone without at least two guardian angels stationed by their side. One is loud and bold, to ensure that you'll work on your Divine life purpose; the other is quieter, and serves to comfort and soothe you. Yet, not everyone clearly hears their angels. If everybody did, we'd have a completely peaceful world!

You can have *more* than two guardian angels, and there are benefits to being surrounded by additional ones. They act like a castle moat, protecting you from negativity. The more angels you have with you, the stronger you'll feel the sensation of their Divine love and protection. It's also easier to hear a whole choir of angels, rather than the voice of just one or two of them.

Invoke additional angels by requesting that God send them to you, by asking the angels directly, or by visualizing yourself surrounded by more of them. You can ask for as many angels as you'd like.

Some people have additional guardian angels because a relative or good friend prayed for them to be surrounded by a number of them. Those who have had near-death experiences have extra angels to help with their adjustment to life following their experiences on the Other Side.

Every time God thinks of love, a new angel is created. That means that there's an infinite number of angels available to everyone.

Archangels

Archangels are managers overseeing our guardian angels. They are one type of the nine choirs of angels (which include angels, archangels, principalities, powers, virtues, dominions, thrones, cherubim, and seraphim). Of these forms of angels, guardian angels and archangels are the most involved with helping Earth and her inhabitants.

Compared to guardian angels, archangels are very large, loud, and powerful, yet they're also extremely loving and egoless. As nonphysical celestial beings, they don't have genders. However, their specific fortes and characteristics give them distinctive male and female energies and personas.

The Bible names Archangels Michael and Gabriel. Some versions of the Bible also list Archangels Raphael and Uriel. Ancient Jewish texts expand this list to 15 archangels.

You'll notice in the list that follows that all but two of the archangels' names end in the suffex "el," which is Hebrew for "of God" or "from God." The two exceptions were Biblical prophets who lived such exemplary lives that they ascended to archangeldom following their human lives.

These archangels are sometimes called by different names, but here are their most common ones, along with their specialties, characteristics, and brief histories:

Ariel (pronounced *AHR-ee-el*), which means "lioness of God." She helps us provide for our physical needs (such as money, shelter, and supplies). Ariel also assists with environmental causes, and the care and healing of animals. Ariel works with Archangel Raphael (who also heals and helps animals), and the angelic realm called the "thrones." Historically, she's associated with King Solomon and the Gnostics, who believed that Ariel ruled the winds.

Azrael (pronounced *Oz-rye-EL*), which translates to "whom God helps." He helps bring departed souls to Heaven, heals the grief stricken, and also assists those who are consoling the bereaved. Regarded as the "angel of death" in Hebrew and Islamic tradition, Azrael is associated with Archangel Raphael and King Solomon.

Chamuel (pronounced *SHAM-you-el*), meaning "he who sees God." He eases anxiety; brings about global and personal peace; and helps find lost objects, situations, and people. He's considered to be the leader of the angelic realm known as the "powers." Chamuel is one of the ten Sephiroth archangels of the Kabbalah, which means that he governs a pathway of the Kabbalistic Tree of Life (a mystical explanation of creation).

Gabriel (pronounced *GAB-ree-el*), which means "messenger of God." This archangel helps messengers such as writers, teachers, and journalists. Gabriel also helps parents with child-rearing, conception, or adoption.

Some faiths believe that Gabriel is a male persona, while others perceive her as feminine. Gabriel delivered the annunciation to Zacharias and Mary, as recorded in the book of Luke, announcing the forthcoming births of John the Baptist and Jesus. In the Old Testament, Gabriel saved Abraham's nephew Lot from Sodom's destruction. Mohammed said that Archangel Gabriel dictated the Koran to him.

Haniel (pronounced _Hawn-ee-EL_), meaning "glory of God." She heals women during their monthly cycles and helps with clairvoyance. She's associated with the planet Venus and the moon, and is one of the ten Sephiroth archangels in the Kabbalah. Haniel is often credited with escorting the prophet Enoch to Heaven.

Jeremiel (pronounced _Jair-ah-MY-el_), which translates to "mercy of God." He deals with emotions, helping us review and take inventory of our lives so that we may forgive, and also helps us plan for positive change. Ancient Jewish texts list Jeremiel as one of the seven core archangels. Because Baruch, a prolific first-century Jewish apocryphal author, was assisted by Jeremiel, this archangel is believed to help with prophetic visions.

Jophiel (pronounced *JO-fee-el*), which means "beauty of God." She heals negative and chaotic situations; and brings beauty and organization to our thoughts, homes, offices, and other environments, as well as lifting negativity in these areas. Some traditions call her Iofiel or Sophiel. Jophiel is known as the "patron of artists," and the Torah describes her as an upholder of Divine law.

Metatron (pronounced *MET-uh-tron*). He was the prophet Enoch, who ascended after living a virtuous life of sacred service. Metatron heals learning disorders and childhood issues, and helps with the new Indigo and Crystal Children. In ancient Jewish tradition, Metatron is an extremely important archangel, and the chief of the Sephiroth Kabbalistic archangels. The Kabbalah credits Metatron with helping Moses lead the Exodus from Egypt to Israel. The Talmud says that Metatron watches over children in Heaven, in addition to the children of Earth.

Michael. His name means "he who is like God." He releases us from fear and doubt, protects us, and clears away negativity. Usually considered the most powerful of all archangels, he's described in the Bible and other Christian, Jewish, and Islamic sacred texts as performing heroic acts of protection. Michael is the patron saint of police officers because he protects and lends courage to those who invoke him. He oversees the angelic realm known as the "virtues."

Raguel (pronounced *Rag-WELL*). His name means "friend of God." He brings harmony to all relationships, and helps to heal misunderstandings. The book of Enoch describes Raguel as the overseer of all the angels, ensuring harmonious interactions between them. Raguel is credited with assisting the prophet Enoch's ascension and transformation into Archangel Metatron.

Raphael. His name means "he who heals." He heals ailments and guides healers and would-be healers. He's one of the three presently sainted archangels (the others being Michael and Gabriel, although at one time seven archangels were canonized). In the book of Tobit (a canonical Bible work), Raphael describes himself as a servant before the Glory of the Lord. He is believed to be one of the three archangels who visited the patriarch Abraham. Because he assisted Tobias on his journey, Raphael is considered a patron saint of travelers. His main role, though, is in healing and assisting healers.

Raziel (pronounced *RAH-zee-el*). His name means "secrets of God." He heals spiritual and psychic blocks, and helps us with dream interpretations and past-life memories. Ancient Jewish lore says that Raziel sits so close to the throne of God that he hears all of the universe's secrets, which he has written down in a book called *Sefer Raziel* (which means *The Book of the Angel Raziel* in English). Legend says that Raziel gave this book to Adam as he was leaving Eden, and to Noah as he was building the ark. The Kabbalah describes Raziel as the embodiment of Divine wisdom.

Sandalphon (pronounced *SAN-dul-fon*). He was the prophet Elijah, who ascended into an archangel. He serves many purposes, including helping people to heal from aggressive tendencies and delivering our prayers to the Creator. In addition, Sandalphon helps musicians, especially those involved in using music for healing purposes. Since he was one of the two humans who ascended into archangel status, Sandalphon is considered the twin brother of Metatron (who was the prophet Enoch). Ancient Hebrew lore speaks of Sandalphon's great stature and says that Moses called Sandalphon "the tall angel."

Uriel (pronounced *YUR-ee-el*). His name means "God is light." He's an angel of wisdom and philosophy who illuminates our mind with insight and new ideas. In Hebrew sacred texts, Uriel's roles are varied and vast. As the angel of light, he's often associated with the angelic realm of the illuminated "seraphim," who are closest to God in the nine choirs of angels. Uriel is believed to be the angel who warned Noah of the impending flood. Uriel is usually identified as one of the four major archangels, including Michael, Gabriel, and Raphael.

Zadkiel (pronounced *ZAD-kee-el*). His name means "righteousness of God." He heals memory problems and assists with other mental functions. Many scholars believe that Zadkiel was the angel who prevented Abraham from sacrificing his son Isaac. The Kabbalah describes Zadkiel as a co-chieftain who assists Michael in protecting and releasing us from lower energies.

The archangels are nondenominational, meaning that you needn't belong to a particular religion in order to elicit their attention and help. Since archangels are limitless nonphysical beings, they can help everyone who calls upon them simultaneously. The archangels will respond to your requests, whether they're spoken, thought, or written. You can even ask the archangels to be permanently stationed by your side, and they're very happy to do so.

What Do Angels Look Like?

I'm often asked this question. As a child, I saw angels primarily as twinkling white and colored lights. As I grew older and my sight adjusted, I saw their shape and form. Now I see angels around everyone, everywhere I go. Their beauty is breathtaking and awe-inspiring.

Angels are translucent and semi-opaque. They have no skin, so they don't have racial colorings to their body, eyes, or hair. They glow in different colors, according to their energies. Their clothing looks like opalescent chiffon coverings.

Angels have large swanlike wings, although I've never seen one flap its wings to fly. The angels taught me that the artists who originally painted them mistook their glowing aura for halos and wings, and so portrayed them in this way. Now we expect angels to look like those paintings, so angels often appear to us as winged beings.

Angels come in all shapes and sizes, just like people. The archangels, not surprisingly, are the tallest and largest of the angels. The cherubs look like small babies with wings. Guardian angels appear three to four feet tall.

Angels are on higher-frequency wavelengths than we are. It's similar to television or radio stations being on parallel yet different bandwidths—the angels live next to us on an energy level that we can feel, and that many of us can see and hear. Whether you can sense your angels' presence right now or not, you can definitely connect with them and immediately receive their assistance, as we'll explore in the next chapter.

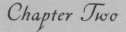

Chapter Two

CONNECTING
WITH YOUR
ANGELS

After you ask for your angels' help, they immediately go to work on your behalf. They'll do one or more of the following:

- Directly intervene and manifest your desires at exactly the right time.

- Give you a sign that they're with you.

- Give you guidance and instructions so that you'll take the appropriate steps to co-create the answer to your prayer, with their help.

Guidance and instructions are the most common ways in which angels answer our prayers. This process is called *Divine guidance.* When you receive such guidance, you must take action so that your prayer will be answered. Many people who believe that their prayers go unanswered are ignoring the information they've received.

Divine guidance is repetitive, loving, uplifting, and encouraging, and always asks us to improve a situation. It can come in one (or a combination) of four ways:

1. Physical or emotional. You get gut feelings, tingling sensations, goose bumps, an intuitive hunch, or feel the presence of an angel with you. These feelings guide you to make positive changes. This is called *clairsentience,* which means "clear feeling."

Those who receive their Divine guidance through feelings tend to be extra-sensitive to energy, other people's feelings, and chemicals. If this applies to you, you'll need to be discerning about who and what you spend time with, as you're more deeply affected than the average person.

One way to handle sensitivity is by shielding and clearing. *Shielding* means praying for spiritual protection, or visualizing protective light surrounding you. *Clearing* means asking the angels to release any negativity that you may have absorbed during the day.

After you ask your angels for answers or assistance, notice your repetitive or strong feelings. Honor these feelings and avoid any tendencies to say, "Oh, it's just my feeling." The primary way that God and the angels speak to us is through our feelings. True Divine guidance makes you feel safe and loved.

Follow any feelings that guide you to make positive changes, even if they seem illogical or unrelated to your prayer request. If you're unsure whether the feelings are true guidance, ask your angels for signs to validate them.

2. Visions and dreams. You see an image in your mind's eye, you have a very clear visitation in a dream or while awake, you see sparkling or flashing lights, or see mind movies that give you information. This is called *clairvoyance,* which means "clear seeing."

Those who receive their Divine guidance visually tend to be very sensitive to light, colors, and beauty in the physical world. If you're visually oriented, you feel best when engaged in artistic and creative expressions. You can visualize your desires being manifested, which helps you be successful in many areas.

Many people mistakenly think that clairvoyance means seeing angels with your eyes open, as three-dimensional opaque beings. While that happens occasionally, most clairvoyants see angels as fleeting ethereal images in their mind's eye. These mental images are just as valid as what you might see outside your mind's eye.

After you ask your angels for help, notice any images that come to mind, or any signs that you see with your physical eyes. If you see a vision of a "dream come true," ask your angels to guide you one step at a time toward its realization.

3. Knowingness. You know things without any rational reason, as if God has downloaded the information to you; you say or write with wisdom exceeding your present knowledge; you know how to fix an item without having to read instructions. This is called *claircognizance,* which means "clear knowing."

Those who receive their Divine guidance as "wordless words" tend to be highly intellectual and analytical. If you're thinking oriented, the answers to your prayers will come as brilliant ideas that ask you to start a business, invent something, write a book, and so forth. You're a natural channeler filled with wisdom beyond your years.

When you receive revelations and ideas, avoid the mistake of thinking that this is common knowledge or something that everyone knows. Be confident that you can awaken these Divine gifts and bring them to fruition. You can ask the angels to give you the instructions and confidence to do so.

4. Words and sounds. You hear your name called upon awakening, you hear a strain of celestial music, you overhear a conversation that seems tailor-made for you, you hear high-pitched ringing in one ear, or you hear a song in your head or on the radio that holds special meaning. This is called *clairaudience,* which means "clear hearing."

Those who receive their Divine guidance as words are very sensitive to noise and sound. If you're auditory, you'll actually hear a voice inside your head or just outside your ear. The angels always use positive and uplifting words, and it sounds as if someone else is speaking to you.

You may also hear a high-pitched ringing sound in one ear, which is the way angels download helpful information and energy. If the ringing is annoying, ask the angels to turn down the volume.

When you hear messages that ask you to take positive action, it's important to listen to them. In an emergency or time-urgent situation, the angels talk in a loud, to-the-point voice. During ordinary moments, their voices are softer, which requires you to maintain a quiet mind and environment. As you become increasingly sensitized to hearing the sweet sound of angels, you'll want to protect your ears from loud noise.

Examples of Divine Guidance

Whether they speak to us through feelings, words, visions, or thoughts, the angels' messages are always uplifting, loving, and inspirational. The angels are like air-traffic controllers who can see far ahead, behind, and to each side of us. In other words, they have more of a perspective on how our actions today will affect our future. So if the angels guide you to do something that seems unrelated to your prayers, it's because they can see how such actions benefit your future.

Here are some examples of Divine guidance topics that angels often give us:

- **Health and lifestyle:** Improving your diet; detoxing; exercising more or differently; spending time outdoors in nature

- **Spirituality:** Meditating more; doing yoga; quieting the mind, body, and home

- **Career and finances:** Following your passion; releasing money fears; reducing work stress

- **Emotions:** Letting go of worries; forgiving yourself and others; overcoming procrastination

A Reminder to Ask

There's an old adage that says "Those who write letters are the ones who receive the most mail." Well, it's the same with the angels. If you'd like to hear from your angels more often, then talk with them more often.

Share your dreams, disappointments, fears, worries, concerns, and joys with them. Tell them everything. Ask them about *everything,* as the angels want to help you with every area of your life.

Your personal relationship with your guardian angels will deepen as you speak to them regularly. One way to get to know your angels even better is to ask them their names. Just think or vocalize the request: "Angels, please tell me your names," and then notice the word that comes to you as a thought, sound, feeling, or vision. It's best to write these names down so you'll remember them (some of them may sound unusual). If you don't receive any names, it usually means that you're trying too hard to hear. Wait until you're relaxed, then ask again.

Next, say to your angels: "Please send me signs in the physical world that I'll easily notice, to help me validate that I've heard your names correctly." You'll then notice the names that you've received in people that you meet, conversations you overhear, and so forth.

Practice asking your angels questions and then listening to their replies. In time, you'll learn to instantly distinguish the voice of the angels from the voice of ego (the fearful part of us). It's similar to picking up the phone and immediately knowing whether it's a loved one or a solicitor who's calling. Also with practice, you'll learn to trust and lean upon the angels' guidance as you find success as a result of following their loving advice.

Tips for Increased Clarity

You can ask your angels to help you hear them better, or to understand the meaning of their more cryptic messages. Here are some other ways to increase the clarity of Divine communication with your angels:

— **Breathe.** When we're stressed, we often hold our breath. This blocks us from hearing the messages that could relieve our stress. So, remember to breathe deeply when you're conversing with your angels. The angels have told me that their messages are carried upon the molecules of oxygen, so the more fresh air we breathe, the louder their messages seem to be. That's why it's easier to hear your angels when you're outside in nature, or near water sources (including your shower or bathtub).

— **Relax.** Trying too hard prevents clear Divine communication. You needn't strain to hear your angels, as they're more motivated than you are to communicate. Instead, relax your body with your breath. Be in a receptive state, and ask your angels to help you release any tension in your mind or body.

— **Follow their guidance.** If your angels are asking you to improve your diet, it's probably because they know that processed foods and chemicals create static on the Divine communication lines. Your angels are your best teachers in guiding you on how to better hear their voice. Ask for their assistance in this regard, and then follow whatever guidance you receive.

— **Ask for signs.** If you're unsure whether you're accurately hearing your angels, ask them to give you a sign. It's best not to specify what type of sign you want. Allow the angels' infinite creativity to devise a wonderful sign that you'll easily recognize. You'll delight in the loving sense of humor that angels display in their use of signs, as you'll read about in the following chapter.

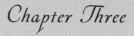

Chapter Three

SIGNS
FROM THE
ANGELS

he angels give us signs so that we'll know that they and their messages are real. Signs can be anything that you see or hear in the physical world three or more times, or receive in a very unusual way. For instance, if you hear the same book title from three or more different sources, then it's probably a recommendation from your angels to read that book.

The angels also leave us feathers in unusual places as a sign of their presence, probably because we associate feathers with angel wings. In the two stories that follow, the angels left feathers as a sign of reassurance of a positive outcome to stressful situations:

When Sandra's cat, Jerry, became ill, she took him to the veterinary hospital. Jerry's condition grew worse, and he went into a coma. But Sandra wasn't about to give up on her beloved cat, so she asked her angels for help. As she stepped out her front door to visit Jerry, Sandra found a white feather lying on her porch. She took this as a positive sign that the angels were helping her cat to recover.

During the following week, each time Sandra and her husband left their home to visit Jerry at the hospital, they'd find a new white feather on their porch. Sandra laid the eight feathers she'd collected on a photograph of Jerry, and continued asking God and the angels to heal her beloved cat. Finally, Jerry recovered enough to come home. His health has been wonderful for the past six years since the angels signaled Sandra through feathers that everything would turn out fine.

Like Sandra, Kathryn received so many feathers that she knew her situation would be resolved:

Kathryn had a misunderstanding with a friend, and she was considering ending the relationship, so she asked for guidance from her angels. As Kathryn sat in her backyard crying about the situation, a feather floated right past her. She took this as a sign that the angels were working on her relationship, and for her to take no action at present.

That afternoon as Kathryn walked to her children's school, she again asked her angels for a sign that her relationship would heal. She looked down and saw a feather, and then another. By the time she arrived at her destination, Kathryn had collected 35 feathers, which she took as a very positive sign. Sure enough, Kathryn and her friend resolved their misunderstanding, and they now remain very close to each other.

Another common sign is seeing angel-shaped clouds, as the following story relates:

> While riding in an ambulance on her way to have emergency heart surgery, Mary was naturally frightened. She prayed for help, and as she looked out the ambulance's back windows, Mary saw a cloud in the clear shape of an angel kneeling in prayer. Mary instantly knew that she'd be okay. She remembered the vision throughout her surgery and recovery process, with complete faith that the angels were watching over her. They were! Mary is now recovered, and very thankful for the reassuring sign that the angels sent her.

Sometimes the signs we receive come in the form of a fragrance, rather than something we see or hear. Many people report smelling perfume, flowers, or smoke when their angels are nearby:

Kathleen desperately wanted to sell her house so she could move near her daughter who was expecting her first baby in August. Frustrated one evening after buyers backed out of purchasing her home, Kathleen sat in her kitchen and cried. Suddenly her entire kitchen filled with the scent of roses. Kathleen couldn't understand this, but a friend explained to her that it was a common sign from the angels that everything would be okay. It *did* turn out fine, and Kathleen's home soon sold.

Then Kathleen needed the angels' help in finding a new place to live near her daughter. Once again, the angels came to her aid and guided her to a beautiful home at a good price. Kathleen knew that it was the right place when she saw a beautiful red rosebush in front of the home. She recalls, "There was one bright red rose standing way out among all the others, and I knew that I was home."

Angel Lights

About 50 percent of my audience members worldwide report seeing flashes of light with their physical eyes. These lights look like camera flashbulbs or shimmering sparkles. Sometimes they're white lights, and other times they're bright jewel-like shades of purple, blue, green and other colors. Several people have told me they've had their eyes examined because they worried that their visions of sparkling lights were abnormal. However, their eye doctors told them that their physical eyes were perfectly healthy.

That's because these lights have nonphysical origins. I call this phenomenon *angel lights* or *angel trails*. When you see these lights, you're seeing the friction or energy of angels moving across the room. It's a little like seeing sparks fly from a fast-moving car.

The white lights are from our guardian angels, and the colorful lights originate from archangels. Here's a list to help you know which of the archangels you're encountering when you see colored flashes or sparkles of light:

- **Beige:** Azrael, the archangel who helps us heal from grief

- **Blue** (pale, almost white): Haniel, who helps women with their feminine health, and assists with clairvoyance

- **Blue** (aqua): Raguel, who helps with relationships

- **Blue** (dark): Zadkiel, the archangel who helps us improve our memory and mental functioning

- **Green** (bright emerald): Raphael, the healing archangel

- **Green** (pale): Chamuel, the archangel of peace who helps us find whatever we're looking for

- **Green with dark pink:** Metatron, who helps children retain their spiritual gifts and self-esteem

- **Pink** (bright fuchsia): Jophiel, who helps us beautify our thoughts and life

- **Pink** (pale): Ariel, who helps with animals, nature, and manifestation

- **Purple** (bright, almost cobalt blue): Michael, who gives us courage and protection

- **Rainbows:** Raziel, who heals spiritual and psychic blocks and teaches us esoteric secrets

- **Turquoise:** Sandalphon, the musical archangel

- **Violet** (reddish purple): Jeremiel, who helps us heal our emotions

- **Yellow** (pale): Uriel, the archangel of wisdom

- **Yellow** (dark): Gabriel, who helps messengers and parents

Angel Numbers

Another common way in which the angels speak to us is by showing us number sequences. Have you ever noticed that when you look at the clock, a license plate, or a phone number that you see the same numbers repeatedly? This is not a coincidence, but rather, a message from above.

Since the era of Pythagoras (the esteemed Greek philosopher), we've known that numbers carry powerful vibrations. Musical instruments and computers are based upon mathematical formulas, and the angels' number messages are just as precise.

The basic meanings of the numbers you see are as follows:

0: This is a message of love from the Creator.

1: Watch your thoughts and only think about your desires instead of your fears, as you will attract what you're thinking about.

2: Keep the faith and don't give up hope.

3: Jesus or other ascended masters are with you and helping you.

4: The angels are assisting you with this situation.

5: A positive change is coming up for you.

6: Release any fears about the physical/material world to God and the angels. Balance your thoughts between the material and spiritual.

7: You're on the right path, so keep going!

8: Abundance is coming to you now.

9: Get to work on your life's purpose without delay.

When you see a combination of numbers, simply "add" the meanings above together. For instance, if you see 428, this would mean: "The angels are with you, so keep the faith, as abundance is coming to you now."

(See my book *Angel Numbers* for more detailed information.)

The angels speak to us in varied and creative ways, so if you feel that you're receiving an angel message, then you probably are. Ask your angels to help you recognize their signs and messages, and you'll begin to notice them all around you. The more you take note of and follow these signs with success, the more confidence you'll have in the angels and yourself.

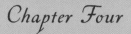

Chapter Four

ANGELIC
PROTECTIONS

It's a good idea to call upon your guardian angels and also Archangel Michael for protection while driving. I also recommend visualizing your car surrounded by white light, which is the energetic essence of angels. In crowded conditions, ask the angels to protect the other cars driving near you.

The angels will protect your loved ones while they're driving even if you're not accompanying them. Simply ask the angels for whatever specific assistance you'd like, and they're happy to provide this for you.

Before you begin driving, simply ask the angels to watch over you and the other drivers, protecting everyone and ensuring a safe and pleasant journey. If you forget to do so, you can ask the angels anytime during your trip. I've even talked to people who have called upon the angels in the midst of a collision, with miraculous results.

Since the angels are above and beyond the physical world, they can intervene in mysterious ways, as Doris discovered:

Doris was driving about 50 miles per hour on a long bridge when her car's hood flew up, completely blocking her view. She felt the car swerve down the embankment and then stop inches from the deep water. Other drivers stopped to help Doris, and they all asked her if she was okay. Then they asked how her passenger was.

Doris explained that she didn't have a passenger, that she had been driving alone. The 12 people who'd witnessed the accident all said they'd seen another person in the front passenger seat. They figured that Doris was delirious from the impact and went to look for the person in the passenger seat.

Stunned, Doris thought, *Was it my guardian angel? My car just seemed to be lifted up and set back down without a dent or a scratch, and no injury came to me.*

Doris's story is fascinating in that 12 people reported seeing a person riding with her, someone who Doris concluded must have been her protective angel. I've received many stories from people who report that their cars have defied gravitational laws in inexplicable ways. After hearing so many of these stories, I believe that the only explanation is that the angels are able to move cars out of harm's way:

Estelliane was driving in the pouring rain when a semitrailer crashed into her driver's side door. She glanced at the silver angel clipped to her rearview mirror and said a prayer. Suddenly, Estelliane felt her car lift up into the air and gently land on the shoulder of the road. Remarkably, Estelliane and her passenger suffered no injuries and the car was drivable.

She says, "The car did something that is not physically possible in terms of the law of dynamics. I got hit sideways, so the car should have spun forward and hit the other cars in front of me. The little angel attached to my car mirror disappeared, but I know that my guardian angels who protected me that day are always with me."

Sometimes the angels protect us from accidents by making sure that our vehicle doesn't work. I've received many stories of car engines suddenly stopping just in time to avoid a collision:

Donna was at a three-way intersection awaiting the green light. When the light changed, she felt a force push her foot from the gas pedal. The car then stalled. At that moment, a large truck sped through the intersection, running the red light. Had Donna proceeded, she would've been sideswiped. Donna says, "I knew that the force that took my foot off the pedal was an angel. I was shaken, but grateful."

The angels can temporarily stall our cars to help us avoid accidents. In this next case, the angels disabled a car overnight while its driver sobered up:

Kathryn was upset because her boy-friend, Ben, insisted on driving, even though he'd been drinking alcohol throughout the day. As they got into the car to make a 90-mile trip, Kathryn silently prayed for protection. So she was grateful that when Ben turned the key, the car wouldn't start at all. The alternator broke at the very moment of Kathryn's prayer, ensuring that Ben wouldn't be able to drive.

I've also received many stories from people who talked about feeling an invisible pair of hands help them. The hands push them out of harm's way, hold them tightly as a car tumbles through the air, or take over turning the steering wheel:

Jacqueline lost control of her car after making a sharp U-turn. Her vehicle bounced and a rollover seemed inevitable. As she desperately tried to correct her steering, a voice said to Jacqueline, "Let go of the wheel."

Jacqueline thought, *I'll crash if I let go of the wheel,* but the voice repeated its firm but loving command. So Jacqueline relented and took her hands off the steering wheel. Ten seconds later, the car miraculously ceased skidding and stopped at the side of the road.

She says, "It was as if someone had taken over and was driving the car for me. Traffic was heavy, but during the entire time I was bouncing all over the road, no cars had passed me. It was clear that my angel had held back all of the other cars in order to keep us all safe."

Roadside Assistance

Angels not only protect us from accidents, they also help us en route. I frequently receive stories from people who were able to drive miles on empty gas tanks or flat tires, thanks to the angels. People also tell me that the angels help them get to appointments and airports on time without speeding. Angels can turn traffic signals green and find you wonderful parking places . . . just ask them!

Brenda was driving home late at night in the pouring rain. She could barely see her own headlights, much less the road. Brenda feared for her safety, but couldn't see well enough to pull off the road. Out loud, she begged the angels to give her enough light to get home safely.

Brenda explains what happened next: "I suddenly saw a brilliant light from the sky shine down." Although the rain continued to pour, the light illuminated her path and she had no problem driving. The light began to dim after 30 minutes. So Brenda again asked the angels for more light.

She says, "As if in answer, the brilliant light came back. It stayed that way until the rain finally stopped and I didn't need it anymore." The whole way home, Brenda continually repeated "Thank you" to the angels. This experience motivated Brenda to incorporate angels more fully into her life.

The angels can keep your car going even when it seems impossible, such as when your gas tank is empty, a tire is flat, or the vehicle is having mechanical problems. Of course, the angels would never ask you to drive under unsafe conditions. They'll either fix your car for you or guide you to a service station or wonderful mechanic who can help you:

Barbara was driving on an icy road when another car skidded into the front of her car. After filing the police report, she said a prayer of gratitude that she wasn't injured and asked the angels to help her car make it to a service station that she was familiar with and trusted.

Barbara recalls, "When I arrived at the service station, my car zonked out. The attendant examined the car, looked at me in awe, and said he didn't know how I'd managed to drive it anywhere. But I knew that it was the angels answering my prayers for help."

Angelic Help in the Air

My husband, Steven, and I travel worldwide giving workshops, and I depend on the angels to take care of all aspects of our arrangements, from start to finish.

For an airplane trip, you can ask your angels to:

- Help you get an extremely nice, warm, friendly, and competent customer-service representative when calling an airline to book reservations.

- Guide you on what to pack for a trip. (*Hint from personal experience:* If the angels tell you to take along an umbrella or some other item, do so even if you think it's illogical. The angels know best.)

- Arrange transportation to the airport. If you're driving yourself, they can help you find a wonderful parking space close to the terminal.

- Help you avoid lines at check-in, and work with sweet and competent airline personnel.

- Let you sail through airport security without being searched.

- Get you a wonderful seat and great seatmates (or an empty seat next to you!)

- Make certain that the airplane is mechanically safe and sound.

- Have the airplane take off and land on time.

- Ensure that you and your luggage make your connecting flights.

- Protect and deliver your baggage so that your suitcases are the first ones on the luggage carousel when you're there to collect it.

- Find you reliable transportation to your hotel.

- Help you avoid lines at hotel check-in.

- Upgrade you to a quiet and comfortable hotel room.

If you encounter turbulence on your flight, ask the angels to smooth the ride. Hundreds of them will hoist the plane and its wings on their backs, and you'll be riding on a cushion of angels. By employing these methods, Steven and I have enjoyed wonderful travel experiences for years.

Helen's* airport story is one of my favorites. It's another reminder that angels are everywhere:

It was 16-year-old Helen's first airplane trip alone, so her mother and grandmother prayed fervently for her protection.

Helen flew from Pittsburgh to Dallas, where she was to change airplanes for her final destination of Los Angeles. An older gentleman wearing plaid pants who strongly resembled Helen's grandfather approached her at the Dallas airport and asked her how she was and where she was going. Normally, Helen would have been cautious around strangers, but there was something about the man that Helen felt she could trust.

Since she was very nervous about the flight, Helen opened up to the man. Strangely enough, he seemed to already know details about her. He told Helen not to worry, that everything would be okay, and that he'd talk to her later.

Helen boarded the airplane and put the gentleman out of her mind. When she landed in Los Angeles, no one was there to meet her, so she was very frightened and confused. As Helen waited for her father, the older gentleman with the plaid pants sat next to her! This surprised her, as she hadn't seen him anywhere on her plane from Dallas to Los Angeles.

The man said, "I thought you'd still be here. I'll just wait until your father comes so you aren't alone." When her dad arrived, Helen turned to introduce her father to the man, but he'd disappeared. Helen told her father that she was talking to the man just a moment before he'd arrived. Her father replied, "I saw you talking all right, but I just thought you were talking to yourself."

A few weeks later, Helen was back home in Pittsburgh attending her church's fund-raiser. She felt a tap on her shoulder, turned around, and was astonished to see the old gentleman wearing the same bright plaid pants smiling at her. He said, "I told you everything would be all right, and now you're home safe." No one else at the church bazaar saw the man.

Helen ran home and related the whole story to her grandmother, who said, "I prayed for you to have a guardian angel, and my prayers were answered."

Helen says, "I know that it sounds unbelievable, but it's true. I've never, ever doubted angels, and now that my grandmother is in Heaven, I also feel that she's with my angels, too."

Protection in Other Ways

In addition to protecting us while we're traveling, the angels also keep us safe at home, work, and school. It's a good idea as you fall asleep to ask the angels to stay posted at your windows and doors throughout the night. You'll sleep soundly knowing that you're completely protected.

You can also ask the angels to watch over your loved ones (even when they're in a different location):

Lassie asked the angels and Archangel Michael (the protective angel) to watch over her son Quinn when he entered the military. When he was deployed to Afghanistan in 2003, Quinn and his team were headed up a steep embankment when he fell and injured his leg. Because of this injury, the team had to take another route. When they arrived at their post, they discovered that an ambush had been waiting for them atop the embankment where Quinn had fallen. If they'd climbed to the top, they could have all been killed.

Two years later, Quinn fell 55 feet out of a helicopter without a parachute and landed on his back. Yet his only injury was a scraped elbow.

Lassie says, "Oh yes, I believe in angels, and I know they saved my son's life."

Not only do angels protect us from harm, they also bring us peace by making our lives a little easier, which includes helping us find lost items or whatever else we're looking for, as you'll read about in the next chapter.

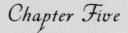

Chapter Five

ANGELS HELP US FIND WHAT WE'RE LOOKING FOR

Nothing is ever lost in the eyes of God. Even though we may not know where an item is, God does. Acting as God's messengers, the angels can bring the item back into our possession, replace it with something better, or lead us to the location of the item.

Archangel Chamuel is the chief "finding angel," who helps us locate missing items. If you misplace your checkbook, keys, or sunglasses, call upon Chamuel and the angels for help. Sometimes the angels will guide you to the location of the item. Other times, the angels will bring the item to you and place it in a location where you'd previously looked for it, as Altaira experienced:

Altaira was cross-stitching one evening when her needle fell onto the floor. She searched everywhere but couldn't find it. Worried that her son or cat would step on the needle, she asked her angels to help her find it. She threaded another needle and then left the room.

When she came back, the first needle was sitting right next to her chair. She says, "I know I looked there because I even felt over the area of the carpet with my hand." Even more remarkably, the second needle that Altaira had threaded was placed in a thread holder so that it wouldn't fall out—something that Altaira knows she didn't do.

Many people have told me that they've been able to locate long-lost valuables after they called upon the angels. I've heard countless stories of people finding their wedding rings, heirlooms, and other valuables. Sophia's story is especially poignant:

Sophia treasured her moonstone and silver earrings, especially since she'd worn them during happy times with her son and other family members. So she grieved when she returned from the grocery store and discovered that one of the earrings she'd been wearing was missing.

She thoroughly checked her hair, clothing, purse, shopping bags, the kitchen, and her car. She worried that the earring had fallen off at the store or in the parking lot. Sophia said to her angels, "Please help the earring find its way back to me." She didn't know how it would happen, but something told her that her faith would be rewarded.

Two weeks later, after Sophia returned from the same grocery store, she walked through the garage to water the plants in her backyard. As she crossed by her car, a flash of silver caught her eye. It was her earring, slightly bent, but not in any way damaged. As she reached down to pick it up, tears of gratitude filled her eyes and she said, "Thank you, angels!" aloud. Sophia says, "I truly believe now, if I didn't before, that with a little bit of faith and lots of help from the angels, anything is possible!"

Not only can the angels locate missing objects, they can also negotiate their return in miraculous ways. After you ask the angels to return something to you, let go of the request and don't worry about how they'll answer your prayer. If you receive a feeling or a thought to go somewhere or do something, be sure to follow this guidance, as it may lead you directly to the object of your prayers, as Karen discovered:

After a long day at work, Karen was looking forward to going home. First, she needed to mail some bills and deposit checks at the bank. So on her way home, she stopped at the post office and headed toward the bank. But as she prepared to make her deposit, she realized that the checks were missing! Karen asked her angels, "Where could the checks be?" A soft voice replied, "Breathe in deeply, listen with your heart, and you will know." So Karen took in three deep breaths and listened.

She immediately heard, "You accidentally picked them up with the bills you mailed, and they're in the post office box." Karen's heart sank with the realization that the mail must have already been picked up by the mail carrier, and that her checks were already long gone.

The voice said to her, "Breathe in deeply and listen to your heart." Once Karen did so, her fears were calmed enough to hear the angels' next set of instructions: "Go to the post office. He was running late and he is there now collecting the mail. He will help you find the checks." So Karen raced to the post office, and sure enough, the mail carrier was pulling out the mail bins to place in his truck.

Karen explained the situation to him, and the man kindly obliged by saying,

"Oh, don't worry, we'll go through the mail together." Very soon they found the checks. As Karen thanked her angels, she heard them say, "Thank you, Karen, for listening. We did this together!"

In addition to finding lost objects, the angels can also guide you to the right job, a great home, wonderful friends, or anything else you need:

Joanie was driving by herself at night, en route from California to visit her mother in Texas. It was getting late, so Joanie decided to pull off the highway and find a hotel for the night. Out in the middle of nowhere, there only seemed to be seedy, unsafe motels along the route. So Joanie said aloud, "Okay, angels, please help me find a safe and comfortable place to stay tonight." She was guided to an exit where she found a newly constructed hotel. The hotel's lobby was lavishly decorated with angel statues, and they had a wonderful room available for Joanie.

The angels can help you with everything—from the seemingly trivial to matters of life and death. In the next three chapters, we'll look at ways to work with your angels to heal and improve your relationships, career, and health.

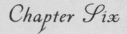

Chapter Six

ANGELIC HELP
WITH
RELATIONSHIPS

It's easy to be at peace when you're alone in meditation. Yet, real spiritual growth comes from learning how to navigate relationships peacefully. How do you stay centered and loving when people around you seem to pull you down? Once again, the angels offer very practical and effective help.

As a former psychotherapist, I've studied relationships for decades. Although many types of therapy geared toward this area are highly effective, I've found that the angels' work in this area far exceeds what humans can do when it comes to manifesting and healing relationships. So whether it's a romantic, familial, parent-child, or friendship relationship in question, you're very wise to work in partnership with the angels.

Your Love Life

The angels can help you with romance, whether you're in a committed relationship or single. If you're looking for your soul mate, the "romance angels" can help you find your special someone. A powerful method for invoking the angels' help is to find a quiet location where you won't be interrupted, and write a letter that starts like this:

Dear Guardian Angels of My Soul Mate,

Then, pour out your heart to these angels in the body of the letter. It doesn't matter whether you know who your soul mate is, because the angels do. Then conclude the letter by saying something like:

I know that my soul mate is looking for me with the same fervor as I am looking for him/her. Thank you for guiding us to meet, love, and experience a joyful and harmonious relationship based upon mutual respect, integrity, shared interests, and passionate romance. Thank you for clearly guiding me in ways that I can easily understand so that I may enjoy this relationship now.

Several couples have met at my workshops, and their relationships have blossomed as a result of the shared goal of working with the angels together. Usually at my workshops I ask audience members who are seeking a soul mate to raise their hands and then look around the room to see who else has their hands raised. Then I invoke a group of angels known as the "romance angels," Cupid-like cherubs who help us recover our playful delight in life. Between these angels and the hand-raising exercise, at least five couples who met at my workshops are now married as a result.

The romance angels can also infuse new passion into existing relationships. Ask them to help you and your partner recover your playful side, which is an important ingredient of romance. The angels say that many couples become overly focused on work and responsibilities, and they need to make time for playful and loving interactions. The romance angels can help you find time for this important endeavor, and also give you the energy to carry through.

Relationships with Friends

Our relationships sometimes change when we commit to a spiritual path, which includes working with the angels. If you have a friendship that began when you were focused on the material world, you may feel yourself pulling away from that friend as your focus becomes more spirit-centered. For one thing, your interests may grow apart. For another, the Law of Attraction says that we're attracted to people who are on the same wavelength as we are. So, someone who's focused on love and peace won't be attracted to someone whose focus is fear.

Ask your angels to help you through these shifts and changes in your relationships. Ask them to bring peaceful resolutions to any relationships that are ending. The angels can also bring you wonderful new friends, if you'll simply ask.

Relationships with Family Members

In the same way, your family interactions may change as you become more spiritually focused. If you come from a more traditional family, they may at first worry about your spirituality. Don't try to convince or convert anyone to your new way of thinking. The best way to handle this sort of situation is to be peaceful and happy. In that way, you're a walking advertisement for the benefits of living on the spiritual path. As people notice your peacefulness, they'll soon ask you about the secret to your happiness.

The angels guide us to release resentment and anger as an avenue to peace. Most of us have experienced pain in our relationships with family, friends, and lovers. The angels ensure that this pain doesn't ruin our present and future health and happiness.

If someone has performed an action that you feel is unforgivable, the angels won't ask you to change your mind and say, "What they did is okay." Instead, the angels want you to release the poisonous anger within your mind and body. When we hold resentment, we attract similar relationships and situations to us.

If you're tired of unhealthy relationship patterns, the likely culprit is unforgiveness toward a family member. The word *forgiveness* is a synonym for "releasing toxins," and replacing them with health and peace. The angels can help you with this, if you'll ask.

One effective way to release emotional toxins is to call upon Archangels Michael and Jeremiel as you're falling asleep. That's because when you're sleeping, you're more open to angelic intervention. When you're awake, your ego's fear can block the angels' help.

Say to the archangels, either silently or aloud:

"I ask that you clear away any old anger, pain, resentment, judgments, bitterness, or unforgiveness from my mind, body, and emotions. I am willing to exchange pain for peace. I now release to you anything that may be blocking my awareness of peace, especially within my relationships."

When you awaken, you'll notice a positive shift. It doesn't matter whether you recall your dream interactions with the archangels or not, as their work is on the unconscious level.

The angels can clear old issues with people who are living or deceased. These healings don't mean that you have to reignite a relationship with the person. The intention is to clear the path for you to feel love, peace, and harmony in all areas of your life.

Children

Dozens of parents have told me that they were successfully able to adopt a baby or conceive after they asked for the angels' help, such as in Mary's example:

> Mary and her husband were frustrated by the process of applying for and waiting for a baby to adopt. Still, they didn't give up hope. One morning as Mary was leaving work, she noticed an angel pin in its original packaging on the ground near her car door. She wondered why an angel pin would be at the construction company where she worked, since she was the only female employee.
>
> She pinned the angel on her purse and hoped that it was a positive sign. That evening, Mary asked her angels for help with the adoption. The next morning, the adoption agency called with the good news that they had a baby for Mary and her husband. They brought home their son, John, the following day, and he just celebrated his fifth birthday.

After a baby is brought home, the angels continue to offer support. The two archangels who specialize in children-related issues are Gabriel and Metatron. Gabriel tends to the early part of childhood, from pregnancy through the toddler stage. As the child matures, Metatron takes over as a firm but loving custodian. His chief role is to develop and protect the child's spiritual nature.

Parents can call on Gabriel and Metatron for extra support with childhood behavioral issues. For health or dietary concerns, Raphael is the archangel to call upon. For any serious behavioral difficulties such as drug use or aggressive tendencies, ask Archangel Michael for help. Many of these difficulties occur when highly sensitive youths unwittingly absorb negative energy from their surroundings. Ask Michael to "vacuum" your child, which is a term the angels use to describe their process of clearing someone of these lower energies. I've seen complete behavioral turnarounds occur as a result of Michael vacuuming a person—with results exceeding the psychotherapy methods I studied in my university and hospital training.

Perhaps it's the angels' pure love, or maybe it's the fact that they're completely unrestricted by fear or Earthly concerns. Whatever it is that effects miracles, I've seen and heard of many of them concerning children helped by angels. This story, which I first wrote about in my book *The Care and Feeding of Indigo Children*, is an example:

A woman named Josie approached me at my workshop with tears in her eyes and her arms outstretched, waiting to embrace me. She exclaimed that after reading my books about working with angels, she'd experienced Divine intervention with her 13-year-old son, Chris.

"Chris was out of control before I began working with his angels," Josie explained to me. "He wouldn't come home on time, and he was using drugs. His schoolwork was a mess. Then my aunt brought home one of your books, and I read how to talk to Chris's angels. I really didn't believe in angels at the time.

I thought they were like Santa Claus: a myth. But I was desperate to help my son, so I gave it a try.

"I silently talked to Chris's guardian angels, even though I wasn't really sure I was doing it right. I wasn't even sure that he had angels, the way he was acting like a devil and all! But I saw results almost immediately. I kept talking to those angels every night."

I asked Josie how Chris was doing these days.

"He's great!" she beamed. "He's happy, off drugs, and he's doing well in school."

Relationship Healing with the Angels

You can heal misunderstandings by talking to the other person's guardian angels. Although the angels can't violate anyone's free will, they will intervene into any situation that's affecting your peace—including relationship woes.

In these situations, close your eyes and center yourself through breath. Then, hold the intention of talking with the other person's guardian angels. You can't make a mistake and do this incorrectly, as the intention is more important than the method you use.

Then, pour out your heart (either silently, in a letter, or aloud) to that person's angels. Tell them about your fears, anger, disappointments, and desires. Next, ask the angels to bring about peace in the relationship. Don't tell the angels how to do so, or you'll slow or miss the answer to your prayer. Allow the infinite creative wisdom of God's Divine Mind to come up with an ingenious solution that will delight everyone involved in the situation.

Have you ever wished that you could go back in time and take back something you said, or handle a situation differently? Well, the angels can help you with this desire through a process called "undoing." Think of the actions or words that you'd like to rewrite, and say to the angels:

"I ask that all effects of this mistake
be undone in all directions of time,
for everyone involved."

This method often results in those involved forgetting about what happened, as if it had never occurred. It puts a new meaning to the phrase "Forgive and forget."

The angels say that when another person annoys or angers us, it's because we're seeing something in them that we don't like about ourselves. In other words, we're projecting our ego issues that we aren't aware of, or don't want to admit to. Everyone has ego issues, so they're nothing to feel ashamed of. In fact, projection is a wonderful tool that helps us become aware of our own ego issues so that we can work on them.

The angels recommend that if we become annoyed or angered at someone, we can say:

"I am willing to release that part of me that
irritates me when I think of you."

This doesn't mean that your own actions resemble the actions of the person who annoyed you. It simply means that some shadow within you recognizes the shadow within the other person.

When we admit honestly to this projection process using the angel's affirmation above, we're able to shift to a higher perspective. We can then see ourselves and other people through the eyes of the angels.

The angels overlook people's surface personalities and ego issues. They instead focus upon the light and love that's within every person, regardless of outward appearances. The more we see the goodness within others, the more we can see it within ourselves.

The angels say that every relationship serves an ultimate purpose, even short-lived ones. When the purpose of the relationship has been served, the attraction between the two people diminishes. This is one reason why relationships sometimes end.

The angels can help us with relationship endings, including making difficult decisions about leaving, giving us the courage and strength we need to endure a breakup, providing for everyone involved, and helping us heal.

When Annette's husband left her and her two small sons, she was devastated emotionally and financially. Almost symbolic of how helpless she felt, her toddler's stroller was locked in her dilapidated car's trunk and no one could open it, so she had to carry her toddler in her arms wherever they went. After six months of struggling, she finally decided to ask the angels for help. In particular, Annette called upon Archangel Michael, whom she'd worked with previously.

Annette was guided to release her hurt and anger toward her ex-husband by writing him a heartfelt letter and then burning it. After the letter was in ashes, Annette began seeing bright blue flashes of light that told her that Archangel Michael was with her.

The next day, Annette was guided to remove all of her ex-husband's belongings from her car. She asked the angels to remove any negativity from herself, her children, her home, and her car. As Annette was cleaning the last of her ex-husband's papers from the car, the trunk of the car popped open on its own. Annette couldn't believe it! She gratefully removed the stroller from the trunk, thanking the angels profusely for helping her.

She went in the house and the telephone rang. It was her nephew, who rarely called, saying that he'd told his neighbor about her situation. The neighbor was selling a beautiful white car in perfect condition for $5,000, but he was willing to let Annette have it for $2,000. Annette cried when the car was delivered, as it was beyond anything she'd hoped for.

She says, "I knew when I saw the white car roll into my driveway that it was a gift from the angels. I am overwhelmed by how much 'luck' I've had since I asked the angels to help my life. They still look after me on a daily basis, letting me know that they're with me through their flashing blue, violet, and green lights. I never want for anything, as all of my day-to-day needs are met, thanks to the angels."

The angels can help us with every relationship issue, whether it's with a spouse, family member, friend, or even a stranger. The angels also guide and protect our relationships at work. After all, we spend a lot of time with co-workers, employers, clients, and other people we come into contact with at our workplace. In the next chapter, we'll explore how the angels want to help us with our career and life purpose.

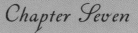

Chapter Seven

ANGELIC HELP
FOR YOUR
CAREER
AND
LIFE PURPOSE

One of the main questions I'm asked by audience members is: "Can the angels tell me about my life purpose?" The underlying question in this query is usually: "What career would be most meaningful for me?"

Since we usually spend eight or more hours of each day working, it makes sense to want meaningful employment. This is something more than a job that pays the bills. It's a career that you feel passionate about, and that you believe is making a positive difference in the world. And if it pays a good salary, well, that's even better.

We each have an important and much-needed life purpose involving our natural talents, passions, and interests. Our life purpose helps other people, animals, or the environment in some way. The angels ask us to focus on providing some type of service, and not to worry about the money or accolades we'll receive. They say, "Serve a purpose, and your purpose will then serve you in return." The angels can bring you whatever support you need in this area.

The Archangels and Careers

The archangels are happy to help you with all aspects of your career. Here are some of the roles that specific archangels can fulfill:

Ariel: This archangel helps those interested in environmental, nature, or animal-related careers. Ariel also helps in the manifestation of money or other supplies needed for your life purpose and day-to-day expenses.

Azrael: If your career involves grief counseling or guiding people through losses (such as working at a hospital, hospice, counseling center, and the like), this archangel can guide your words and actions to comfort and empower the bereaved.

Chamuel: The "finding archangel" will help you locate the career or job you're seeking. Chamuel will also help you retain your peacefulness, helping you find the best job.

Gabriel: The messenger archangel helps teachers, journalists, writers, and those who want to work with children. If you feel guided to write, Gabriel will motivate and guide you. If you'd like to help children in some way, ask Gabriel for a Divine assignment.

Haniel: The archangel of grace is wonderful to invoke when going out on a job interview, attending meetings, or any-time you want to be extra-articulate and graceful.

Jophiel: The archangel of beauty helps to keep the energy clean and high at your workplace, and to keep your thoughts about your career positive. She also helps artists, creative types, anyone involved in the beauty business, and feng shui practitioners with all aspects of their careers.

Metatron: If your career involves ado-lescents or energetic children, Metatron can help you. He can give you a Divine assignment if you'd like to work with adolescents; and Metatron is also a won-derful motivator and organizer, so call upon him if you need assistance with your get-up-and-go.

Michael: Archangel Michael can help you discern your life's purpose and the next step to take in your career. One of the best ways to start the process is to write him a letter, inquiring about your best career or educational choices. Michael is one of the loudest archangels, so you probably won't have any trouble hearing him. Write his replies below your questions in your letter, so you have a record of his career guidance.

Michael's speaking style is very much to the point. He's quite loving, but he's also very blunt. For this reason, Michael is a wonderful archangel to call upon for the courage to change or improve your career. He'll help you change to a better job; start your own business; and speak your truth lovingly to co-workers, bosses, and clients.

Michael is also amazing at fixing electronic and mechanical items such as computers, cars, fax machines, and such.

Raguel: If your work involves relationships with clients, co-workers, and mediation (such as marriage counseling), Archangel Raguel can ensure harmonious interactions.

Raphael: If you're in a healing career, or feel guided to be a healer, Raphael can help you. As the chief healing angel, Raphael assists with all aspects of healing careers. Raphael can guide and help you to select the healing modality that you'd most enjoy, manifest tuition for your healing education, open and run a healing center, find the best employment in a healing field or establish a successful private practice, and guide you with the best actions and words during your healing sessions.

Sandalphon: This archangel helps with careers in the arts, especially music. Call upon Sandalphon as a muse to inspire you, as a teacher to guide your creative process, and as an agent to market your creative projects.

Uriel: The archangel of light can illuminate your mind with wise ideas and concepts. Call upon Uriel for problem solving, brainstorming, or important conversations.

Zadkiel: This archangel helps you improve your memory, and he's a wonderful helpmate for students or anyone who needs to remember names, figures, or other important information.

The Angels at Work

The angels will work overtime to help you with your career. Just ask, and they will screen your phone calls and keep away unnecessary time-wasters.

Angels can also guide suitable customers to your business. A wonderful prayer to say in the morning is:

*"I ask that everyone who would receive blessings
from my product (or services) be given the time,
money, and whatever else they need to
purchase my product (or services) today."*

I've spoken with several successful shop owners who use a similar prayer with great success. In visiting these stores, I'm thrilled to see that they're filled with happy, paying customers.

Ask the angels to help you have fun at work, and they'll inject each day with joyful, meaningful moments. If you need something, such as a new computer, new inventory, or a bigger office, ask the angels for help in this regard. If you need ideas, connections, or energy, again the angels can come to your aid.

The angels can help you with every big and small detail connected to your work life because they love you and care about you. They want you to be at peace, and they also know that you're happiest when you feel good about the way you spend your day.

The angels want to help us feel good all the time, and that includes healing our loved ones if a health challenge arises. In the next chapter, we'll discuss some of the ways in which angels watch over our health, ensuring continued peace of mind, body, and spirit.

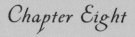

Chapter Eight

HEALING
WITH THE
ANGELS

Nothing is impossible for God and the angels. They can heal any condition, increase our motivation to exercise, and eliminate or reduce cravings for unhealthful foods or substances. All that's required on our part is a crystal clear decision that we want to heal, and a willingness to surrender the situation entirely to God and the angels.

The angels work in conjunction with Jesus, Buddha, or other deities, so you needn't worry that angelic healing interferes with your religious beliefs or constraints.

You can ask God to send healing angels to another person. As stated earlier, the angels won't violate someone else's free will by imposing an unwanted healing upon them (remember that not everyone wants to heal for various personal reasons known only to themselves). However, the *presence* of the angels has a calming effect that is always helpful and healthy, so it's a good idea to invoke angels for those dealing with health challenges.

Archangel Raphael is the primary angel who conducts and oversees healings. He's assisted by "healing angels" who work in precise concert with him to orchestrate miraculous healings. Raphael's halo is emerald green, which is the energetic color of pure love. Raphael surrounds injured or diseased areas with emerald green light.

Sometimes the angels heal by guiding us to wonderful human health practitioners. After you ask for the angels' help, pay close attention to repetitive ideas or feelings that ask you to contact certain doctors or health facilities. Remember that you can always ask the angels to speak louder, or to explain anything that you don't understand.

Holly's story illustrates how the angels can miraculously heal us, provided that we ask for their help and then get out of the way so that they can do their work:

Holly survived a head-on automobile collision, but with her right ankle completely shattered by the impact, she felt as though an important part of her life had died. An avid hiker, jogger, and dancer, Holly was now barely able to stand and walk. She couldn't wear the pointy high-heeled shoes she'd always loved, and she wasn't able to dance around the kitchen as she'd regularly done while fixing her family's dinner.

Without the use of her right ankle, life seemed colorless, and Holly became depressed. She was limping, in pain, and her doctor was recommending surgery to permanently fuse her ankle with a screw to completely restrict the movement of her right foot.

Holly had read many books about angels, and she fervently believed in God, yet she'd always been the one in control of her life, never asking others for help . . . not even God. A self-professed "control freak," Holly always believed that if she didn't take care of things herself, they wouldn't get done. However, now she was depressed and ready to ask for help.

After reading the healings described in my book *Angel Medicine,* Holly had an epiphany and realized that she deserved the same help that others had received from God and the angels. She said to herself, *I am worthy of a miracle!* She also realized that her previous method of trying to control everything and use "mind over matter" wasn't working.

She recalls, "For the first time in my life, I let go. I realized I didn't have to handle this alone. I let go of the fear, the hurt, and the depression. The only thing I asked for was that my healing occur while I was sleeping, as I knew I'd ask too many questions if it happened while I was awake!"

After Holly asked God and the angels for a healing, she curled up with her three dogs and fell asleep. Normally during the night, Holly's dogs would stir and ask to be let outside, but this evening was completely different and they slept until daybreak.

Holly, on the other hand, was abruptly awoken by electrical impulses that made her body twitch. She felt both hot and cold as the electrical impulses moved through her body. The room was filled with the same feeling of static electricity.

Holly felt lighter than she ever had before, and she knew in that moment that she'd been healed. A voice said to Holly, "Stand up," so she swung her legs over the edge of the bed. The dogs still slept.

Holly says, "The foot that was for the most part immobilized had regained full range of motion! My right foot matched every angle and rotation of the left. I stood up, and for the first time in a year and a half, I was pain free. I could place all my weight on that foot and walk without a limp."

Holly now dances, jogs, and wears high-heeled shoes again. She remarks, "I'm doing what science says is impossible. I simply had to believe. I simply had to ask for it. Thank You, dearest God, for sending Your archangels to me. I finally have my life back."

In addition to healing human bodies, the angels can also heal animals. Again, it's just a matter of asking:

Andrea's cat, Jesus, was very ill. He wouldn't move or eat, so she took him to the vet, where he was diagnosed with an infection and kidney stones. A few days later, he was still in the animal hospital with a high fever. Around 4:30 P.M., when Andrea called to check on her cat, the vet warned that her cat might not live.

Crying, Andrea hung up the phone and implored the angels to heal her cat. After 30 minutes of talking with her angels, Andrea felt peaceful. She heard a voice say, "Your kitty will get well and be as if nothing happened."

The next morning when she called the animal hospital, a nurse told Andrea that her cat's temperature returned to normal about 5:30 the evening before. This was the same time when Andrea felt peaceful after talking with her angels! Today, you'd never know that Andrea's cat had ever been ill, just as the angels promised.

Healthy Lifestyles

While the angels are happy to help us with health crises, they're also very involved with preventive medicine so that we stay healthy and vital throughout our lives. You've most likely felt or heard your angels nudge you to change your diet, exercise more, or do something else to improve your health.

Many people find that soon after they begin working with angels, their taste for certain foods and beverages changes. Some people even lose the ability to comfortably digest their former dietary favorites.

This is part of the upward energy vibration shift that occurs when you're surrounded by angels. In the same way that the Law of Attraction means that you're attracted to people who hold similar feelings and beliefs to your own, so will you find your attractions to foods and beverages changing.

Some people naturally and easily improve their diet, yet many of us need angelic help. I had terrible headaches soon after I began writing angel books. Since I'd never had them before in my entire life, I knew that something was wrong. I asked Archangel Raphael about this, and I immediately heard (through my feelings and thoughts) that my daily chocolate eating was the culprit. He explained that chocolate was lowering my energy, which caused a clash whenever I connected with the angels. It was kind of like low-pressure and high-pressure weather systems colliding and causing a storm.

I was horrified by this news, as I craved chocolate almost constantly. I wondered how I could go even one day without it, so I asked Raphael to help me. That was in 1996, and I haven't craved or wanted chocolate since that evening. He completely healed me of all desires for it, which was no minor miracle for a former chocoholic like me. The headaches also vanished and haven't returned.

The angels aren't prudes or morality police, but they do know that some of us need to live chemical-free lives for optimal health and happiness, so they often guide us to detoxify and steer clear of alcohol, sugar, caffeine, nicotine, and other drugs. The angels have helped me and many others to be free of chemicals and cravings.

In addition to diet issues, the angels also steer us toward healthy exercise programs that match our interests and energy levels. They often guide us to yoga, because it helps us focus and meditate; as well as strengthen our muscles, clear our chakras, and have more energy.

The angels also love us to spend time in nature, as the magical energy of fresh air, trees, flowers, plants, water, and sunshine refreshes and renews us.

In addition, the angels urge us to get plenty of rest. This guidance also includes ensuring that bedrooms are quiet, beds are comfortable, and that bedding and pillows are allergen free.

If you've had feelings or thoughts urging you to engage in any of these healthy lifestyle changes, that's a sign that you're hearing your angels' guidance. If you need help with motivation, energy, time, money, or anything else in support of making these changes, just ask.

Chapter Nine

ANGELS
ON
EARTH

You may have met an angel in human form who gave you a comforting message or performed a heroic deed. Angels can appear in human bodies when it's necessary to save a life or to help someone really hear what they have to say.

Incarnated angels look like ordinary people. Sometimes they're well dressed, and sometimes they're dressed in rags. These angels usually take physical form temporarily, just long enough to perform a Heavenly function. However, some angels live entire lifetimes as humans, when a family, hospital, school, or other group requires long-term angelic help.

Here's an example of how some angels in human form helped Susan:

> One cold winter, Susan's* furnace went out. She called appliance companies but discovered that she couldn't afford the cost of a replacement furnace, nor repairs. The next day, an unmarked white van pulled up in front of her home. Two men in unmarked uniforms informed Susan that they were sent to deliver and install her new furnace.
>
> When Susan protested that she hadn't ordered a new furnace, the men said that they'd install it and she could later discuss the finances with their office. Susan never heard from the men again, and she didn't know what company to call to inquire about paying for the furnace. She just knew that her angels had arranged for heat for herself and her family.

Angels help us in miraculous ways. Instead of praying for the money to replace her furnace,

Susan simply asked for heat to be restored to her home. If she'd insisted that God give her money because she believed that was her only route to having a furnace, the answer to her prayer may not have readily come.

In the same way, Tracy discovered that the angels are unceasingly generous with time and money:

Tracy and her baby daughter were at the airport checking in for their flight home; however the airline said that Tracy's ticket was invalid and that she'd have to buy another one to be allowed on the flight. She didn't have the money for a second ticket, so she sat down and began crying.

A gentle hand touched Tracy's shoulder. It was a well-dressed elderly woman who asked if she could help. When Tracy explained her predicament, the woman immediately bought her a replacement ticket. Tracy thanked the woman profusely, and then a moment later the woman vanished.

When Tracy boarded the airplane, she was happy to find that this same woman was seated next to her, and she comforted Tracy and her baby during the flight. When they landed, Tracy again thanked her benefactress for the ticket and comforting words. Yet, immediately after they disembarked, the woman again vanished. Tracy has no doubt that the woman was an angel in disguise.

An angel may come into our lives in human form for a brief relationship, to provide us with protection, to steer us through a major life intersection, or to give us support and guidance. These beings may exit our lives as quickly as they entered, because they've fulfilled their angelic function:

Anna had been styling Betty's hair every Friday morning at 9 A.M. for three months. One Thursday evening, Betty called Anna to change the next morning's appointment to 8 A.M. As a result, Anna arrived at her shop an hour earlier than normal. Ten minutes later, a 6.0-magnitude earthquake shook her shop (it was the Whittier Narrows earthquake of October 1987).

During the quake, Anna's mobile home fell over and a utility pole crashed into her awnings. If not for Betty's earlier appointment, which got her out of the house, Anna would have likely suffered injuries or worse. Betty never arrived for her appointment, and Anna never heard from her again. After all, Betty had served her Heavenly function of protecting Anna's life.

Sometimes Heaven asks us to fulfill the function of an angel. Have you ever counseled a friend or client and said something so wise and comforting that you wondered where those words came from? That's an example of God speaking through you as a messenger angel.

Other times, it's very clear when you're being tapped on the shoulder to act as an Earth angel, which is what happened to Kathy:

A licensed nurse, Kathy thought about stopping to help when she saw a terrible auto wreck on the other side of the interstate. But she worried about getting across the fast-moving traffic. Something inside of her told her to stop anyway. As she got out of her car, a woman approached and called Kathy by her first name, although they'd never met before. The woman said that the people in the accident needed her assistance. When Kathy replied, "I can't get across the road," the woman said, "I will help you."

The woman stepped out in the middle of the busy interstate and put her hands up to stop the big semitrailers. She grabbed Kathy's arm and led her across to a young man lying in the road who desperately needed medical attention. Kathy looked over her shoulder to thank the woman, but she'd disappeared.

Kathy administered CPR to, and prayed with, the young man until the ambulance arrived. She later inquired about the woman, but no one else had seen her. Kathy is sure that she was a guardian angel, and that she herself was used in the service of an angel that night.

Most people who meet an angel in human form don't initially realize that the helpful person is an angel. It's only afterward when the angel vanishes from sight that its true identity becomes known:

One extremely foggy night, Barbara and her friend Lorraine worried about driving home from school safely after a day of teaching. The fog was so thick that they had difficulty finding their car in the school parking lot. Just as Barbara was reluctantly getting behind the wheel to drive, a well-dressed man appeared from out of nowhere.

"Move over," he said authoritatively. Neither woman felt afraid, and somehow trusted the man and his judgment. On the drive home, they both felt sleepy, as if in a dreamlike stupor.

Barbara recalls, "I came back to reality just as we pulled into the driveway to find that my husband and Lorraine's husband were waiting for us, relieved that we'd made it home safely." Lorraine dashed into the house, while Barbara pondered what had happened. The man had disappeared, and Barbara was seated behind the steering wheel without any recollection of how she'd gotten there. To this day, Lorraine and Barbara are both puzzled, but they believe that an angel came to their rescue that night.

Angels take on human form to provide physical assistance, like the angel-man who drove Barbara and Lorraine safely home through the fog. They also briefly incarnate during times of stress and crisis, when we can't hear the still, small voice of Spirit. In those cases, angels take human form so that we'll pay attention to their important messages and warnings, as in Patricia's case:

Patricia was driving through an intersection when she heard a huge crash. As she opened her eyes, she realized she'd been in an accident. Patricia slowly sat up and noticed a woman standing at her car window. "Turn off the car!" the woman said. "It's off," Patricia replied, not realizing that the engine was still running. The woman repeated, "Turn the key to turn it off." Patricia complied, and the woman disappeared.

Firefighters and paramedics used the Jaws of Life to pull Patricia from her car. One of the men remarked, "Good thing you turned off your car. It was leaking gas all over the road, and one spark from the ignition would have blown you sky-high." When Patricia explained that the woman had instructed her to turn off the car, the man said, "What woman? No one was at your car before us. They couldn't have gotten to you until the car was towed out of traffic, off to the side of the road." That's when Patricia realized she'd been saved by an angel.

Whether they're incarnated in human form or in the spirit world, the angels are here to implement God's plan of peace, one person at a time. That means the angels want to help you with whatever will bring *you* peace. If you don't know what that is, you can ask the angels for guidance on setting healthy intentions for yourself. The angels can also give you the time, motivation, energy, and whatever else you need to act on your Divine guidance.

The angels love you more than words can convey. They love you unconditionally, and they appreciate and value your gifts, talents, and Divine mission. More than anything, your angels wish you to enjoy utter peace and happiness. They're available around-the-clock to help you with this endeavor. All you need to do is ask.

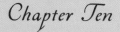

Chapter Ten

FREQUENTLY ASKED QUESTIONS ABOUT ANGELS

Here are some of the questions that are frequently posed by audience members at my lectures, and by readers of my books. While I don't claim to know all the answers, I'm a good listener, and these responses are the ones I received by asking God and the angels. I encourage you to ask them your questions and listen to the replies you get as well.

Q: Why can't I hear my angels?

A: The two main reasons why people can't seem to hear their angels is that they're trying too hard to make something happen, and they're unaware of or unsure about the angelic messages they're receiving.

It's important that you don't strain, or try too hard, to hear them. Easy does it. Remember that the angels are more motivated than you are to have a conversation. Let them do the work, while you stay in a receptive state instead of chasing after their voice.

Quiet your mind through breath, then close your eyes and ask your angels to help you feel peaceful. Then, ask your angels a question. Notice the impressions that come to you in the form of ideas, physical or emotional feelings, visions, or words. It's impossible to get nothing, since angels always reply to every prayer and question, and because you're always thinking and feeling—two channels of angelic communication.

Honor the thoughts and feelings that come to you, especially if they're repetitive, loving, and inspiring. Often the angels' messages are very simple and seemingly unrelated to your question or prayer. If you're still unsure about the validity or meaning of the message, ask the angels to give you a clear sign or additional information.

Sometimes people can't hear their angels because of lifestyle habits. Possible interference to clear Divine communication can include a noisy environment and chemicals or animal products in the diet. If you've been getting strong feelings or ideas to clean up your lifestyle, ask the angels for motivation and help in doing so.

Q: I've asked my angels for help, but nothing seems to happen.

A: The most frequent reason why prayers seem to go unanswered is because Divine guidance (the angels' response to your prayers in the form of instructions and advice that will lead you to your desires) hasn't been noticed or is being ignored. If you expect one specific type of answer to a prayer, you may not notice something that differs from your expectations. For instance, when I prayed to meet and marry my soul mate, I received Divine guidance to go to a yoga class, which is where I ultimately met my husband. If I hadn't listened to the Divine guidance to attend this class, I may have assumed that my prayers were going unanswered.

Some people don't trust the Divine guidance they receive. For instance, if you pray for an improved financial situation, you may get strong impressions to open a business or change jobs. Yet, if you feel intimidated by the idea of changing jobs or running a company, you may ignore this guidance and assume that the angels aren't helping you financially.

A third reason falls under the category of "Divine timing." Some prayers are instantly answered, while others need time to "cook" before all the factors fall into place. Prayers may not be answered until we feel ready or deserving of receiving their fulfillment.

Q: Do you worship angels?

A: No. The angels don't want us to worship them. They want all glory to go to God.

Q: Why don't the angels save everyone, especially innocent children?

A: This question speaks to one of life's deep mysteries, and the answer may be unknowable. Some people choose not to fight for their lives during illness or injuries, and other people don't listen to their Divine guidance that might spare them. It seems that we all have a "time" to return home to Heaven, which our souls predetermine prior to our incarnation. While we wish that everyone would choose healthy and long lives on Earth, apparently that's not part of every soul's path or desires.

Q: What if what I'm asking for isn't God's will for me?

A: Some fear that God is *willing* their suffering, and they're afraid of violating a greater will than their own. Yet, if we truly believe that God is loving, and if we trust that God is good, then why would the Creator will anything but love and goodness for us? One who is all love would never "test" us, or use pain as a way to make us grow. Wouldn't we be more useful to God's plan if our energy and health were vibrant and radiant?

God is omnipresent, within each of us. This means that God's will is everywhere, overlapping your own. And a loving God would never want you to suffer in any way, just as you'd never will your own children to suffer. It's true that you can grow through pain, but it's also true that you can grow through peace.

God usually has higher standards for us than we do for ourselves. Very often, we ask for too little, while God stands by, unable to offer more lest our free will be violated. Ask for whatever will bring you peace, and Heaven will happily help you.

Q: I was raised to believe that I should only talk to God or Jesus. Is it blasphemous to talk to angels?

A: This fear stems from some organized religions' interpretation of spiritual texts. If you truly believe that you should only speak with God, Jesus, or some other spiritual being, then don't violate that belief. To do so would cause unnecessary fear, and we certainly don't want to add to that negative emotion.

However, do consider this: The word *angel,* as stated earlier, means "messenger of God." Angels are gifts from the Creator who act like Heavenly postal carriers, bringing messages to and from the Creator and the Created. They operate with Divine precision in delivering trustworthy guidance to us. And just like any gift, the giver (the Creator) wishes us to enjoy and use the gift. The Bible and other spiritual texts are filled with positive accounts of people talking to angels, and this natural phenomenon carries into the present day.

Q: How do I know that I'm really speaking to an angel and not just making it up?

A: True Divine guidance is uplifting, inspiring, motivational, positive, and loving. Angel messages always discuss how to improve something: an outlook, one's health, relationships, the environment, the world, and so on. Angels generally repeat the message through your feelings, thoughts, visions, and hearing until you take the advised action. If you're unsure if a message is real or not, wait awhile, as true Divine guidance repeats itself, while false guidance eventually fades away if ignored.

Watch out for the very common "impostor phenomenon," in which the ego tries to convince you that you're not qualified to talk to angels and that you don't have intuitive or psychic abilities. Know that this message is fear and ego based.

God and the angels all speak in loving and positive words. If you ever hear negative words from anyone, living or not, stop talking to them and immediately pray for the assistance of Archangel Michael. He'll escort lower energies away and protect you from negativity.

Talking with angels is a pleasant, joyful experience. Whether you hear them, see them, feel their presence, or receive new insights, you'll certainly enjoy connecting with them.

Q: If I work with angels, am I shirking my responsibility for taking control of my own life and my own personal growth?

A: Some people feel that they're "cheating" by requesting Divine intervention. They believe that we're supposed to suffer in order to learn and grow, and that we're responsible for getting ourselves in and out of jams. Yet the angels say that while we can grow through suffering, we can grow even faster through peace. And our peacefulness inspires others in ways that suffering cannot.

The angels won't do everything for you, though. They're more like teammates who ask you to pass the ball as you collectively move toward each goal. As you ask them for help, the angels will sometimes create a miraculous intervention. But more often, they'll help you by delivering Divine guidance so that you can help yourself.

～～

ABOUT
THE
AUTHOR

*D*oreen Virtue, Ph.D., is the author of the *Healing with the Angels* book and oracle cards, *Archangels & Ascended Masters,* and *Angel Therapy,* among other works. Her *Messages from Your Angels Oracle Cards* deck was the #1 best-selling nonfiction work in Australia in 2002. Her products are available in most languages worldwide.

A lifelong clairvoyant who works with the angelic realm, Doreen holds Ph.D., M.A., and B.A. university degrees in counseling psychology.

Doreen has appeared on *Oprah,* CNN, *The View,* and other television and radio programs. For more information on Doreen and the workshops she presents throughout the world, to subscribe to Doreen's free e-mail angel-messages newsletter, to visit her message boards, or to submit your angel healing stories, please visit **www. AngelTherapy.com**.

You can listen to Doreen's live weekly radio show, and call her for a reading, by visiting **HayHouseRadio.com**®.

HAY HOUSE TITLES
OF RELATED INTEREST

ASK AND IT IS GIVEN:
Learning to Manifest Your Desires,
by Esther and Jerry Hicks (The Teachings of Abraham)

BORN KNOWING:
A Medium's Journey—Accepting and Embracing My Spiritual Gifts,
by John Holland, with Cindy Pearlman

THE DISAPPEARANCE OF THE UNIVERSE:
Straight Talk about Illusions, Past Lives, Religion, Sex, Politics,
and the Miracles of Forgiveness,
by Gary R. Renard

THE GOD CODE:
The Secret of Our Past, the Promise of Our Future,
by Gregg Braden

POWER ANIMALS:
How to Connect with Your Animal Spirit Guides (a book-with-CD),
by Steven D. Farmer, Ph.D.

SACRED CEREMONY:
How to Create Ceremonies for Healing, Transitions, and Celebrations,
by Steven D. Farmer, Ph.D.

SPIRIT MESSENGER:
The Remarkable Story of a Seventh Son of a Seventh Son,
by Gordon Smith

TRUST YOUR VIBES:
Secret Tools for Six-Sensory Living,
by Sonia Choquette

❧

All of the above are available at your local bookstore,
or may be ordered by contacting: Hay House USA (see next page)

We hope you enjoyed this Hay House Lifestyles book. If you'd like to receive a free catalog featuring additional Hay House books and products, or if you'd like information about the Hay Foundation, please contact:

Hay House, Inc.
P.O. Box 5100
Carlsbad, CA 92018-5100

(760) 431-7695 or **(800) 654-5126**
(760) 431-6948 (fax) or **(800) 650-5115 (fax)**
www.hayhouse.com® • **www.hayfoundation.org**

❧

Published and distributed in Australia by: Hay House Australia Pty. Ltd., 18/36 Ralph St., Alexandria NSW 2015 • *Phone:* 612-9669-4299 *Fax:* 612-9669-4144 • www.hayhouse.com.au

Published and distributed in the United Kingdom by: Hay House UK, Ltd., 292B Kensal Rd., London W10 5BE • *Phone:* 44-20-8962-1230 *Fax:* 44-20-8962-1239 • www.hayhouse.co.uk

Published and distributed in the Republic of South Africa by: Hay House SA (Pty), Ltd., P.O. Box 990, Witkoppen 2068 • *Phone/Fax:* 27-11-467-8904 orders@psdprom.co.za • www.hayhouse.co.za

Published in India by: Hay House Publishers India, Muskaan Complex, Plot No. 3, B-2, Vasant Kunj, New Delhi 110 070 • *Phone:* 91-11-4176-1620 *Fax:* 91-11-4176-1630 • www.hayhouse.co.in

Distributed in Canada by: Raincoast, 9050 Shaughnessy St., Vancouver, B.C. V6P 6E5 • *Phone:* (604) 323-7100 • *Fax:* (604) 323-2600 • www.raincoast.com

❧

Tune in to **HayHouseRadio.com®** for the best in inspirational talk radio featuring top Hay House authors! And, sign up via the Hay House USA Website to receive the Hay House online newsletter and stay informed about what's going on with your favorite authors. You'll receive bimonthly announcements about Discounts and Offers, Special Events, Product Highlights, Free Excerpts, Giveaways, and more!
www.hayhouse.com®

CROSSING HOFFA

Crossing

A TEAMSTER'S STORY

STEVEN J. HARPER

**BOREALIS
BOOKS**

Borealis Books is an imprint of the Minnesota Historical Society Press.

www.borealisbooks.org

The Minnesota Historical Society Press is a member of the Association of American University Presses.

Manufactured in the United States of America

10 9 8 7 6 5 4 3 2 1

∞ The paper used in this publication meets the minimum requirements of the American National Standard for Information Sciences—Permanence for Printed Library Materials, ANSI Z39.48-1984.

International Standard Book Number 13: 978-0-87351-580-1 (cloth)
International Standard Book Number 10: 0-87351-580-3 (cloth)

Library of Congress Cataloging-in-Publication Data

Harper, Steven J., 1954–
Crossing Hoffa : a Teamster's story / Steven J. Harper.
   p. cm.
Includes bibliographical references.
ISBN-13: 978-0-87351-580-1
   (cloth : alk. paper)
ISBN-10: 0-87351-580-3
   (cloth : alk. paper)
   1. Harper, James Henry, 1928–
   2. Hoffa, James R. (James Riddle), 1913–
   3. International Brotherhood of Teamsters, Chauffeurs, Warehousemen and Helpers of America. Minneapolis. Local 544.
   4. Labor unions—Minnesota—Minneapolis.
   5. Labor unions—Corrupt practices—Minnesota—Minneapolis.
   I. Title.

HD6519.M62I584 2007
331.88'11388324092—dc21
[B]   2007000399

For Kit: Everyone has a story—
She and our children have been mine

CROSSING HOFFA

CROSSING HOFFA

Prologue

IT WAS TIME FOR ME TO OPEN THE BOX.

Less than an hour earlier, in the predawn December darkness that enveloped Chicago, my father, James Henry Harper, had died in his home at the age of seventy-three. When he had begun his battle with cancer two years earlier, his handsome six-foot frame had carried about 170 pounds. My father had always disdained his physical appearance, but he was truly proud to have retained a relatively full head of hair. The tight black curls that were the curse of his youth relaxed just enough in later years to create silver waves that distinguished him. He regularly flashed a warm, broad grin that squeezed the corners of his lively blue eyes into a squint behind his bifocals. When he laughed—which was often—the effect was deep, sustained, and infectious. For the last decade of his life, that laugh usually transitioned into a smoker's cough. Sixty years of smoking Camel cigarettes will do that to a person.

My parents had lived together in a small, brick ranch house near the end of a cul-de-sac. During my father's final eighteen months, the dominant item of furniture in the living room was the mechanized bed that we'd acquired after the surgical removal and reconstruction of his esophagus. His most frequent trips from his new bed terminated at the La-Z-Boy recliner about three feet away; he took those journeys less often during his final days. Next to the recliner stood a floor lamp with a flat surface just large enough to hold a glass of water, a small disposable cigarette lighter, his open pack of Camels, an unopened pack lying faithfully in ready reserve, and a half-consumed bottle of Snapple Iced Tea. He hated iced tea and never drank it, but the bottle served as the receptacle for his cigarette butts, which floated there until someone—never Dad—liberated them into a garbage can.

Next to the lamp was a chest of drawers upon which a metal safe-keeping box rested. Latched and secured with a miniature padlock, it

lay within easy reach of his recliner, which for his grandchildren had become the seat of all wisdom. As he spoke with them, he sometimes opened the metal box and leafed through its contents. Only rarely did he remove an item for brief inspection or display, and he always returned it when he finished. No one really knew the complete contents of what he called his "treasure chest."

As his oldest son and the family's only lawyer, I was now responsible for handling the legal aftermath of his death. As I sat in his recliner and slowly unclipped the lock from the box, I realized that it almost certainly contained symbolic milestones of his life. He knew I would be the first to open the box upon his death because I would need his birth certificate for the funeral director. He had told me that the certificate was in the box. I drew a deep breath and opened it slowly. With ceremonial care, I lifted each item as if it were a museum piece:

- ▸ His 1928 birth certificate, as promised.
- ▸ My mother's 1935 birth certificate.
- ▸ His 1948 army discharge papers.
- ▸ A certified copy of the 1950 court order dissolving his short-lived first marriage, to his high school sweetheart.
- ▸ A series of 1960 letters between my father, the Louisiana State Board of Pardons, and the state's attorney general. Relating to my father's 1951–52 imprisonment at Angola, an episode so horrendous he was sure its scars would endure for generations, the letters discussed his "Pardon, with Full Restoration of Citizenship," a document that had become trapped somewhere in the Bayou State's bureaucracy.
- ▸ His 1953 marriage certificate signed by his new father-in-law, who had conducted the wedding ceremony in the Mankato, Minnesota, Lutheran church where he was the senior pastor.
- ▸ Copies of birth certificates for me, my two younger sisters, and my younger brother.
- ▸ Two handmade Father's Day cards from my sisters—dates unknown, but certainly works from their early childhood.
- ▸ A boyhood note from my brother, thanking my father for taking care of him.
- ▸ A key case I had made during my Leathercraft Kit period at the age of thirteen. I smiled as I remembered that everybody in the family received a "leather something" from me that Christmas.

But four other items in the box puzzled me.

- A union dues booklet, fifty years old. The 3¾- by 2⅛-inch ledger recorded James Harper's July 20, 1954, initiation as a member of the International Brotherhood of Teamsters, Chauffeurs, Warehousemen and Helpers, Local 544 in Minneapolis, Minnesota. Several fragile pages filled with postage-like stamps bore the ink imprint "Dave Morris" and confirmed my father's status as a "Teamster in good standing" for every month that he had paid his dues. Dave Morris was a name that I remembered.
- His 1956 and 1957 Teamsters identification cards, signed by Sidney Brennan as secretary-treasurer of Local 544. I'd never heard of Brennan.
- His 1961 Teamsters identification card, this one signed by Fred V. Snyder, who replaced Brennan as secretary-treasurer and became my dad's mortal enemy in 1959. From my early childhood, his name had been synonymous with evil.

The last discoveries were remarkable. Why had he kept these artifacts? My father hadn't been a Teamster for forty years. I sat back in

Jim Harper's 1954 union dues booklet

Two of Jim Harper's union cards

his recliner and closed my eyes as memories flooded my mind, entire scenes from my childhood emerging in vivid detail.

Almost from the moment of my birth, my dad had taken me everywhere. When he drove the two of us around town, I sat next to him in my toy "car seat," complete with a small steering wheel that I turned whenever he turned his. When he carried me on his shoulders, I usually clutched his short, tightly curled hair for dear life while he gently urged me to hold his sloping forehead instead. When we walked together, I wrapped my entire small hand around his little finger as I ran three steps for every one of his.

I remembered our trips to Werner, the trucking company where he worked as an over-the-road driver. There I regularly visited the driv-

ers' room, the loading dock, and the business office. I recalled illicit truck rides that had violated the law and company policy because I had ridden as an unauthorized passenger and a minor.

"Quick, get down on the floor," he would whisper to me if a police car appeared while he drove the truck with me as his wide-eyed passenger. Of course, I quickly obeyed. Sometimes his sly smile and the gleam in his eye caused me to wonder if he was just teasing. If so, it didn't matter because as long as I was with him I would have cheerfully remained on the floor for our entire trip.

I recalled, too, my nicest childhood home, where we had lived for eighteen months beginning in the spring of 1960. Ours was the only house in the neighborhood with large floodlights capable of blanketing all sides of our half-acre lawn. With the flip of a single inside switch, my friends and I could play night baseball in our yard. As young as I was, I sensed that he had installed our unique illumination system for reasons he wasn't telling me. Certainly, those lights weren't required for protection against potential thieves who might wander onto a dead-end street in a crime-free middle-class suburb of Minneapolis.

I probed the recesses of my mind to extract darker images: my father's snub-nosed .38 caliber pistol, the sounds of gunshots from his homemade firing range in our basement, his reel-to-reel tape recorders and telephone monitoring devices. I remembered asking him about something he called a "wire recorder," which he often wore under his trucker's jacket. I will never forget the uncharacteristic intensity of his reaction when I posed one question too many about it.

"Where'd you get that, Dad?" I wondered.

"You must never tell anyone I have it," he responded with surprising firmness. "No one. Understood?"

At the age of six, I had understood the words but not what lay behind them.

I remembered the day he brought home our first family pet, a German shepherd he named Fritzie. The dog would always protect us, Dad said, even if there came a time when he could not. Protection from whom or what was never explained, and I did not ask for clarification.

I remembered the fervor with which he had told me never to accept a ride from anyone—ever. "Someone might even tell you that Mom and I've been hurt and that you should get in their car to see us at the hospital. That won't be true. Only Mom or I will ever come to get you.

If, for some reason, neither of us can, the only other person we would send is Grandpa. No one else. If anyone else tries, run away—and scream as loud as you can."

This was not your typical stranger-danger discussion with a six-year-old child.

All of this and more had been locked in my memory bank for four decades; now the door to that vault opened wide.

As I got older, I never missed an opportunity to spend time with my father. Starting at the age of ten and continuing through high school, I spent summers and school-year Saturdays working with him in the trucking industry. By then, he had left driving and entered management. We rode to work together at seven, broke at noon for lunch at his favorite diner, and sat throughout the day at adjacent desks in the small office we shared. I typed documents for him and occasionally answered the second telephone line when he was on the first. I watched his rhetorical magic in handling drivers in the office and customers over the telephone. He called it his "line of bullshit," but whatever it was, it worked. During the summers, we left for home every night at six. "No bankers' hours for me," he often told others with pride. On Saturdays, we worked from eight until noon, went to lunch, and then saw a movie. Through our times together, I came to know him in ways that were extraordinary for a child. He had revealed himself to me completely, warts and all—or so I thought.

I always assumed that my father had closed the Teamsters chapter of his life when he stopped driving a tractor-trailer rig for a living. I also believed he had told me all the essential elements of the union story that led to his involuntary change of occupation. Dad regarded himself as an ordinary guy, just a trucker who tried to rid his local of what he saw as the corrupt leadership of its secretary-treasurer. In doing so, he hoped to make the Teamsters better for the rank-and-file members and their families. One man in particular, International Brotherhood of Teamsters vice president Gordon Conklin, initially urged him on. Another, *Minneapolis Morning Tribune* labor reporter Sam Romer, promised to keep his struggle in the public eye. Countless fellow workers pledged their loyal support for his cause.

Then came the extraordinary part. Only after it was too late to turn back did he realize that he had crossed swords with one of the world's most powerful men, James Riddle Hoffa—a man known everywhere simply as Jimmy. As the local insurgency succeeded, Hoffa himself

visited Minneapolis for a private meeting in a downtown hotel room where he told my father to stop his crusade.

For some reason, Dad refused.

My father's coalition of enthusiastic supporters abandoned him, and, sure enough, his collision with Hoffa was almost lethal. But he had moved on long ago—or had he? However unambiguously he had finally left Hoffa's Teamsters in 1961, it was becoming clear to me that the Teamsters had never completely left him. I needed to understand more fully than I had—and perhaps more fully than Dad himself had—the story of his early years leading to the union battle that remained with him to the end. Something about that struggle had made it a defining event—perhaps *the* defining event—of his life. I also wanted to consider the period from 1959 to 1961 from Hoffa's perspective, so I might gain some insight into his reasons for caring so much about a lowly over-the-road driver's effort to clean up Minneapolis Local 544.

My task became obvious: I had to write this book. There was a message in the collection of artifacts in my father's treasure chest. If anyone in the world could discern the meaning of his final communication to the living, I could. There were no other candidates; my father had known it and now I knew it. The box had been opened, and my search for the message began.

ONE

THE EARLY YEARS

1

Flashpoint

My father was on television only once in his life. I was five years old and I still remember it, although I didn't know at the time what had put him on the evening news. As I thought about that episode forty years later, I realized that it must have been related to his "union fight," as everyone in our family would forever call it. Trying to imagine what led to Dad's television appearance, I recalled the folder of papers he'd handed me about ten years before his death.

"These might interest you some day," he said as I took the materials without comment. Because I thought he had already told me the story they contained, I didn't bother to read them. Now that he was gone, I was desperate to find the collection. I hoped that I'd placed it where I kept most of my life's treasures: in my bottom dresser drawer.

Underneath a potpourri of my own mementos, there it was. As I paged through his seventy-six-page collection of "union fight" materials, I knew immediately that he had given me a head start on what would become my final project with him. He had assembled articles from the *Minneapolis Morning Tribune, Minneapolis Star, St. Paul Dispatch,* and *St. Paul Pioneer Press* as they were published from 1959 to 1961; I was surprised to see that some had appeared on the front page. Here, too, were the formal charges he had filed against Fred Snyder and others at Local 544, several letters to Jimmy Hoffa (along with Hoffa's terse replies), and his handwritten notes on typed memoranda documenting his crusade.

Unable to avoid the tendencies I had developed over two decades as a trial lawyer, I ordered the papers chronologically and read them carefully. Then I read them again. I grabbed a yellow legal pad and wrote an outline of the events, knowing I would add more as my project continued. The exercise made the subject and timing of his 1959 television appearance much clearer to me.

My father had organized an insurgency in what was, I soon learned, one of the largest and historically most controversial Team-

sters strongholds in the country. He recruited a slate of candidates to run against the three incumbent trustees who, along with the local's four elected officers, comprised Minneapolis Local 544's governing board. The focus of his attack was the local's top officer, secretary-treasurer Fred Snyder; even the newspapers called him "Fritz." One of the articles included a photograph of him: a middle-aged man with thinning black hair, thick lips, and a rough countenance. He looked like someone who could summon a smile only with great effort.

The trustees were supposed to oversee Snyder and his fellow officers, but my father didn't think that was happening. As long as the

Fritz Snyder, 1961

trustees were Snyder loyalists, he retained wide discretion to run the local and spend its money. Too much discretion, perhaps: my father had privately documented Snyder's supposed misuse of about $2,000 in union funds. As Christmas 1959 approached, my father prevailed against odds that had seemed insurmountable only six weeks earlier when he had first pitted his slate of "Rank-and-File Group" trustees against Snyder's. He thought that deposing the Snyder trustees would create huge problems for Local 544's secretary-treasurer. He also believed that he had secret help from two important people: *Minneapolis Morning Tribune* labor reporter Sam Romer and International

Teamsters vice president Gordon Conklin of St. Paul.

My father was right about the problems his reform effort would create for Snyder, but it eventually created even bigger problems for himself. In any other city, Hoffa would not have cared about any special scrutiny given to a local leader's use of union dues because he considered most such men expendable. But this was Minneapolis, where Hoffa had secrets known to neither Fritz Snyder nor Jim Harper. When it was all over, my father apparently thought his seventy-six-page collection of materials constituted the entire story of his entanglement with Snyder and, ultimately, Hoffa. But slowly it became clear to me that he was wrong in ways I had not remotely expected and he would never know. My father's saga was bound up with some little-known history about Hoffa himself, an untold story of the union leader's pervasive connection to my hometown of Minneapolis, and a

tale of personal betrayal. At another level, the saga also reflected my dad's search for personal redemption. But I had not yet discovered any of those truths when I studied his materials for the first time. I was simply trying to reconstruct the chronology of events from 1959 to 1961. His television appearance was a key moment in that period.

After his candidates won all three trustee elections on December 22, 1959, my father became a celebrity. He fielded questions from media representatives who were anxious to hear his insights as the architect of the successful rebellion. Among them was a Minneapolis television newscaster. When the program aired, I watched with my mother and three younger siblings on the black-and-white set in our rented two-story home in South Minneapolis. As Mom and I reconstructed the episode from our memories more than four decades later, we both recalled the professionalism with which he had presented himself. The reporter introduced the segment:

"Over-the-road driver Jim Harper is the leader of a dissident faction at Minneapolis Teamsters Local 544. The insurgents call themselves the Rank-and-File Group. The local itself has over 3,000 members and is one of the largest Teamsters locals in the country. Harper's group backed three challengers in a hotly contested trustees' election. The three incumbents were supported by Local 544 secretary-treasurer Fritz Snyder. Ironically, Snyder ousted his predecessor, Sid Brennan, about a year ago in a similarly heated battle for the top spot in the local. In a stunning upset, all three of Harper's Rank-and-File trustee candidates defeated Snyder's incumbents. We're here to find out what this means for the future of Local 544. Jim, this is a big victory for your Rank-and-File Group, isn't it?"

"It's a victory for all rank-and-file members of Local 544," he responded. "We wanted fair and honest elections. That's what we got and now you see the results." According to my mother, Dad had mastered a way to speak so people couldn't see his missing upper teeth. Only months earlier, an incompetent dentist had removed all of them, and my father didn't have the time, money, or desire to order dentures.

"What's next?" the reporter continued.

"We want what General President Hoffa wants for all Teamsters. We want our union rights to be respected. We want an independent audit of the books to make sure members' dues are going where they're supposed to go. We want honest leadership for Local 544, just

as President Hoffa wants a clean, strong, honest, and democratic union for all of us."

"Jim, how did you wind up in this position—challenging the top officer at Local 544?"

The answer to that question was a longer story than my father could have told on a news segment. Indeed, it would become the central question of my research. Even though my dad was only thirty-one years old at the time, I knew as I began this project that he had already experienced more defeats than most men endured in a lifetime. What I had underestimated were the depths to which he had previously descended and the importance of the "union fight" in his effort to claw himself out of his own personal abyss.

2

The Sins of the Father

I decided on a straightforward approach. I wanted to understand how my father's life had developed to the place where he found himself in December 1959. I would then approach Hoffa's life in the same manner. My goal was to learn what had led each man to the precise moment their lives intersected, and then to follow them for the ensuing eighteen months of their entanglement over Minneapolis Local 544. Both men's behavior during these seemingly minor events seemed irrational to me, and I hoped to find the reasons for it. When I began the project, I had no idea if the resulting story would interest anyone other than me, but that was enough.

That folder of "union fight" materials framed the focal period of my father's battle with Hoffa. He had thought those papers told the complete story, but I was not so sure. I also wanted to trace the story's roots much earlier than 1959, so I could understand the overreactions on both sides of the controversy. Why did an inconsequential Minnesota insurgency eventually get Hoffa's personal attention? Why did Jim Harper press ahead after Hoffa personally told him to stop? Why did he persist in challenging the world's most powerful labor leader over matters that now seemed almost trivial? After all, his claims that Snyder misused union monies involved only about $2,000. For the answers to some of those questions, I began with a reconsideration of my father's early life; that meant taking a close look at his parents.

Fortunately, I had been an attentive and inquisitive child. I already knew quite a bit about Grandpa and Grandma Harper because I had also benefited from an open, close, and loving relationship with both of them. My grandfather, James Rhodes Harper, or "Jim Sr.," had given my sisters, cousins, and me weekly violin lessons in our homes. He and I also played chess before, after, and sometimes during those Sunday afternoon sessions. He never spoke much, but as we sat in silence and studied the board, I discovered that you could learn quite a bit about a person when few words were exchanged. His wife, Alice,

was the opposite; there was no quieting her. We shared interests in coin collecting and Scrabble. She and I also enjoyed watching old movies on the color television that we acquired in 1967.

I had always known that both of Dad's parents were highly intelligent and that Jim Sr. was a musical genius, but some things never added up. The simplistic explanation that "Grandpa is an alcoholic and it ruined his life" was insufficient to explain a man who was a series of confusing contradictions: he had never graduated from high school and now cleaned rugs for a living, but he spoke three languages fluently and could make a violin sing. He also pulled his own cavity-ridden teeth with a pliers. Alice, too, was proficient in multiple languages including French, Spanish, and German. She had a college degree, and it always seemed strange to me that a woman of her abilities spent most of her working career at the University of Minnesota's campus information desk. One of her favorite pastimes was taking periodic trips to the bank, where she would ask a teller to update her passbook savings account and post the latest accrued interest on her meager funds. As a teenager, I explained that she received interest every month regardless of whether it was typed into her little book. She didn't believe me.

Somewhere in their experiences, I now hoped to find insight into what I knew to have been my father's profoundly troubled early life, as he himself had described it to me. I turned to a large box containing Alice's photo albums. Until I had intervened shortly after Dad's death, my mother had planned to discard the carton as part of her effort to move on. I opened the first album to find photographs and old newspaper clippings in no particular order. Items from different decades shared the same page. Photographs had been cut—sculpted would be a better word—and collaged with others. It was as if Alice had dissected her entire life, then put it back together in a way that pleased her. I soon discovered that the resulting mosaic bore little relationship to the reality she, Jim Sr., and their son had experienced together. As I returned to my lawyerly penchant for reordering materials chronologically and searched my own memory, pieces of my father's puzzling life fell into place.

As young and immature parents, Alice and Jim shaped my father's early years, mostly for the worse because they had not overcome their own difficulties. My grandfather was the product of an illicit affair. His

mother, Harrie Brown, was thirty-four at the time; his father, Harrie's next-door neighbor Louis Harper, was fifty-two. Both were married with children. Even after my grandfather's birth in 1905, his biological parents tried to keep their secret. The baby was named Harold after his strong-willed mother, and of course he carried the surname of her lawful husband, Chester Brown. As a young boy, he didn't know the truth because he lived in the Brown home where all of the children believed they shared the same parents. Eventually, both families fractured, and the boy attended his actual parents' wedding when he was eight years old. He was also given a new name: James Rhodes Harper. But by the time he was twelve, his real parents, too, were divorced. It left him without any meaningful adult male influence and tethered him to a tenuous emotional post in his mother, who was a faith healer.

Jim retreated into music. His genius included a "perfect musician's ear," which meant, he later told me, that he heard inside his head every note as it was supposed to sound when properly played in heaven. It also meant an involuntary grimace would cross his face whenever I failed to hit a note in the violin lessons he gave me decades later.

As a youth he mastered new instruments without instruction and within days of picking them up: clarinet, saxophone, drums. His favorite was also the most difficult—the violin. For it, he had teachers. Throughout his teenage years he trained with illustrious professionals; among them were current or former first violinists from the symphony orchestras of Prague, Chicago, Los Angeles, and Minneapolis. During my own lessons, I often saw my grandfather's profound sensitivity emerge when his hands touched the violin. With a fervor that somehow made the instrument an extension of his soul, he could make it sing, weep, or squeal with delight. He usually made it cry.

The newspaper clippings in Alice's albums confirmed what my father had told me. By the time Jim Sr. was twenty-one, his mentors had concluded that their prodigy was ready to tour Europe with his violin. He would polish his art under the tutelage of the world's most distinguished masters. He was on his way to classical musical stardom, until he derailed that overseas trip and the dream that went with it. The cause? A woman: Alice.

My father first heard the story when he was ten years old; he told me when I was about the same age. In Jim Sr.'s view, his dreams of greatness vanished when Alice tricked him into marriage. She was from the small rural town of Blue Earth, Minnesota, and was brilliant,

although neither her husband nor her son would ever so regard her. Only as an adult did Dad learn—as Alice one day told me—that Columbia University had offered her a full scholarship. For any woman in 1923, this was the opportunity of a lifetime, but it was more than she could handle. After the long train ride from Minneapolis to New York, she arrived at Grand Central Station, gathered her bags, climbed the station stairs, looked at the crowd outside, walked back down the stairs, and rode the next train back to Minneapolis.

Meanwhile, the largest Minneapolis radio station was broadcasting Jim Sr.'s violin recitals. He had also fallen in love, but not with Alice—yet. As he later recounted the story to his son, who in turn told it to me, Alice pursued him relentlessly for years. They had first met at a northern Minnesota resort where he was performing at the age of nineteen; she was a year younger. As he described it, when he and his supposed true love had a falling-out three years later, Alice took advantage of the situation, seduced him in a weak moment, and became pregnant. As I now reflected on this version of the story, it seemed to me that Alice could not have been the villain her husband and son described to me. I also knew my grandfather to be far from innocent or naïve when it came to members of the opposite sex. Perhaps their own retellings of the story ultimately convinced them it was true.

My grandparents were married on November 15, 1927, four months after Alice had graduated from the University of Minnesota. My father first heard the story behind his birth when he was ten. Even then, he told me, he was aware of the usual nine-month duration of a woman's pregnancy, and of course he knew his own birthday. He found the puzzle regrettably easy to solve: fewer than eight months after my grandparents' wedding ceremony, my father, James Henry Harper, entered the world on July 11, 1928. Jim Sr. was forced to cancel his previously planned European trip for advanced violin study; soon the Great Depression intervened to prevent it from ever being rescheduled. My dad concluded that his very existence had killed his father's professional musical aspirations.

Aware of his unwanted origins, my father found special misery in listening to his dad play the violin. The instrument always sounded as if it were sobbing. It made him want to weep as well, but Jim Sr.'s command eliminated that option: "Harper men do not cry after the age of ten." My dad later told me the same thing during one of my crying

episodes at age eleven, which meant I'd already blown that deadline. Over time Dad expanded the rule to encompass all emotional displays. Surely it helped shape his distorted definition of manhood.

My father sometimes wondered what tragedy might lay behind the birth of his sister, Ruth, in 1931. She was born during the family's three-year stint in Chicago, where the matriarch Harrie had moved after marrying yet again, this time to a wealthy real estate speculator. The young violinist, Jim Sr., now a new father, chauffeured his stepfather's Lincoln limousine while still trying unsuccessfully to revive his musical career. As an early metaphor for his son's proximity to the dark side of life, the Lincoln was housed at 2122 North Clark Street on February 14, 1929—the day Al Capone tried to eliminate Bugs Moran and his gang in that very garage. The shootout would become known as the St. Valentine's Day Massacre.

After the effects of the continuing economic collapse wiped away the Lincoln and the wealth accompanying it, the family returned to Minnesota. They arrived in time for the 1934 Minneapolis Teamsters strikes led by Socialist Workers Party member Farrell Dobbs. Jim Jr. turned six during the summer that city business owners armed themselves with private security forces. The hired guns engaged in violent and deadly confrontations with workers who fought at the vanguard of the burgeoning worldwide labor movement; among them were twenty-three-year-old Fritz Snyder and his brother. Proprietors believed they were locked in a death struggle for the very survival of capitalism; workers sought only a living wage and humane working conditions.

As death and injury in the streets escalated, governor Floyd B. Olson declared martial law and called out the Minnesota National Guard to restore order. The Teamsters eventually gained recognition as the organization with which owners had to deal when setting their employees' wages. The events made Dobbs a national celebrity in the Teamsters union. A few years later, young Jimmy Hoffa joined him in Minneapolis—a pivotal step in the Detroit union leader's career.

3

Minneapolis Launches Hoffa's Career

Jimmy Hoffa was twenty-four when he walked the streets of Minneapolis in 1937. The aftermath of the successful 1934 labor strikes had generated unprecedented worker interest in Farrell Dobbs's fledgling local. The International Teamsters' general president had sent Hoffa there to help recruit over-the-road truck drivers, the constituency that was Dobbs's only area of labor-organizing weakness. As young as he was, Hoffa had already proven himself among the best at that particular task, undoubtedly as a consequence of early years that were at least as difficult as my dad's.

Hoffa was born on Valentine's Day 1913 in a southern Indiana coal town. His father died when Jimmy was seven. Two years later his mother moved the family to Detroit, where the growing automobile industry held improved prospects for work. Hoffa's formal schooling ended somewhere around the ninth grade. He lied about his age and found a job working the dock for Kroger Grocery and Baking Company when he was fifteen. He was and would remain only five foot five, but powerfully strong.

Hoffa's charismatic leadership qualities and instinct for the jugular became evident when he helped lead his first labor walkout at the age of eighteen. As the Great Depression deepened and working conditions worsened, he and his fellow dockworkers took action: one day they simply refused to unload trucks filled with fresh strawberries. Rather than risk spoilage, management acceded to their demands within an hour. Hoffa and his fellow strike leaders received a local charter from the American Federation of Labor, and he became vice president of the new single-company union local. While devoting the daylight hours to his new union, Hoffa continued to work nights at Kroger. After he threw a crate in the direction of his supervisor, Hoffa quit before he could be fired. He then became a full-time organizer for an affiliate of the International Brotherhood of Teamsters.

Hoffa's wages came from the dues that his new recruits paid to the

union. He searched for over-the-road drivers, listened to their concerns, and talked their language. A sign he posted in his union hall said it all: "If it moves, sign it up." When he urged men to join the Teamsters because it would help them, they believed it—because Hoffa himself believed it. They identified with him because he had the same physical strength, rough exterior, and down-to-earth demeanor they possessed. Throughout his life, most people assumed incorrectly that Hoffa had been an over-the-road driver himself. It didn't matter that he had never driven a truck; he generated respect and loyalty from workingmen throughout Michigan.

Minneapolis would soon propel Hoffa into the Teamsters' national spotlight. The union's general president, Dan Tobin, wanted someone to assist organizer Farrell Dobbs there—someone who would also keep an eye on Dobbs as he gained power throughout the Midwest. A Detroit labor leader recommended young Hoffa, who had recently married. He had met Josephine Poszywak, his new wife, in the spring of 1936 while she was walking an International Laundry Workers picket line in Detroit. In September a justice of the peace performed their marriage ceremony in Bowling Green, Ohio. The newlyweds' honeymoon was brief because Hoffa wanted to get back to work on the following Monday. Shortly thereafter, he accepted the fateful assignment in Minnesota that would determine the course of his life—and my father's.

Hoffa thought socialists and "commies" like Minneapolis's Dobbs were "screwballs," but he acknowledged Dobbs's innovative approach, one that was making him one of the most successful labor organizers in history. Dobbs's idea was to take a purely local craft union—the Teamsters' name derived from their original jobs driving horse-drawn wagon teams—and add workers from all industries in all cities. Over-the-road drivers were the critical links among such potential new union members from across the country. Hoffa had the rapport with these men that Dobbs lacked. He went to Minneapolis and helped Dobbs establish what was to become the Central States Drivers Council, which represented most over-the-road Teamsters in twelve midwestern states.

After Hoffa left Minnesota in 1938, friction intensified between Dobbs and International Teamsters general president Tobin. Dobbs's Local 544 became one of the country's largest, and its independent

power became a threat to the International leadership. By 1940, Dobbs concluded that his members would fare better if they separated from the larger Teamsters organization. At about the same time that the general executive board voted to place the local under International trusteeship and, therefore, under the International's control, Dobbs and his colleagues in Minneapolis voted to secede the local from the larger union.

At that point, one of the Teamsters' competitor unions, the Congress of Industrial Organizations, entered the fray. Organizer Denny Lewis sent a telegram inviting Dobbs to move Local 544 into the CIO, which was run by his flamboyant brother, John L. Lewis. The Lewis raid infuriated Tobin, who dispatched Hoffa back to Minneapolis. After overcoming his initial reluctance to undermine Dobbs, Hoffa soon found himself playing a central role at one of the largest Teamsters locals in the country. As he eliminated socialist domination of the local and gained control in Minnesota, Hoffa earned the confidence of the International Teamsters' leadership while significantly supplementing his Detroit power base.

There was little doubt about Hoffa's success on his return mission to Minneapolis. He had his own skills, the full backing of the nation's top Teamsters, and the help of Tobin's friend, Franklin D. Roosevelt. By the time Hoffa left Minneapolis again in 1941, he had destroyed Dobbs, who, along with his socialist colleagues, was imprisoned for conspiring to overthrow the U.S. government in the first civilian incarcerations under the Smith Act of 1940. At a dinner honoring Tobin a few years later, Roosevelt announced his intention to seek a fourth presidential term. Hoffa would long remember how an ostensibly neutral federal government could quietly take sides in what the public might perceive to be a wholly private matter.

With his victory in Minneapolis, Hoffa became a vice president and negotiating chairman of the Central States Drivers Council he had helped to establish. From his Detroit base, he coordinated the actions of Teamsters in the twelve states under his jurisdiction, enabling them to speak with a single and more powerful voice. James Riddle Hoffa was on his way to the pinnacle of America's labor movement—thanks to Minneapolis.

4

Jim Harper's Story Unfolds—And Unravels

The first message from my father's box seemed to be emerging from his own father's thwarted musical ambitions. Perhaps even more powerful than a dream is the aftermath of its loss. Unfortunately, in my grandfather's case the resulting wake swallowed his son, too.

The return of my dad's family to Minneapolis shortly before Hoffa arrived there didn't change the dominant themes of the household. For as long as my father could remember, drinking away the family's limited income had been part of his own father's daily routine. He was rarely home for dinner and usually staggered through the front door during the early morning hours, at which point Alice would "pick a fight" with him—at least that was how my dad described it later. He and his little sister, Ruth, heard it all. If they felt particularly brave, they could actually peer through the steel grate in their upstairs bedroom floor to observe what was happening in the living room below.

"Why doesn't she just leave him alone?" he wondered, as he later described his reaction to the verbal warfare between my grandparents. "I won't do this to my kids," he thought, assuming he would gain the power over his life as an adult that was eluding him as a child. Through it all, he kept everything buried deep inside because that was what Harper men did.

Alice had no idea that her behavior worsened her son's growing emotional crisis, but he made that clear to me in our later conversations: "When I was little, she wouldn't let me cut my curly hair, so it grew long. She made me wear hand-me-down knickers from my rich nephews. Between the hair and the goddamned knickers, I looked like a damn girl." Jim Sr. was often out at night, and Alice sometimes left her two young children home alone while she went to see a movie: "She thought we were asleep, but we weren't. So my job from a very young age was to be ready to keep my sister calm and defend our home against any intruders."

He often related another incident that occurred when he was six years old: "My mother locked me out of the house because she didn't want my dirty shoes leaving tracks on her newly scrubbed floors. When I couldn't get inside, I tried to cross the street and was hit by a car. I can still see the scared look on the face of the poor bastard who hit me, but I was okay." Well, sort of—forever after, he detested the sound of a honking horn.

Alcoholism continued to fuel Jim Sr.'s depression, and the family languished with the world in continuing economic crisis. Jim Jr. worked after school in the local hardware store to earn enough money to replace his knickers with long pants. Jim Sr. worked a full-time day job and accompanied a Minneapolis vaudeville show at night, earning a grand total of less than thirty-five dollars for a sixty-hour workweek. As the 1930s ended, he tried to keep his musical career going, but life was not meaningful for him. Alcohol expanded to fill the void. Shortly before his son's thirteenth birthday, Jim Sr. left home. No one knew where he was going or if he would return. Jim Jr. was crushed; something inside him silently snapped.

"I couldn't understand why he would leave," he later told me. "I thought maybe I should've done something different so he hadn't gone, but I couldn't for the life of me figure out what it was. Then I got angry. I decided that if my old man didn't care enough about me to stick around, why should I care about him or myself?"

Even so, he was concerned that his father's departure was the culmination of his own failures as a son, coupled with his mother's constant nagging. He thought that the two of them had driven his father away forever. He also learned by example: when things got bad, running away might be the answer.

Jim Sr. surfaced in Seattle, where he worked for several months at various manual labor jobs, including the night shift at a lumber mill. Meanwhile, young Jim found a job in a neighborhood grocery store. Although he was only fourteen, wartime conscription created opportunities normally reserved for older boys, and he used the store owner's small truck to make home deliveries. It was his first driving experience, and he loved it. He controlled the vehicle, escaped from the travails of his life, and achieved the solace eluding him everywhere else. He long remembered these feelings and the place—alone behind the wheel of a truck—where he had first known them.

When Jim Sr. ran out of money after about a year, he sent Alice a

simple telegram that captured the essence of their relationship. I found it in one of her albums: "Quit mill. Will return when you send money." She complied, he returned to Minneapolis, and his downward alcoholic spiral continued.

My dad later described to me his futile attempts to gain his father's approval: "When he went to a bar, I was at his side and took sips from his beer whenever he'd let me. When he visited his girlfriend, I went along. When your grandma and I took the streetcar past the apartment where that girlfriend lived, my job was to keep your grandma busy so she wouldn't notice our car parked outside." When he described these scenes from his youth, it was always clear to me that he loved his father, but it was equally clear that he hated his habits. He could not reconcile his conflicting emotions and feared sharing them with anyone.

So Jim Jr. looked outside his immediate family for reaffirmation. Somehow, somewhere, life had to be better than this. The pursuit of his dreams would take him to places he could never have imagined, even in his worst nightmares.

Dad had told me two different stories about the demise of his first marriage. When I was thirteen, he initially explained that his first wife was overly demanding and he could not maintain the lifestyle to which she was accustomed. When I was older, he provided a much different version, placing the blame for the failed relationship solely and squarely on himself. I think the truth probably lies somewhere in between, but closer to the latter formulation. Either way, his rendition of the essential facts never changed.

The girl was a year behind him in high school and from the other side of the economic tracks. Her father owned the neighborhood drugstore, and Jim Jr. truly believed she was out of his league. To his great surprise, he won her over and, at last, found the love his own parents had not provided. Without warning, his emotional world soon collapsed again. Shortly after his high school graduation in 1946, he was shown a letter his girlfriend had written, suggesting that his devotion was unrequited. Unable to deal with yet another rejection from someone he loved, he resorted to his father's time-tested remedy: he got drunk. The next day he enlisted in the army. A few days later he learned that he had misinterpreted his girlfriend's note. Unfortunately, Uncle Sam didn't care that Jim Jr.'s recruitment had resulted

from a mistake compounded by an adolescent overreaction and topped with a hangover.

He reported to Fort Benning, Georgia, for basic training and decided to make the best of a bad situation. He hoped that in the army he could finally prove his worth to his girlfriend, his father, and himself. At every turn, he pushed himself as he sought out the most difficult obstacles and then tried to overcome them. For an eighteen-year-old enlisted man who was afraid of heights, only one path seemed obvious to him: he would become a paratrooper, one of the elite of the armed forces whose heroic feats during World War II were already legendary. So in early 1947, it was off to the 82nd Airborne at Fort Bragg, North Carolina, and paratrooper school, for which he easily qualified. If he became a hero, it would make up for everything.

Jim Harper upon entering the army in 1946

On the day he was supposed to take his final jump, he awoke with a searing pain in his left ear. He naïvely assumed that a short trip to the infirmary would yield medicine to get him through the final requirement for his paratrooper wings. What he got instead was a written directive from the base physician: "Grounded until further notice."

"I was supposed to take that slip of paper to the co," he proudly told me years later. "Instead, on the way back to the barracks, I ripped it up and threw it away. I was going make my final jump with my squadron, period. I did, but my eardrum burst as a result. That gave me a problem. If I'd gone back to the infirmary with my bleeding ear, I thought for sure they'd court-martial me and send me to Leavenworth for disobeying the grounding order. So I kept stuffing cotton in my ear until it stopped bleeding. No big deal." But for the rest of his life he could hear almost nothing with his left ear.

The army provided him a forum for success. After earning his wings, he became an instructor at Fort Bragg's paratrooper school. As a private first class, he trained not only enlisted personnel but also senior officers attending his classes to learn the new art of jumping from airplanes. Among his students for one training session was a brigadier general. Fully aware of his rank, the general periodically interrupted the class with witty remarks. The other students were amused; Jim Jr., the teacher, was not. After warning the recalcitrant senior officer, he walked directly to the general, stood in front of him, nose to nose, and without equivocation said, "Sir, drop and give me twenty, now, sir."

The general was startled, but he did the twenty pushups as ordered. The class of junior officers and enlisted men watched in stunned silence. Jim assumed he was in trouble when a week later he received a note summoning him to the general's office. He arrived to hear the general admit to his own mistake: he had been out of line in disrupting the class. In a story my father loved to tell, the superior officer commended him for challenging misguided authority:

"The general told me he could count on one hand—make that one finger—the number of privates who would have the guts to tell a general to drop and give him twenty. I was the one. Then he said, 'Private Harper, I want to send you to officers' candidate school.' He said I was officer material. He said I was top officer material! I learned an important lesson from this episode. Stand up for what is

right, even when the odds are against you. Character and courage will be rewarded."

As he considered his unexpected opportunity, the world seemed to turn against him once again. To attend his girlfriend's high school prom, he drove nonstop from Fort Bragg to Minneapolis on a weekend pass, attended the dance, and then drove nonstop back again. Chicago traffic delayed his return trip and he reported to duty several hours late. The blemish on his record eliminated his chances for the officer corps; in a single stroke, he had converted his success into failure. He viewed it as a reversion to his fundamental and immutable form. He consoled himself with beer—and alcohol tightened its cruel grip on his life.

At least he still had his girlfriend. By the time he left the army in 1948, they were married, having secretly exchanged vows in a civil ceremony near Fort Bragg. After his discharge, her parents held a large formal wedding in a Minneapolis Catholic church. He tried to forget his prior defeats and move forward with his new wife. He enrolled as a part-time student at the University of Minnesota, where he hoped eventually to earn a journalism degree. He dreamed of entering the emerging field of television broadcasting. With his handsome appearance, extraordinary intelligence, and remarkable speaking skills, it was a dream well within his reach.

While attending classes, he worked part-time jobs that didn't pay a living wage. As the marriage faltered, he thought that buying his wife expensive things might help. He passed a bad check to supplement his income and immediately panicked. Fearing shame would follow the discovery of his deed, he drove his spouse to her regular morning bus stop and then fled town. The final decree of dissolution and annulment of the marriage was entered in April 1950.

He often told me that he embodied the "Harper jinx." He must have developed that view from these early episodes in his life, when one failure led inevitably to the next. Life seemed hopeless even though he was only twenty-one years old. Then things got even worse.

5

Angola

Cast adrift on emotional seas that became rougher as he got older, young Jim Harper careened toward disaster. He would blame only himself for his failures, but that judgment was far too harsh. Everyone has a background story that helps explain who and what they are; my father never fully understood his own. Perhaps none of us does. And perhaps that was the next message from his box.

He talked to me often about what he called the mistakes of his youth, hoping I would avoid them. The worst of his errors came with unexpected consequences that almost killed him. After he deserted his wife and left Minneapolis, he fell into a deep depression. He sold his car for beer money and hitched rides with truckers across the country. When he found a town of interest along the way, he would stick around and do odd jobs for a time. Once he had earned enough pocket money to move on, he usually did. Alcohol remained his escape, just as it had been and continued to be for his own father.

As he later described it to me, his ritual was always the same: "I sought out the roughest area of town. I found the roughest bar and then went inside to see if I could get someone else to start a fight." As I heard these stories, it always seemed to me that he had some kind of death wish causing him to take risks that were either remarkably stupid or uncommonly courageous, depending upon the situation. During his youth, stupidity dominated.

To supplement his income, he passed more bad checks. By the time he reached Louisiana, he'd concocted a more complicated scheme, one that ultimately landed him in jail for a year. He went into various flower shops with the same routine.

"I'd tell the shop owner that I wanted to send some flowers to my mother for her birthday," he recounted, undoubtedly flashing the same broad grin that he had used at the time. "'Sure,' the owner would say. 'What a fine son you are. Let's see what we can find.' Then after spending several minutes trying to decide what to send, I'd ask *him,* 'Which

one do *you* think is best?' After the owner made the final selection, he'd ask me for a delivery address. I'd make up a name and destination while he filled out the forms."

Whenever he told this story, his eyes always twinkled when he described what happened next: "'How much do I owe you?' I'd ask. Then I'd ask if a personal check was okay, even though I knew there was no money in my account. Hell, I wasn't even using my real name on the checks. As I filled out the worthless check, I'd look surprised as I opened my wallet and told him I didn't have enough cash for bus fare. Then came the best part. I'd ask *v-e-r-r-y p-o-l-i-t-e-l-y* if I could I write a check for five dollars more than the price of the flowers. He'd say yes and . . . bingo!"

The scam was accomplished and he would exit the store five dollars wealthier than when he had entered. He used the same line—asking permission to write a check for a little more than the amount he owed—to pay for hotel rooms across the South. Unfortunately, his scheme worked too well and he ran his program for too long. He failed to keep track of the shops he had previously "hit." On his second trip to one of his earlier victims in Baton Rouge, he was recognized and arrested. Oddly enough for a man prone to self-destructive confrontation, he put up no resistance as the machinery of law enforcement had its way with him. He was twenty-two years old, terrified, and embarrassed. He should have called for help, but he didn't.

His offense of passing a few bad checks totaling less than a hundred dollars would have been a misdemeanor punishable by a small fine in his home state, but he was not in Minnesota. With a lawyer, he might have avoided Louisiana's much stricter penalties for the felony conviction looming before him, but he went it alone. The result was his first experience with the dark side of his country's criminal justice system. It occurred during his interrogation in a Baton Rouge police station. "Two cops beat the living daylights out of me," he later told me. "They had a bunch of open cases and wanted me to take the rap for them. After knocking me to the ground, they kicked me in the gut until I threw up blood. But I refused to confess to crimes I hadn't committed."

Life had not prepared him for this. The world was upside down. The cops with their guns and uniforms were actually the bad guys. Was it just Louisiana? he wondered, but he knew the answer had to be no. Who were the good guys? Were there any good guys?

"Except for childhood spankings, even my old man had never hit me," he had often told me. "Sometimes he was mad enough to. I once told him he could hit me if he wanted and I wouldn't hit him back. But he never did."

Without family, friends, or anyone to help or vouch for him, his guilty plea to the crimes he had committed—forgery and defrauding a hotel—resulted in a sentence of three years' probation and a one-way ticket back to Minneapolis. One condition of his probation required him to stay out of taverns. But he was already well on his way into the abyss of alcoholism, and no one nearby helped him out. When his mother heard about his conviction, she formally disowned him and told him so. Although Jim Sr.'s alcoholism and depression now dominated his life, he tried to follow his son's new trail of bad checks in Minneapolis and cover them. Jim Jr.'s drinking worsened; he slept most nights during the fall of 1951 on the flat roof of his parents' back porch. In an unfortunate coincidence, he was drunk one night when his local probation officer joined him at the bar.

"Well, look who's here," Jim Jr. announced. "Let's all toast the man who has the impossible job of trying to keep me straight!" Confronted with this blatant probation violation, the officer had no choice but to take him immediately to the police station. He was processed, jailed, and eventually put on a plane to Louisiana.

The state flag hanging in the East Baton Rouge parish courthouse showed a white pelican feeding its nesting young over the slogan "Union, Justice, & Confidence." Jim saw it as he completed the final leg of his trip on November 9, 1951. "What a joke," he thought. "Justice—Some justice you got in a goddamned state where the cops beat the shit out of a guy until he confesses to crimes he didn't commit. Bullshit." The judge revoked his probation and remanded him to the custody of the Louisiana State Penitentiary at Angola to serve a three-year term. Jim knew nothing about his new home, but he would soon learn things he would spend a lifetime trying to forget.

Until I reviewed more closely his letters to Louisiana governor Earl Long and the state's parole board, I didn't focus on the fact that Angola had been Dad's prison home. In our periodic discussions about his criminal indiscretions, he had always minimized his prison experience, so I had assumed it to be a few months, most of which he served in a special trusty status that kept him away from the general

prison population. After he died, I learned I was wrong, which must have been the way he wanted it.

I researched the history of Angola and, in a remarkable coincidence, found several books about the prison that included photographs and descriptions from the late 1940s and early 1950s. They were staggering. My father had given me only brief glimpses into the horror that his life there must have been; he had given my younger brother, Michael, a few more. Between our recollections and the published materials, I developed a relatively complete understanding of his prison time. The specific buildings that had housed him were demolished long ago, but even with its newer facilities, Angola today remains one of America's most dangerous prisons. Before undertaking this project, I never suspected that as my father entered the facility in 1951, there was not a close second-place finisher for the title of "America's worst prison."

If there was a hell on earth in the United States during the middle of the twentieth century, this was it. The relatively narrow Mississippi River flowed under hundred-foot-high bridges near my father's upper Midwest home, but it had widened into the gigantic "Old Man River" by the time it merged with adjacent lands at sea level in the Tunica Hills of Louisiana. Angola had retained the name of the African country from which its earlier slave inhabitants had come. Where the state's border met the southwest corner of Mississippi, it had grown from its first days as an 8,000-acre cotton plantation, infamous for its brutality, to a massive 18,000-acre prison camp that continued the tradition.

As the Louisiana criminal courts doled out their special brand of justice in 1951, newly sentenced convicts from parishes throughout the state were collected in Baton Rouge. Every Monday, the prison bus took the men north along U.S. Highway 61 for thirty miles until it reached a dirt road that meandered another twenty miles to a dead-end at the final secluded destination—the state's only penitentiary. The entire trip took about two hours.

As his bus left the capital city limits, my father must have found it ironic that he was traveling on the same U.S. Highway 61 and next to the same river that flowed southward from the Minnesota home he wouldn't see for a long time. He probably wondered if the two-lane pavement was called the Great Mississippi River Road in Louisiana as

well. As he rode through small towns, he would have observed pictur-
esque natural surroundings, as bright sunshine and lush vegetation
contrasted sharply with the barren winter beginning to descend upon
his home state. He might have thought the whole experience wouldn't
be as bad as he had feared. After all, he'd survived boot camp at Fort
Benning; how much worse could this be? He would soon learn the answer: a lot worse.

At the end of the road, the bus arrived at the prison entrance. Concrete blocks supporting a curved iron arch held foot-high letters
spelling out STATE PENITENTIARY. To the right was a white brick
guardhouse; above it stood a manned tower. The only other artificial
barrier surrounding the perimeter of the grounds was a series of tall
wood posts webbed with barbed wire, but nature had done all the remaining work necessary to assure confinement. Levees that inmates
had constructed and maintained on three sides of the compound held
the Mississippi River and its strong currents at bay, while a swamp
filled with reptiles blocked any attempt to escape on the fourth. Because of the physical isolation that rendered unauthorized flight unthinkable, it was called the Alcatraz of the South. Unfortunately, it
shared other attributes of that notorious institution.

My father would have expected a traditional prison, like those in
the movies, complete with high brick walls and razor wire along the
top. Louisiana's sprawling complex at Angola was unlike anything he
could have pictured. The two-story concrete administration building
was at least three city blocks long. The segregated prison population
of 2,700—about two-thirds black—was divided into eight camps.
Identified alphabetically, each camp was surrounded by a ten-foot
barbed wire fence and run by camp captains. Administrators and staff
lived in separate houses within the prison's borders but outside the
barbed wire surrounding the camps. The grounds also housed a sugar
mill and a vegetable cannery.

The facility had fallen into disrepair as it went largely ignored and
without funding through governor Huey Long's corrupt administration during the early years of the Great Depression. Long had told taxpayers that Angola was draining a million dollars yearly from the
state's treasury but that the labor of its captives in the sugar cane and
vegetable fields should have made it self-sufficient. With those words,
he had established a public attitude about the prison that still prevailed when Jim Harper arrived almost twenty-five years later. Beat-

ings and brutality created a workday running from "can to can't" and brought the institution into marginal profitability. In the 1940s, the state constructed a prison hospital; that was particularly ironic because there was no permanent doctor and only a single nurse. In 1948, Huey's brother Earl Long, now governor, made the Angola superintendent's job a political patronage position to which he appointed a distant relative.

Twenty-five guard towers surrounded the perimeter of the compound. Guards in four of the towers had standing orders to shoot to kill because they surrounded the notorious "red hat" cellblock. That structure was built after an escape attempt in 1933 and named for the red enamel paint on the caps of its residents whose distinctive headgear made them readily identifiable in the fields as troublemakers. It contained thirty cells, each measuring six by three feet and sealed with a solid steel door. Only a single foot-square window slot near the roof allowed ventilation to the outside; the slot was covered by a guard-controlled steel flap. Each red hat cell contained an iron bunk but no mattress. A bucket serving as the prisoner's toilet and basin was emptied every morning of the prior day's accumulations. Meals consisted of the nearby camp E prison mess hall leftovers, dumped into a wheelbarrow and delivered to the red hat occupants.

Although all red hats were regarded as agitators or incorrigibles, some were just inmates the warden didn't like. In theory, their block was a disciplinary area to be used only for punishment. The reality was that any significant prison disturbance resulted in a red hat cell block packed with several inmates to each cell. Twenty years after my father was there, a federal court finally ordered long overdue reforms to the prison because the "obviously deplorable conditions . . . shocked the conscience" in violation of the U.S. Constitution. As a result, the red hat cellblock was converted into a dog kennel.

After "processing" in the massive administration building and receiving a new black-and-white wardrobe, each new inmate was eventually escorted to his living quarters. On the ground floor of most two-story camp buildings were the mess area, kitchen, and showers. The second floor consisted of a barracks-style dormitory with wood planking. For each camp, all three to four hundred prisoners lived and slept together in a single common area filled with endless rows of wooden double and triple bunk beds whose mattresses were only three inches

thick. The camps were racially segregated but did not distinguish convicts based upon their offenses. Petty thieves shared accommodations with rapists and murderers.

The lavatory toilets contained no partitions or doors; they operated with a pull chain hanging from the water receptacle overhead. Even in 1951, they appeared to be fifty years old. The inmates got clean clothes once a week. Most meals consisted of corn bread and vegetables; prison guards usually kept the meat.

From his first day at Angola, my father's overriding anxiety would have been sexual assault. His handsome and youthful appearance would have marked him as a "pretty boy," destined for life as some other inmate's companion. He must have searched for a way to avoid becoming either a victim of that violence or a participant in it—and quickly. As he later described that part of his prison life to me, he got lucky, relatively speaking.

"The child molesters were at the lowest rung of the ladder," he said in outlining the prison's social hierarchy. "Even cons knew that you shouldn't mess with innocent little kids." He always spoke with disgust about the terrible things that adults did to children. "Con artists like me were at the top. We were smarter than the other cons. Hell, I even prepared court papers for other cons to try to get them out of the joint. But there was a special group of cons that no one crossed: the convicted murderers. I had one in my lower bunk."

For some reason that he never understood, this much older man, who was regarded by the general prison population as the father of his camp, took a paternal interest in him. Equally important, his protector made clear to the other prisoners that he was to be left alone. Although the old con's protection had been a start, it was not a complete solution. During this period, my father developed his icy stare.

"I had to convince myself that I was capable of killing the target of my gaze," he told me. "I then projected that anger through my eyes whenever another con approached. It made me look 'crazy mad.' If some con wanted to hurt me, even a con bigger and stronger than me, but believed from the wild look in my eyes that I was willing to die hurting him in return, that con would think twice. He might leave me alone altogether, or he might hesitate long enough to matter. But I had to act as if I had nothing to lose. And to act as if I had nothing to lose, I had to believe it myself—deep in my heart."

Angola Prison in 1951

Angola's main gate

Prison bunks

Angola Prison in 1951

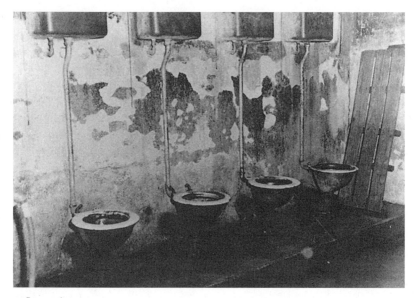

Prison toilets

Prison showers

That must have been easy for him, given the progression of his life to that point.

To complement his special form of method acting, rage also activated a small, irregularly shaped birthmark at the top of his forehead. Usually it wasn't visible, but when he became angry the mark turned bright red. The icy stare and blazing birthmark created a primal early warning system for potential antagonists observant enough to notice. He also put out the word that his icy stare implied: anyone who had designs on him had better plan to be a corpse when the fun was over, because he intended to kill any such attacker. The time, place, and manner of death were undetermined, but he made clear that it would happen. For added insurance, he always slept with one hand clutching a small steel pipe that he kept under his pillow. Only once did he have to threaten its use when a would-be attacker approached: Jim displayed the pipe, the stare, and the birthmark. The attempted assault immediately ended as the inmate turned and walked away.

In addition to physical jeopardy, his surroundings inflicted profound and continuous emotional damage. He didn't tell me about the violent rapes that I now know he must have witnessed. Victimized inmates were chattel to be used, bartered, sold, or even auctioned. The slavery that prevailed at Angola's founding as a cotton plantation more than a century earlier continued in a different form, but still a poisonous one. The guards did nothing to stop it. In fact, those charged with maintaining stability at the prison thought that such outlets for the release of sexual tension helped to encourage a calm environment, especially among the most physically violent inmates.

Jim initially worked in the fields that produced sugar cane and vegetables marketed throughout Louisiana and much of the South. Angola utilized inmate trusty guards, a system the prison's general manager adopted in 1916 to save money on security. About one-fifth of the inmates reached trusty status after a period of good behavior. One of several trusty assignments entailed the armed supervision of other convicts in the fields. Black convicts supervised black worker lines and whites supervised whites. My father had never told me about the warden's standing offer: a six-month sentence reduction went to any inmate trusty guard who shot another inmate during an escape attempt. When that happened, only the word of the trusty shooter stood against that of his victim in determining whether the reward should be given. "Yes, sir, captain" and "No, sir, captain" were the only appro-

priate salutations by which any inmate was permitted to address his keepers. Any departure from the script assured a beating.

About half of the prisoners were "wide-stripers" serving life terms; however, Louisiana law made such inmates eligible for commutation and parole after ten years and six months of good behavior. Even so, the combination of age, prison conditions, and sentence caused many to end their lives in confinement. Some of the dead convicts were buried at Point Look-Out, the prison cemetery on the grounds. But over the years, hundreds more had disappeared from the ranks of the incarcerated than could be counted in that graveyard. The state itself acknowledged a number of prisoners who died of "sunstroke," but that was code for fatal collapse under the weight of an excruciating workload and physical abuse.

My father had always said that he thought most incarcerated offenders in all prisons came from society's poorest ranks. He also believed that the state's attitude toward taking a man's life for capital crimes was unforgivably casual and callous. He must have developed those views at Angola. The prison stored the state's only electric chair. As a designated execution date approached, guards loaded it onto a truck carrying the oak chair's electric generator. They then drove the self-contained instrument of death to the town where the condemned man had committed his offense. In that way, the local citizenry could experience firsthand the state's unique form of retributive justice. In addition to Louisiana's official executioner, the death squad included an inmate electrician, a prison chief electrician, and a camp captain. Angola's portable electric chair performed about 4 percent of the executions in the United States from 1950 to 1954, even though Louisiana held only 1.5 percent of the country's total population. Every convict knew that whenever the fateful switch was flipped, the executioner's final words were always the condemned man's first name, preceded by a one-word salutation: "Goodbye."

The prison was no bargain for the living, either. Brutality was an institutional theme: inmate against inmate; guard against inmate; even inmates selected as trusty guards joined in the action. Beatings were commonplace and gave way to more imaginative pursuits. Guards tied prisoners to posts before administering castor oil to stimulate involuntary bowel movements. To enhance the experience, the torturers wrapped a convict's pants tightly at his ankles so his trousers collected the accumulating body waste.

"No one on the outside could believe what went on in there," my father said to me cryptically long afterwards. I am now sure he could not believe it himself.

Nevertheless, I learned that if anything relating to my father's experience could be so characterized, the timing of his entry into the institution was auspicious. Only nine months before his arrival, thirty-one protesting inmates had used razor blades to sever the Achilles tendons connecting their left calf muscles to their heels. Once those tendons had been cut, running was impossible and walking was extremely difficult. In the public hearings that occurred in the aftermath of this amazing event, a few convicts explained that the incident had less to do with social protest than with survival.

One of the original cutters told an investigating commission that the episode had begun with a camp captain's threat: the warden had ordered the death of eight inmates who had been caught digging a tunnel out of the prison. The captain told the workers that the warden was planning to kill the troublemakers while they were working in the fields "so he can close y'all's records." The targeted inmates thought that if physical disability prevented them from working, then the warden could not so easily and permanently "close their files." By cutting their own Achilles tendons, the prisoners hoped to save their own lives. When word of the first cutters spread, other inmates followed the example and the prison hospital was packed with convicts seeking the attention of the facility's only nurse. The event brought national attention to Angola, including a November 22, 1952, *Collier's* magazine article titled "America's Worst Prison."

In addition to the continuing newspaper and magazine coverage, Jim caught another break at Angola. The most recent of Angola's superintendents had become the first to accept rehabilitation as a goal of incarceration and adopted a new system of evaluating inmates' intelligence and abilities before assigning them to prison jobs. Along with the other new arrivals, my father received a battery of tests. His typing and clerical skills from his army days paid off: after a short time working in the fields, he was given an administrative job in the office.

The lesson of a prison sentence did not deter him from taking reckless and even suicidal risks in pursuit of affirmation and as a distraction from his horrifying environs. Given his strong performance and good behavior generally, he became a trusty in record time. His posi-

tion gained him relative freedom within the prison environment—more freedom than was good for him, in fact. While working in the office, he became acquainted with the wife of an administrator. She regularly visited the building and noticed the unusually handsome young inmate with striking blue eyes set in prominent cheekbones. He sometimes flashed her a wink to accompany his seductive grin. The charm that had ultimately landed him in jail remained, and he took every opportunity to flatter the woman who was more than twenty years his senior. Searching for some aspect of her appearance that would lend itself to favorable comment, he resorted to the line he'd seen his own father use with consistent success: "You have the most beautiful eyes I've ever seen."

Eventually, the result was an ongoing sexual affair with her. Because a trusty was not confined to the fences of his camp, he pursued the relationship at her home on the prison grounds. He took special satisfaction in the irony of his dangerous liaisons: he was having sex with the wife of a man who kept him incarcerated. If he had been discovered, he surely would have died in the red hat cell block or as the victim of an imaginary escape attempt. If he understood the risks, he didn't care. At the time of this particular youthful insanity, death may have seemed like an attractive alternative for him.

He celebrated only one birthday in prison: his twenty-fourth. In my later research, I learned that Louisiana made July 11, 1952, memorable by conducting the state's only double electrocution for aggravated rape on that day. The *Times-Picayune* covered the story on page 24, while the front page reported on the selection of Dwight Eisenhower and Richard Nixon as presidential and vice presidential candidates at the Republican convention—a world away in Chicago. Eisenhower was promising he would "go to Korea" in an effort to end that conflict. Dad once told me it was probably just as well that he never made it to officers' candidate school because he "probably would've died in some swamp over there."

Except for local newspapers that came into the office and occasional letters from his sister and grandmother—but never his mother—he was physically and emotionally isolated from everything outside Angola. He was grateful for his father's communications, although they consisted only of short notes accompanying packs of cigarettes. His

sexual affair was a purely physical and death-defying diversion; the woman offered him no emotional support. No one visited him. He was alone in a place whose impressions would last a lifetime.

Some of his conclusions would have been obvious. The unspeakable brutality of the place was incomprehensible and indescribable, even if there had been someone on the outside with whom he could have shared his observations and reactions. As difficult as it would have been for him to believe, old-timers must have convinced him that earlier conditions had been worse. As Jim arrived in November 1951, the man who would become the state's governor a year later was already making the prison's reform his biggest campaign issue. Shortly after that election, a massive program would transform the institution for awhile. My father saw the role of the press in exposing social injustice and thereby setting in motion the forces necessary to remedy it. The phenomenon must have made an enormous impact on him. A decade later, he certainly thought press coverage would help him clean up his union.

Other lessons he would have learned only from an intimate understanding of the people in prison with him and those who kept him captive. In our later discussions about it, he seemed to place almost all inmates into one of three general categories, each of which had its counterpart among those who were on the outside.

First, there were the animals. These men had intentionally committed violent crimes against others and took their criminality to new lows at Angola. Whatever they had been before imprisonment, these creatures could no longer be considered members of the human race. The guards and camp captains who tortured inmates certainly belonged in this category, too. So did the two cops who had tried to beat a false confession out of him. No one could ever convince him that government law enforcement officers consisted only of the good guys.

Nor were all cons bad guys. Like him, a second group of inmates had committed crimes against property but weren't violent. From these men, he must have developed the corollary he often expressed to me: "Always be careful not to judge people too quickly. A guy might not be what you first think he is—or what other people tell you he is." A good example would have been his inmate-protector. Although the man was a convicted murderer, that crime hadn't been his intent. The death had been the unexpected consequence of a robbery gone bad. The killer was after money, and the crime had produced an unexpect-

edly poor result for his victim. But my father would have focused on how his fellow prisoner treated him: he protected him and that alone would have removed the inmate from the animal category, even though he'd ended another man's life. With this criminal as with all men, everything depended upon circumstances that Dad would evaluate for himself. He wouldn't judge any man based upon accusations, labels by others, or even a conviction. He'd never trust the system to judge anything or anyone. He undoubtedly hoped that people would do the same for him in return.

He worried most about a third group of prisoners: the ones who didn't belong there. Although he told me that most convicts were guilty of something, he also believed that prisons held innocent men. He had withstood beatings from cops who sought false confessions; not all others could. He also saw men who would have avoided jail time if they had gained access to better lawyers or, in some cases, any lawyer at all. As a trusty assisting in the preparation of usually futile petitions for release, he became convinced that every prison housed those who had been falsely accused, inadequately represented, wrongly convicted, and unfairly imprisoned. He saw courtroom results dictated by wealth and social class. He also saw stakes that were sometimes very, very high.

Regardless of the category, he always said prison usually made any convict worse. His assessment in that regard was borne out by the prison's nurse who testified in public hearings shortly after her 1951 resignation following seven years of service: "I have seen almost 7,000 men discharged from this institution and I have never seen a man discharged . . . who was as qualified [for a place] in society as he was the day he was admitted."

Jim Harper was no exception to the nurse's observations. He learned the lessons all prisons taught best: how to be a better criminal. His life finally had a purpose. Once he got out, he'd be more careful next time: "I decided that I'd become the best con man in the United States."

6

Leaving Angola and Finding Mary

I steeled myself before I telephoned Angola's prison administration office. Riddled with anxiety and trepidation, the researcher in me had to determine if any records of his incarceration still existed. My study of the institution had been completed, except for this one last call that would mark the end of my travels with my father through Angola. The voice at the other end of the line confirmed that there was no file for the prisoner number I had given her, but she also said it was from such a distant past that I should speak with another person who had access to an old index card file. After I read his number to that person, she asked me to hold for a moment and then returned to tell me that she had found a card: "James H. Harper?"

My heart raced. "That's it," I said as the adrenaline coursing through my body caused my hands to tremble. "What information is on it?"

She read to me his name, parish ("East Baton Rouge"), crimes ("defrauding hotel and forgery"), sentence ("three years"), sentencing date (November 9, 1951), and parole date (December 16, 1952). That was it; nothing else. All other written record of his presence there had been expunged from the official files, just as he had first told me when I was thirteen years old.

"The slate has been wiped clean," he had said firmly.

I paced in my office for ten minutes after I hung up. He had really been there. It had never seemed real until that moment. I cannot imagine how he survived it, but I now realize that in most ways he hadn't. As with virtually all prisons and prisoners, Angola had destroyed and reconstructed him—all for the worse.

After thirteen months in jail, Jim returned to Minneapolis just before Christmas 1952. He was twenty-four years old, six feet tall, and strikingly handsome. Slender at 135 pounds, he had an angular face and sky blue eyes that gave him a strong resemblance to a fast-rising popular crooner from New Jersey named Frank Sinatra. But physically and in every other dimension of his being, he saw only his own flaws. The

quarter-inch gap between his two prominent front teeth made him feel especially ugly. So did the way his feet splayed out; he thought he walked like a penguin. The prison experience had enhanced his physical strength; in all other respects, it had ruined him.

Events immediately following his release alienated him even more. He quickly learned that a felony prison conviction coupled with hard time in the joint limited a man's job opportunities. No one wanted him for anything. During the days, he painted houses with Jim Sr., who had stood by him with regular shipments of cigarettes to Louisiana. His father's loyalty and the redefinition of their relationship had been the only good things to emerge from his Angola experience.

The two spent their evenings together at a Minneapolis tavern called the Grand Buffet Inn, named for its street, not for any splendor of its own. At the Grand, Jim Sr. played saxophone, clarinet, drums, and piano, tended bar, and acted as chief bouncer. It was licensed to serve only beer with an alcohol content of no more than 3.2 percent; no hard liquor of any kind was allowed.

Jim Sr. was also a celebrity look-alike, but of a much different type. He was bald and, because of his resemblance to General Dwight D. Eisenhower, was repeatedly asked if he was the new president's brother. Such inquiries were particularly irksome to a lifelong Democrat. Even so, the image of Ike and Sinatra getting drunk together at the Grand must have caused quite a few double takes.

Beyond a vulnerability to alcohol's addictive properties, Jim Jr. was his father's son in other respects. He was a ladies' man, and Jim Sr. was an eager accomplice to his exploits. Whenever young Jim entered the tavern with one of his many girlfriends, Jim Sr. made sure the band started playing whatever special song had been designated as "theirs."

In April 1953, Jim Jr. was again passing bad checks in pursuit of his ambition to be the best con man around when a striking blonde entered the Grand for the first time. Two escorts accompanied her and a girlfriend. At five foot four, the green-eyed beauty had a perfect figure. Her stunningly good looks reminded him of his favorite female movie star, Ingrid Bergman. When she walked into the Grand, she took her first steps toward becoming my mother.

Mary Margaret Fischer was born in 1935 into a devoutly Lutheran family. Her father, Gervasius Fischer, had followed generations before him into the ministry. In addition to two younger sisters, she had an

older half-brother and half-sister from Gervasius's first marriage to a woman who had died of cancer. Mary's mother, Margaret, had always suffered from hypochondria that masked her otherwise formidable intelligence. When Mary was nine years old, her mother finally gave birth to the son she had always wanted, but he died a few days later. Thereafter, Margaret battled depression that clouded the rest of her life.

Mary became more than her mother could handle, and Gervasius's unwillingness to intercede didn't help. She spent her early childhood in Milwaukee, where her father was a pastor at a downtown Lutheran church. By the age of twelve, she had skipped two grades and was ready academically for high school. Margaret sent her away, insisting that she live with her grandparents about sixty miles to the west and attend the Lutheran high school and college at which her grandfather taught. By the time he died in June 1949—when Mary was fourteen— her parents had moved to Mankato, Minnesota. Gervasius had accepted a "call" to become pastor for the town's largest Lutheran congregation. Although her widowed grandmother was invited to live with the family in Mankato, Mary was sent to board at Dr. Martin Luther High School in New Ulm, a small town about an hour south of Minneapolis. The school's restrictions—no dating outside the academic community, no rides in cars with boys, strict curfews—made her last two years of high school feel like incarceration during the same period that her future husband actually was in prison. She wanted to become a doctor, but Gervasius ordered that she remain at New Ulm for college and become a parochial school teacher.

New Ulm could not hold her. After completing high school at sixteen, she traveled with her older half-sister, Doris, whose marriage to a professional baseball player, Frank Kellert, took the three of them to Cuba and throughout the United States. After returning to Oklahoma City, where Doris and Frank had their permanent home, Mary and a friend made all the arrangements necessary to begin a medical career at the University of Texas. She was forced to abandon that dream when her parents refused to provide any financial support. By her eighteenth birthday in 1953, she had found work as a bank teller in Minneapolis. Gervasius had insisted that she live in a women's residence and she obeyed, but his influence on her was waning and her rebellion was fully under way.

Mary was restless the night she first walked into the Grand. She was looking for some excitement beyond a job that was too easy and

the two nice but dull escorts she and her girlfriend had brought into the bar. She got more than she anticipated as young Jim Harper immediately took notice and marked her for pursuit.

They became engaged two months later. Jim was still on parole and his fiancée's parents were less than enthusiastic about the proposed union, but they had finally given up trying to tell her what to do. She would be someone else's problem now. Jim's personality was so engaging that they actually found themselves liking him anyway. Somehow, Angola had not destroyed his charm.

Alice argued against the marriage, identifying for Mary all of the many flaws and failures that she saw in her son. Mary would hear none of it because she was in love; nothing else mattered. She was confident that she could change all of his imperfections. In August 1953 and only four months after they had met, Gervasius performed

Jim and Mary Harper in 1953

their marriage ceremony in his Mankato church. Jim was twenty-five; Mary was eighteen.

A few weeks later, she announced that she was pregnant—with me. In fact, although she had said nothing previously, she had suspected that she might be pregnant at the time of their marriage. But she was not sure and, in any event, didn't want to be wed solely because someone felt obliged to marry her. How ironic, Jim thought upon hearing the news, that he was actually reliving this aspect of his father's life. But there was a critical difference. Unlike Jim Sr., he had married a woman he loved and with whom he shared the unfulfilled dream of a happy family. He resolved that he would not repeat his own parents' mistakes. This child and any others who followed would become his very reason for living, and they would always know it.

He abandoned his earlier ambition to become the next John Dillinger or Al Capone. He no longer wanted to become America's best con man. He would rather become America's best father. But the injection of Angola's poison left him with an attraction to life's dark side that was not so easily flushed from his system.

So yet another message from my father's box began to emerge: Mary saved him. But for her entrance into his story, it's hard to imagine the depths to which he might have sunk. Through it all, she would never give up on him. She took her "for better or for worse" vow seriously and became the first person in his life to remain at his side through all adversity. He struggled with the conflicting emotions that her devotion caused. On the one hand, allowing himself to be loved was not easy. On the other, it gave him new strength to pursue larger and nobler purposes. Starting with Mary, he began to think that what he could do for others would ultimately determine his view of himself.

With the motivation that his new family provided, he pressed ahead, but it wasn't easy. The nagging failures of his youth still propelled him to seek a new and more reliable father figure. The baggage that went with being an ex-con made him struggle to find some way to make amends, even as it simultaneously pulled him back to society's darker corners. As a confused young man, he searched for a mission to redeem him and for comrades who would accept him for what he was, although he still had no clear vision of that himself. If he had been a religious person, someone like Jimmy Hoffa would have seemed like the answer to contradictory prayers.

7

Hoffa's Supporting Players

As I began to connect the developing timeline of my father's life with key events in Hoffa's career, I would soon learn that Hoffa, too, was a study in contradictions. While my father was scraping the bottom at Angola, Hoffa was rising to the top of the Teamsters. In doing so, Hoffa himself set in motion all of the forces necessary to produce his own destruction; it was only a matter of time.

After vanquishing the Minneapolis socialists from the Teamsters union, Hoffa returned to Michigan and confronted a new challenge: the Lewis brothers' threat that Hoffa had repelled in Minnesota was only one front in a multi-city attack, including several venues in Hoffa's home state. In self-defense, he turned to the underworld for help. His efforts began in the early 1940s, when he sought only survival as a regional Teamsters leader. A decade later, his dark allies would contribute to a national power structure facilitating his climb to the International Teamsters' general presidency. Two decades after that, they would be central characters in theories relating to his disappearance and presumed death.

Dan Tobin decided to retire in 1952. After forty years as the Teamsters' general president, his most obvious successor was Dave Beck, who held the longest tenure of any International vice president on the general executive board. Beck had long been to the western United States Teamsters what Hoffa had more recently become to their midwestern counterparts.

Although he was favored to succeed Tobin, Beck was not particularly popular among rank-and-file members. A "stop Beck" movement surfaced shortly before the 1952 International convention began in Miami; Hoffa's name circulated as an alternative. When the resulting tumult caused Tobin briefly to reconsider his retirement decision, Beck announced that he would not pursue the presidency if Tobin chose to remain. Hoffa saved Beck's day when he pledged all of his

Central, Southern, and Eastern Conference delegates to Beck. As a consolation prize, Hoffa became, at thirty-nine, the youngest International vice president in Teamsters history. His uniquely powerful role as kingmaker to Beck allowed him to function with influence far beyond his nominal office as ninth vice president.

Hoffa's meteoric rise became especially unfortunate for a fellow International vice president, Sid Brennan of Minneapolis. Once again, Minnesota would be at the center of a story that initially revolved around Hoffa and five key characters but continued for a decade before eventually enveloping Dad.

It had all begun innocently enough. After the International had assumed final and complete control of Local 544 following Hoffa's crushing victory over Farrell Dobbs in 1941, Tobin established his own loyalists as the new leadership in Minneapolis. At the top, Sid Brennan became secretary-treasurer, the most powerful position in the local and one that he still held when Hoffa became an International vice president in 1952.

Brennan had begun his Teamsters career in 1933, in his mid-twenties, as a driver for a printing company. Two years after putting him in charge of Local 544, Tobin promoted Brennan to an International vice presidency on the general executive board. That placed him in the highest echelon of national union leaders and allowed him to rule Minneapolis with an iron fist.

Fritz Snyder served as the local's vice president. Snyder was a secondary figure in this early scene but would occupy a lead role in my father's story. He was three years younger than Brennan, about six feet tall, losing hair, and gaining weight. Physically and psychologically, Snyder appeared to be the darker of the two men. His formal schooling had ended after the ninth grade. Although he was not particularly bright, street smarts were far more valuable for his line of work. His father's surname was Schneider, and he told fellow Teamsters that he had lost a brother in the Minneapolis Teamsters strikes of 1934—a martyr in the cause of organized labor.

Brennan and Snyder looked for any opportunity to increase their power in the union, even if it came at the expense of fellow Teamsters. They saw what they perceived to be such an opportunity in the late 1940s, when they tried to take over a neighboring local that Gordon Conklin headed in St. Paul. Conklin was the third key character in the

drama that began to unfold in 1952. He would figure importantly in Dad's union struggle seven years later.

Conklin had a slim frame, and his thin face, light coloring, and dark-framed eyeglasses made him look more like an accountant than a Teamster. Born in 1903, he was four years older than Brennan and seven years older than Snyder. His family had owned the feed store in his native Blue Earth, Minnesota—my grandma Harper's hometown—and he had lived there before moving to Minneapolis when he was thirteen. At seventeen, Conklin was driving a horse-drawn wagon. Three years later, he was behind the wheel of a truck as a Teamsters union driver. In 1927, he left the world of manual labor to spend four years as an insurance salesman. Three years after returning to the union, he was again driving a truck during the Minneapolis Teamsters strikes of 1934. In 1941, the Teamsters at Local 120 in St. Paul made Conklin their leader.

When Brennan and Snyder launched their assault on his local, Conklin sought Hoffa's help. Hoffa obliged, the attack from Local 544 collapsed, and Conklin became one of Hoffa's most loyal supporters. Meanwhile, Brennan and his sidekick Snyder gained a serious enemy in Gordon Conklin. Fortunately for him, Snyder occupied a minor enough position in the Teamsters world that he remained well below Hoffa's radar for the next several years; Brennan was not as lucky. By 1952, Hoffa relished the possibility that his new role as a nationally prominent leader had placed him in a position to accelerate the demise of Brennan, a fellow International vice president he had grown to distrust. That was when Washington, DC, reporter Clark Mollenhoff entered the picture.

Gordon Conklin

Mollenhoff would become the fourth significant figure in my father's union fight, although Dad would never know it or meet him. Mollenhoff was born in 1921. His hometown was Burnside, Iowa, just a few miles south of the Minnesota border and not far from Blue Earth. Cutting a large and imposing figure with his six-foot-four frame and booming voice, he had worked as a part-time reporter for the *Des Moines Register* while attending Drake University Law School. After receiving his degree in 1944, he entered the military.

Upon his discharge from the service in 1946, he returned to the *Register* as a courthouse reporter. In 1950, he was transferred to its Washington bureau.

The publisher of the *Register* also published the *Minneapolis Morning Tribune* and its late-afternoon counterpart, the *Minneapolis Star*. When his editor told him in January 1953 to visit Minneapolis to investigate allegations of "Teamsters racketeering," Mollenhoff was thirty-two and not particularly thrilled with the assignment because he didn't believe that a worthwhile story would result. He was wrong. In his 1965 book *Tentacles of Power: The Story of Jimmy Hoffa*, Mollenhoff detailed his decade-long pursuit of Hoffa, a pursuit that resulted in a 1958 Pulitzer Prize for investigative reporting halfway into his adventure. As I read it, I was surprised to learn that his work

began with that initial 1953 visit to the Twin Cities. Seeking local assistance for his exposé if there was one, he contacted fellow newsman Sam Romer at the *Tribune,* a man Mollenhoff described as one of Gordon Conklin's best friends. Romer would become the fifth important player in the saga that began with Mollenhoff's first trip to Minneapolis and continued until it almost destroyed my father nearly a decade later.

The reference to Romer in Mollenhoff's book gave me pause. My father had told me that he had secretly confided in Romer, who, in turn, had provided extensive early newspaper

Sam Romer

coverage of the controversy at Local 544 that began in 1959. But he had never mentioned any particular connection between Romer and Conklin. Nor had he ever spoken of Clark Mollenhoff. When I told my mother about my discovery of a longstanding Conklin-Romer connection, she said my father hadn't known of it.

From my Chicago office, I used my computer to log onto the online index of collections at the Minnesota Historical Society and typed "Sam Romer" into the "search" field. When the results showed an index of "Sam Romer personal papers," I was breathless. When I traveled to St. Paul and reviewed them, I could not believe my eyes. But I'm getting ahead of the story.

· · · · ·

In January 1953, Romer and Conklin were delighted to help Mollen-hoff expose Brennan's corruption. Each man had his own motive for assisting that enterprise. At thirty-nine, Romer had reached what would remain the peak of his career—and it wasn't very high—and was still waiting for the major story that might make his reputation. At least to that point, it had eluded him. Nine years older than Mollenhoff, he worked the local labor beat for the Tribune.

Conklin would have embraced the opportunity to help Mollenhoff, too. He could introduce him to Brennan's loudest rank-and-file detractors. This would be Conklin's payback for Brennan's earlier assault on his local. Moreover, the union's rising star, Jimmy Hoffa, had spread the word in Minnesota that he supported the dissident Teamsters' complaints and encouraged rank-and-file members to cooperate with the Mollenhoff-Conklin-Romer investigation of Brennan.

The two Minnesotans made certain that Mollenhoff met with the union members who most disliked Brennan and were eager to talk about his wrongdoing at Local 544. By the time he left Minneapolis, Mollenhoff had become convinced of Brennan's corruption. He concluded that the story should be told in all its ugliness, but he feared that the Teamsters could embroil him and his publisher in debilitating litigation. Truth would be an eventual defense to any lawsuits that the union filed, but even a victory would cost money and time. His best protection would be congressional proceedings about which he could simply "report." The only immediate problem was the absence of any such investigation of the Teamsters. Mollenhoff would soon remedy that situation.

A decade later, the fruits of Mollenhoff's efforts would eventually send Hoffa to jail. My father would never know that, along the way, the complicated Minnesota story connecting Hoffa, Romer, Conklin, and Snyder would eventually reach and endanger his own life.

8

A Tangled Web

As I dug deeper into Hoffa's story, it soon became clear to me that he unwittingly sowed the seeds of his own destruction when he unleashed his Minnesota Teamsters allies to assist Mollenhoff's investigation into Sid Brennan's corruption. Upon Mollenhoff's return to Washington, he reviewed his preliminary findings with New Hampshire senator Charles Tobey, who was wrapping up his hearings on wrongdoing in the longshoremen's unions that ran America's shipping docks. He urged Tobey next to look closely at the Teamsters. In a February 14, 1953, letter to Romer, Mollenhoff wrote, "We aren't certain of the hearing we want, but it is almost certain the Tobey Committee on interstate and foreign commerce seems to be the best place. Tell Gordon to keep me posted. The tax material came up faster than I had anticipated and should in itself provide material to put Brennan's activity in proper perspective. Thanks again for help that made a tough job a lot of fun." As I reviewed this letter fifty years later in the reading room of the Minnesota Historical Society with the added context of Mollenhoff's 1965 book, I concluded immediately that "Gordon" had to be Conklin. The intrigue was becoming more interesting than my father could have imagined.

While Senator Tobey concluded his longshoremen's hearings, a House of Representatives committee assumed responsibility for investigating Beck, Hoffa, and the Teamsters in June 1953. Mollenhoff covered the hearings in Detroit, where Hoffa did not enjoy his maiden voyage into the world of congressional scrutiny. He refused to answer questions relating to the presence of his wife's name on the payroll of a Detroit local. Similarly, he refused to discuss her ownership interest (held in her maiden name, Josephine Poszywak) in a Tennessee trucking firm; Hoffa's union had contracts with the company. Fortunately for Hoffa, the House did not appropriate funds to continue those hearings.

But Mollenhoff refused to let the congressional investigation of the

Teamsters die. Because of his tireless efforts, the Senate seemed ready to pick up the House's investigative baton on July 15, 1953. As Mollenhoff had hoped when he had written to Romer in February, Senator Tobey was authorized to convene hearings on the Minneapolis Teamsters. But when Tobey died suddenly nine days later, the anticipated Senate investigation died with him. Three months after that, Ohio's Republican senator John W. Bricker refused to seek additional funding for any continued Senate effort. I would eventually learn that dark dealings in Ohio were almost as important to Hoffa's career as those in Minneapolis.

Because of Mollenhoff's persistence, the House of Representatives was ready to swing back into Teamsters investigative action by the fall of 1953. A special subcommittee convened in Detroit during Thanksgiving week and heard testimony on how members of the Paul Dorfman family—Hoffa's friends in Chicago—came to be running Teamsters' insurance plans despite their limited qualifications for the job. The committee also asked again about the ownership interest that Josephine Hoffa held in the Tennessee truck line, as well as general misuse of Teamsters funds. With Mollenhoff's help, the hearings eventually turned a revealing spotlight onto Minneapolis Local 544.

The testimony that guided the subcommittee's investigation toward Minnesota came from several directions, but all of it originated with Clark Mollenhoff. First, there was Teamsters organizer Jerry Connelly. Although he was not a Local 544 officer, suspicious circumstances surrounding Connelly's 1951 move from Miami to Minneapolis were revealed. He refused to answer questions about his connection to a gun that may have been used in the attempted murder of a Teamster in Connelly's local in Florida—the outcome of what began as an extortion scheme. Next, a Minnesota trucking company president tried to explain away as a "mistake" loans from Sid Brennan that appeared on the company's records, as well as payments made to Brennan. Finally, Local 544 recording secretary Gene Williams refused to testify concerning his handling of a union pension fund, except to say that he had borrowed $10,000 from the fund to finance the opening of his Minneapolis bar, the Williams Bar and Cafe. The momentum to press forward with additional hearings in Minneapolis seemed unstoppable, but it was stopped. The *Detroit News* broke the story:

Terrific pressure is being exerted on congressmen investigating labor racketeering to abandon their investigation and dissolve the special committee.

The pressure is strong, and its sources so highly placed, that members of the House Committee on Labor and Education who were in Detroit all last week feared to name names in publication.

The subcommittee had petitioned to extend its inquiry to Minneapolis, Chicago, South Bend, and Akron.

Rep. Wint Smith (R-Kan), chairman of the subcommittee, was asked about the influence being brought to bear on the investigators.

"The pressure comes from way up there," he said, pointing skyward, "and I just can't talk about it any more specifically than that."

Representative Smith himself offered no further explanation of his "from way up there" remarks, but the *Detroit News* reported that the committee and staff members took several long-distance telephone calls during the hearings "and were not happy when they hung up the phone."

A few months later, Ohio Republican congressman George Bender assumed responsibility for investigating the links between the Teamsters union and organized crime. Bender took his committee to Minneapolis where, again, Mollenhoff supplied the most potent ammunition for the interrogators. When called to testify before Bender's hearings in April 1954, Local 544 officers Sid Brennan and Gene Williams asserted their Fifth Amendment rights in refusing to answer a long series of pointed questions about their personal finances and union activity. Mollenhoff himself was pleasantly surprised at what appeared to be Bender's aggressive approach to the issues.

Coincidentally, congressional hearings on another topic took an important turn in April 1954—and they were nationally televised. My father watched with millions of others as Senator Joseph McCarthy investigated alleged Communists in the federal government, including the armed forces. The U.S. Army fought back, and the beginning of McCarthy's end came when its lawyer, Joseph Welch, defended a young protégé in words that would echo for generations: "You've done enough. Have you no sense of decency, sir? At long last, have you left no sense of decency?" No remotely comparable media coverage attended the House committee's questioning of prominent Minneapolis Teamsters, about whom my father knew little and cared even less.

After a break for the summer, Bender moved his committee to Cleveland, where four days of hearings started in late September 1954. Hoffa's Ohio protégés William Presser and Louis Triscaro also pled the Fifth, refusing to answer questions related to their income. Triscaro was a former boxer who allegedly had connections to the Cleveland underworld; Presser was Hoffa's top Ohio operative. At a brief follow-up session in Washington in November 1954, Bender backed away from questioning Presser, who again pled the Fifth in response to questions posed by other committee members and staff investigators. Bender recessed the hearings "at the call of the chairman," but they never resumed.

What had happened between Presser's September and November appearances that effectively ended Bender's investigation? I think the answer was buried in Ohio. Although Bender was a member of the House, he yearned to sit on the other side of the legislative chamber. He hoped to win a November 1954 special election that would fill the vacancy created by the death of the legendary Robert A. Taft.

During the six-week break between the Cleveland and Washington hearings, Presser announced that the Teamsters union was switching its support to Bender in the upcoming Senate race. Previously, the Teamsters had actively supported Bender's Democratic opponent and had criticized Bender for chairing the congressional committee that was investigating the union. When asked at the October 1954 meeting of the union's Ohio Conference why the Teamsters were now changing their allegiances, Presser reportedly said that Bender was the man to support and refused further comment. The Ohio Executive Board members returned to their locals with instructions to support Bender.

Four days after his Washington appearance the next month, Presser was quoted as having told those attending a meeting of the Ohio Conference of Teamsters, "We found, especially during the latter portion of the hearings, that we had a second friend on the congressional committee, a friend that did a fair job for the people concerned . . . and his name is George Bender and it has taught me a lesson."

The Ohio Teamsters' endorsement made all the difference for Bender: he won his Senate race by only six thousand votes. An Ohio Teamsters leader would tell federal investigators several years later

that his Teamsters Joint Council was asked to make a contribution shortly after Bender's 1954 election: $40,000 was supposedly being raised to cover expenses relating to the congressional appearances of Triscaro and Presser. When asked what the money was for, the leader said he was told that "money was spent to pull certain strings to see that these charges were dropped." He was not told that the money went to Bender: "It may have; it may not."

In 1955, Senator Bender was the guest of honor at an Ohio Conference of Teamsters meeting. Presser personally toasted him, reportedly saying, "To you, George Bender, the Republican whose name has been handled around as an anti-labor Senator, if it weren't for this one man, and his advice and the constant pounding we would have a lot of problems that do not exist . . . and Bill Presser is committed to George Bender anywhere down the line."

It would be several years before federal investigators would find in Presser's Cleveland Teamsters headquarters a file containing two documents that might have connected a few more of these dots. Inside an envelope marked "Christmas list" was a December 8, 1955, invoice for champagne dispensers showing deliveries to those whose names were to be engraved on them. Also included was a separate list of the same names: Beck, English, Hoffa, Brennan, Connell, Bender, Bliss, Dorfman, and Presser. That Presser's "Christmas list" included International general executive board members Dave Beck, John English, Hoffa, and Hoffa's friend Owen Bart Brennan from Detroit (no relation to Sid Brennan of Minneapolis) was not surprising because they were prominent Teamsters officials. The inclusion of Chicago's Paul Dorfman was also understandable, given his link to the Teamsters' insurance business that Hoffa had helped direct to him and his family members. Ray Bliss was chairman of the Ohio Republican Party. Bender was, of course, Ohio's newest U.S. senator.

The remaining name on the list was James C. Connell, a recently appointed federal judge in Cleveland. Because a Republican resided in the White House, such appointments typically followed the recommendation of Republican senators from the appointee's state. At the time of Connell's ascent to the bench in August 1954, Taft's death had left John W. Bricker as the only Republican senator from Ohio. Bricker had refused to seek continued congressional funding for a Teamsters investigation in Minneapolis and elsewhere after Charles Tobey's sudden death in 1953. While in private practice, Judge Con-

nell had been an attorney for Teamsters locals in Cleveland. During his confirmation hearings, the American Bar Association had reported to the Senate Judiciary Committee that Connell had shown an "arbitrary attitude" as a state court judge and expressed concern that "in this instance, the office of United States judge is being used for political purposes and not to enhance the more perfect administration of justice." Years after his confirmation, another Senate committee would hear testimony that Judge Connell knew of his secretary's side-jobs, which yielded monthly payments from an Ohio Teamsters lawyer. In 1958, Judge Connell would preside over a key case involving the Teamsters; he ruled in favor of Hoffa's position.

When the champagne-dispenser documents in Presser's file finally reached the public eye in February 1959, Bender and Connell denied ever receiving any gifts from the Teamsters.

Even with help from people in high places, troubles for Hoffa and the Teamsters grew. Hoffa blamed Mollenhoff for much of the public attention to his difficulties but was powerless to stop him. On November 6, 1955, the reporter met with Hoffa and peppered him with unpleasant questions about the allegations swirling around Minneapolis Teamster Jerry Connelly. According to Mollenhoff, Hoffa eventually said, "Now looka here, Clark. They don't pay newspaper reporters enough for you to be giving me the bad time that you've been giving me. Everyone has his price. What's yours?" Hoffa later denied ever saying those words.

TWO

COLLISION COURSE

9

Harper Joins the Teamsters

For several months before I was born in April 1954, my father supplemented his salary as a clerical worker with occasional nights of door-to-door selling—brushes, magazines, cutlery, and pots and pans. He often returned home after a successful night and literally showered Mom with cash. Despite his talent, sales was not the career he wanted. Shortly after my birth, he found more regular employment as a night clerk-typist for a Minneapolis truck line, Werner Transportation. One of his supervisors was dispatcher Dave Morris.

My father soon realized that compared to his clerical job, the unionized over-the-road drivers of the big tractor-trailer rigs made some real money. The only way to get such a position was to become a Teamster and start at the bottom of the unionized employee ladder: the loading dock. The next step up was to city driver. He hoped that after years of apprenticeship, he would work his way to the top—manning over thirty tons of machinery and payload over the road. Dave Morris would accelerate his climb.

Morris matched shippers with delivery pickups and drivers with their loads. Tall, strong, and dark, he was about five to ten years older than my father. He had connections, although how and to whom no one knew for sure. Jim Sr. rarely offered opinions about anyone, but he told my father that he did not like Morris. My mother told him the same thing, but Dad would hear none of it. He was loyal to the precious few people in his life who were willing to help him; Morris became one of them.

The first step in my father's progression to over-the-road driver came shortly after his twenty-sixth birthday in July 1954, when he joined the other Werner dockworkers and drivers who were among the three thousand members of Teamsters Local 544. As he paid his union dues every month, the stamp placed in his small receipt booklet bore the ink imprint of Dave Morris—a Teamsters organizer and his sponsor.

He soon discovered that he had colorful comrades among his Minneapolis Teamsters. In 1956, Teamster Jerry Connelly was again in the news, this time for his role in a car bombing. The target was the leader of a rival Teamsters local whose members had crossed a picket line established by Connelly's local. A day after Connelly's Minnesota state court conviction, a federal judge in Minneapolis sentenced him to two years in prison for another crime: he was found to be the ringleader of Teamsters extortionists, one of whom was Sid Brennan. Even the union's brilliant young attorney, Edward Bennett Williams, had not succeeded in Brennan's defense. Clark Mollenhoff's 1965 book reported that shortly after his conviction, Brennan secretly offered to help federal investigators "get the goods on Hoffa" because, he said, "Hoffa's the real crook." Brennan told them that Hoffa had "planted" Connelly on him.

As my father read about the publicly reported events in the *Tribune*, he became increasingly concerned about the bad press his local was generating. Mom had given birth to my sister in February 1955 and was again pregnant for most of 1956. The rapid growth of our family reinforced his determination to develop a respectable career. Dirty Teamsters in the newspapers were not helping.

Along the way from the loading dock to a coveted over-the-road position, my father met and became the protégé of the driver of all drivers: Marvin Masteller, who was one of the very first Werner long haulers. I had spent many childhood hours with Dad and Masteller and in 2003 was somewhat surprised to learn that he was still alive. Unaware of the state of his health, I called his home to let him know that Dad had died almost two years earlier. I told him that my father had always spoken very highly of him; a few weeks later I traveled to Minneapolis and we met for lunch.

He looked as I remembered him, only smaller—probably because I was now bigger. Even Masteller's name communicated something about the man. At five foot six, he weighed about 180 pounds: "built like a brick shithouse," as Dad would say. Despite his stocky appearance, there wasn't an ounce of fat on him. Only six years older than my father, Masteller undoubtedly had a presence—even in his early thirties—that made him seem much older as he chomped on fat cigars and bellowed vulgarities. Even in ordinary conversation, his deep, raspy voice sounded like a drill sergeant's barking out orders in a boot camp.

Following a rough childhood, he had served in the Pacific theater during World War II. After the war, he applied for work at Werner Transportation Company, whose owner had acquired a fleet of large diesel-powered tractors. When the owner asked if he could drive one, Masteller was typically direct: "How can I learn if you don't give me the goddamned chance to learn? By the way, do you throw people out on their asses in this company?" He got the job.

Masteller seemed larger than life because he was, and no one could tell him what to do. Uniforms were an example. All other Werner drivers wore them. My dad actually liked the Werner uniform because it helped to offset his feelings of isolation; it made him feel part of a team. Not Masteller, who communicated his views on that subject to the owner: "I'm not a goddamned walking billboard for you or your company. You pay me to drive a goddamned truck, and that's all you pay me to do."

Masteller took a liking to "Jamie," as he called my father. Much like the father-figure convict who had protected my father in prison, Masteller made clear to the other drivers that they should not harass his younger friend. Although rookies usually suffered through pranks during their indoctrination into the driver ranks, there would be no molasses in the fuel tank for this novice over-the-road Teamster. With Masteller giving the orders, everyone complied.

Werner's concerns about any driver's ability to handle its big trucks were well founded. The company's over-the-road drivers had to master the largest and most powerful tractor made: the Autocar—monster of the road. Its flat cast-iron front bumper looked like a battering ram. A single headlight on each side of its three-foot-high radiator grill gave the appearance of an animal snarling at oncoming traffic. Its massive front end dared any other vehicle to test its strength.

An Autocar's idling diesel engine grumbled like a resting lion. When the accelerator pedal fed it fuel, a deafening roar reverberated inside the cab. Dad's partial hearing loss from his final parachute jump actually served him well in this venue. The dashboard was nothing more than a sheet of metal into which a few vital measuring devices had been placed. Except for the leather seats and rubber floor mats, the inside of the cab consisted entirely of metal. The truck was not built for the comfort of its occupants. It was built to perform the job of pulling trailers loaded with freight from point A to point B. For

Dad, that would eventually be from Minneapolis to Mauston, Wisconsin, and back again.

Despite its heft and bulk, the Autocar could move very quickly. It had a 300-horsepower diesel engine, tremendous for its time. The driver had to manipulate the transmission stick through ten gears before reaching top speeds close to 100 miles per hour. More like a railroad train than a highway warrior, the Autocar easily maintained its high speed, even when towing a load that brought the combined weight of tractor, trailer, driver, and shipment to 65,000 pounds. The problem with the Autocar was not getting it under way. The challenge came in stopping it.

Brakes alone were not enough. Particularly when traveling at high speeds or down steep grades, excessive use of the tractor brakes produced friction that would burn them up long before the vehicle came to rest. The trailer also had brakes, but they were of limited use in slowing the behemoth tractor pulling it. The only effective way to slow an Autocar was to use its own power against it in a maneuver called engine braking.

The principle was simple; the execution was more complex. The driver was required at precisely the right moment to engage the clutch, move the gearshift quickly through neutral, and then force it into the next lower gear. Remaining in neutral—drivers referred to it as "idiot gear"—actually worsened the situation in a downhill run because the rig gained speed as it coasted, although the brakes offered some help. If the driver could jam the shift lever so the lower gear engaged, the meshing of the transmission's gear and the engine's crankshaft forced a reduction in speed. Scream as it might, the Autocar's engine could not break the laws of physics that slowed the vehicle.

By the end of 1956, my father had somehow leapfrogged over many others to become an over-the-road driver's helper. He knew that his hard work had contributed to his advancement, but he believed that his enigmatic friend Dave Morris had somehow pulled strings to assist his career. His job as a helper meant riding in the passenger side of the cab as the truck pulled a fully loaded thirty-five-foot trailer. Masteller made sure that he sat in the driver's seat for those trips, during which he told his young charge more than once, "Master the truck, or it'll kill you." What Masteller didn't say was that even if he mastered the truck, it could still kill him.

· · · · ·

Inside an Autocar

For a Werner driver, the Great Mississippi River Road—U.S. Highway 61—was the place where failure to master the Autocar was most likely to be lethal. For most of America, limited-access interstate highways bypassing cities and towns did not yet exist. Congress did not enact federal legislation authorizing the Eisenhower Interstate Highway system until 1956, and it took decades to complete it. The route from Minneapolis to Mauston, Wisconsin, was a two-lane blacktop meandering through several small towns. For half of that run, the treacherous Mississippi River Road was the designated route for all Werner drivers.

The road started near the source of the Mississippi in northern Minnesota, not far from the resort where my grandparents had first met. My dad knew from personal observation that it flowed all the way to Louisiana and the Gulf of Mexico. Just south of Minneapolis, it hugged the winding riverbank separating Minnesota and Wisconsin. In contrast to the open midwestern landscape surrounding it, the Great River Road appeared to belong in the middle of a mountain forest. Huge trees rose from each side of the road to form a cocoonlike tunnel over much of its course. The roadway itself rose and descended with grades that challenged the most skilled drivers. If a vehicle took a downhill slope too quickly, it would speed out of control, the brakes of the tractor and trailer powerless to stop the fully loaded combination from landing in a ditch or flying off a bluff and into the river. Likewise, if a trucker did not reach sufficient speed at the bottom of a valley, he would never be able to climb to the top of the hill ahead.

Most Werner men drove their tractor-trailer rigs at night along the dangerous twists and turns of the River Road. Moreover, there were no highway lights along the way, leaving only the two single-lantern headlights of the Autocar to illuminate the path ahead. A mechanical miscalculation or driver fatigue could carry a man, his tractor-trailer combination, and his load off the road and over a cliff.

Because of its massive bulk, the Autocar barely fit on its side of the Great Road. When two Werner Autocars sped past each other, typically traveling over 70 miles per hour in opposite directions, only six inches separated them. A driver always knew when an oncoming company truck approached at night: the illuminated WERNER sign on the tractor's roof told him. Sometimes, for fun, the two drivers turned off the headlights as their trucks converged in the darkness.

Dad loved it all. Werner's professional over-the-road drivers were

his new comrades. The drivers' union—the International Brotherhood of Teamsters, Chauffeurs, Warehousemen, and Helpers, Minneapolis Local 544—was his new community. He was part of something bigger than himself, and his life seemed to be turning in an unambiguously positive direction.

After his young protégé was promoted from driver's helper to student driver, Masteller sat in the passenger seat for Dad's one and only student driving trip. My father was so excited that he ran a red light early in the journey, but Masteller immediately put him at ease: "Don't worry about it. Sometimes those things just happen."

About halfway into their return trip the next day, they began a steep downhill run. Along the descent, Dad noticed a fork in the road where a gravel path to the right led up a slope from the main thoroughfare but seemed to go nowhere; it simply ended.

"What's that?" he asked.

"Hope to hell you never need it," Masteller answered. "That's the goddamned runaway truck lane. That's for the poor bastard who lets his truck get away from him as he's going down this hill. That's his one and only escape. He can veer off the road and go up that path to save his ass. If he misses it, he'll die right"—he paused as the road took an abrupt turn—"here."

The moment Masteller uttered the word "here," Dad understood exactly what he was talking about. If the rig had not slowed enough before reaching that turn, it would have careened down a steep embankment toward disaster.

As their journey reached its final two hours, Dad was relaxed and driving well within the posted speed limit. Masteller thought he looked too comfortable. Holding the final third of his cigar between his teeth, he turned to my father and said, "When are you gonna drive this goddamned son-of-a-bitch?"

"What do you mean?" Dad was puzzled.

"You're driving like a goddamned pansy. I'll show you what I mean," Masteller barked as he extended his left leg across the floor of the cab, slammed his foot on the accelerator, pushed the pedal to the floor, and held it there.

"Now drive the bastard!" Masteller yelled as he removed the cigar from his mouth with his right hand, flipped its ashes out the window, and placed it back in his mouth.

Dad's eyes barely remained in their sockets; his body levitated from the seat. He threw his half-smoked Camel out the window and grabbed the big steering wheel with both hands. He'd never traveled this fast in a car, much less a thirty-ton rig. He maneuvered around the curves of the Great River Road and glanced at the speedometer: seventy, and still accelerating. He decided he wouldn't look at the dial again.

"How are you gonna slow this goddamned son-of-a-bitch down?" Masteller yelled over the roar of the engine.

"Engine braking . . . downshifting." Dad returned the shout.

"Well, there's a damned sharp curve and a goddamned bridge up ahead. You'd better do it or you'll kill us!"

Although Dad knew the engine-braking maneuver, he'd never actually performed it at these speeds. He grabbed the transmission stick, depressed the clutch with his left foot, and tried to force the truck into a lower gear.

"Better get us out of idiot gear!" Masteller urged. My father struggled to move the stick out of neutral—dangerous limbo for any trucker because the rig coasted without restraint.

He tried again to jam the stick into the lower gear as Masteller let up on the accelerator just enough to allow the transmission to engage before once again slamming the pedal to the floor. The force of Masteller's reapplied pressure on the accelerator had no impact on the vehicle's speed. The truck now traveled at the top speed attainable in its newly found gear.

Masteller smiled as he puffed on his cigar. No such expression graced my father's face because the truck was still going over fifty miles an hour, so he knew that he'd have to continue downshifting. As he did, the vehicle slowed. While beads of perspiration formed on Dad's forehead, Masteller finished his cigar and threw the stub out the window. After ten minutes that felt like ten hours, Masteller finally lifted his foot from the accelerator altogether.

"Now that's called driving the damn truck," Masteller laughed as he lit a new cigar. "You're ready. Now you're a Werner over-the-road truck driver. But remember what I say: Master the truck, or it'll kill you."

10

Hoffa's Ascent — And His Minnesota Connections

As Dad learned the ups and downs of the Great River Road in 1956, Clark Mollenhoff was convincing Robert Kennedy that corruption in the Teamsters union remained a cause worth pursuing. The result: the McClellan committee entered the scene. One of its members was senator John F. Kennedy; his brother, Robert, became its chief counsel and began a dogged pursuit of the Teamsters union, starting with general president Dave Beck. The congressional investigative assault on Beck became relentless, as he refused on Fifth Amendment grounds to testify about his financial affairs and the misuse of Teamsters funds. Overwhelmed by the pressure, Beck eventually said that he would not seek reelection to the Teamsters' general presidency in 1957.

The Teamsters were ready for their long-awaited savior: Jimmy Hoffa. Beck's announcement gave the charismatic Hoffa his opening, but he had to get past an immediate problem: he had been indicted for attempting to bribe a McClellan committee lawyer on Kennedy's staff. Before Hoffa's trial began, the case against him seemed airtight to most observers. In addition to eyewitnesses, the government had incriminating photographs of Hoffa's exchanges with the congressional attorney. According to the committee lawyer himself, the pictures showed Hoffa giving him money in return for committee secrets. Knowing the formidable case the union leader faced, Robert Kennedy remarked, "If Hoffa isn't convicted, I'll jump off the Capitol."

My father read about all of this in his monthly *International Teamster* magazine. He was far more impressed with Jimmy Hoffa than with Bobby Kennedy's effort to imprison him. After the jury exonerated the union leader, Hoffa proclaimed, "It proves once again that if you're honest and tell the truth you have nothing to fear." Rather than focus on the damning evidence against Hoffa or the superior courtroom performance of his trial lawyer, Edward Bennett Williams, my father viewed the whole situation as one more unsuccessful government attack on Hoffa and the progressive labor movement.

He rejoiced in Hoffa's vindication for another reason. Despite my father's continuing effort to live a straight life, he had to acknowledge that anyone who could beat a federal rap of the magnitude directed at Hoffa was worthy of respect for that reason alone. In his heart, he still believed from his Angola year that criminal justice in America was a game. For those who could afford to play, the stakes must have seemed less daunting. As far as he was concerned, Hoffa's alleged crimes did not warrant the severity of the government's assault. He hoped that Hoffa beat every charge. Anybody had to be better for his new Teamsters community than Dave Beck. And Hoffa wasn't just anybody.

After the not-guilty verdict at the bribery trial, my dad read the musings of Hoffa's attorney in *International Teamster:* "I'm going to send Bobby Kennedy a parachute for when he jumps off the Capitol dome." My father would have laughed if he'd known that Hoffa later claimed to have sent Kennedy one, along with a one-word note: "Jump!"

Hoffa waited only ten days after his acquittal on bribery charges to announce his candidacy for the International Teamsters general presidency at the upcoming Miami convention. A month later, he gained all the publicity needed to win the election when he made his first appearance before the McClellan committee. In the nationally televised hearings, Hoffa struck a sharp contrast to the weak and corrupt image of Dave Beck. Careful to avoid what he regarded as Beck's biggest mistake, Hoffa never invoked the Fifth Amendment to refuse answering any of his interrogators' questions. Instead, he appeared to enjoy his verbal dance with his congressional inquisitors. Hoffa's popularity among the rank-and-file Teamsters grew with every assault on the embattled underdog. Dad was impressed: not even the highest government officials could push Jimmy Hoffa around.

Just as his path to the general presidency seemed wide open, Hoffa confronted a surprising obstacle from within. On September 17, 1957, thirteen rank-and-file Teamsters from a New York local filed a lawsuit seeking to enjoin the impending International Teamsters election. The insurgents claimed that Hoffa had violated the union's constitution. Among their charges was a conspiracy to "fix" the national election, as well as misuse of union funds. F. Dickinson Letts, an elderly judge who had been appointed by president Herbert Hoover, granted their request to enjoin the election at which Hoffa was certain to be-

come the Teamsters' next general president. Hoffa's appeal of the ruling produced a partial victory. The injunction was lifted and the election was allowed to proceed, but the appellate court said that the challengers retained the right to pursue their remedies afterwards. So even if Hoffa won at the convention, Judge Letts could undo that victory in subsequent legal proceedings. In their final effort to stop the election, the rebels went to the U.S. Supreme Court.

As I read about these events, I was gaining new insight into Hoffa's hostility toward local union insurgencies. I also noted my father's unfortunately ironic choice in later naming his own renegades the "Rank-and-File Group" only two years after a New York group of "rank-and-file" Teamsters had tried to obstruct Hoffa's rise to power.

As the International Teamsters convention began in Miami, outgoing general president Beck went to the podium with his dramatic proclamation: "The chair desires to announce at this time that Chief Justice Warren has, as of this date, decided not to block the election."

Before he became the nation's chief justice, Earl Warren had been the governor of California. In that role, he had welcomed the Teamsters delegates to their last national convention in Los Angeles, stating his "increasing admiration for the Teamsters union . . . not only something great of itself, but splendidly representative of the entire labor movement." Five years later, Hoffa now treated the unwillingness of Warren's Supreme Court to involve itself in the current fray as a personal victory. He jumped to the front of the stage, smiled broadly, and lifted Beck's arm to form a victory salute. The auditorium erupted with wild applause and cheers.

International Teamsters general secretary-treasurer John F. English took the podium. As the union's elder statesman, he had been an International officer for twenty of his more than fifty years as a Teamster. Even Robert Kennedy had grown to respect English as a man of integrity who was seemingly above reproach. He walked to the center stage podium, where he told the convention that it was a critical time in the Teamsters' history. He said that the union was under continuous assault from the left and the right—the FBI, the Senate's McClellan committee, and the Teamsters' parent union, the American Federation of Labor. Describing Hoffa as a champion who'd done more than anyone else for the Teamsters, English nominated Hoffa for the general presidency. He urged the members to take care of Hoffa because Hoffa was taking care of them.

In his 1960 book *The Enemy Within*, Robert Kennedy reported that he later asked English why he maintained continued enthusiasm for Hoffa at the 1957 convention in the face of mounting evidence against the charismatic leader. According to Kennedy, English replied, "And what do you want me to do? I've been with this union all my life. I've been a Teamster for fifty years. What do you want me to do? . . . Do you want me to lose my pension, everything?" During his rise to power, Hoffa seemed always to present his Teamsters with an easy choice: support Hoffa's ascent to the top of the union or risk the ire of the world's most charismatic labor leader once he got there. Hoffa appeared to have friends and foes—and virtually no one in between.

A more interesting story of the convention—and its Minnesota connection—was secretly developing outside the auditorium where the delegates had gathered. In addition to the general presidency, the election would also decide the composition of the entire Teamsters general executive board of vice presidents drawn from various regions of the country. Minnesotan Sid Brennan had served on the board since 1943, but Hoffa now wanted Gordon Conklin representing that state instead.

A few days before the convention delegates voted, Clark Mollenhoff had a private conversation with Hoffa on the subject of Conklin's proposed new leadership role. Mollenhoff later reported that conversation in his 1965 book. Although Sid Brennan's extortion conviction was an ongoing spur to congressional examination, that was not the reason Hoffa wanted to replace Brennan. He told the reporter that any and all opposition on the executive board would be eliminated, which meant Brennan would be out and Conklin would be in.

"I've got one guy you'll approve of," Hoffa reportedly told Mollenhoff privately. "I'm putting Gordon Conklin from St. Paul on my ticket in place of Sid Brennan. I understand you kinda like Conklin." Hoffa knew that Conklin had helped Mollenhoff back in January 1953, when the reporter first began his investigation into Minneapolis Teamsters corruption.

Mollenhoff's 1965 book also revealed his conversation with Conklin the next day. "Haven't you been reading the papers?" he asked the International Teamsters' vice president-to-be. "Don't you know what the McClellan committee has put on the line about Jimmy?"

"I don't like it, Clark," Conklin supposedly replied. "I don't see what

I can do. Jimmy has always treated me okay. He backed me when I had my back to the wall in the fight to keep Brennan's boys from taking over St. Paul. You gotta support the guys that supported you. Even if I wanted to object, I can't see where it would do any good. Jimmy has the organization, and he has the votes. I could end up on the outside—and with nothing gained." Perhaps the seductive power of a position on the general executive board was irresistible. Maybe the prospect of spending the rest of his life perched comfortably atop the Teamsters hierarchy drew the fifty-four-year-old Conklin ever closer to Hoffa and his new regime, however troubled it might be.

On the same day that the Soviet Union launched Sputnik into outer space in October 1957, Hoffa won the general presidency of the Teamsters with 73 percent of the vote. His landslide victory was accompanied by a wholesale turnover in the International's top leadership as Hoffa's personal selections, including Gordon Conklin, dominated the new general executive board.

My father believed every word of Hoffa's inaugural speech, reprinted in full in *International Teamster*. Hoffa pledged that the Brotherhood would be a model of trade unionism. He asked for time and the support of each and every Teamster to accomplish his task. He told his 1.5 million-man membership that he wanted to hear from them; he wanted their advice; he wanted their guidance; he wanted their help. If a member was dissatisfied with the union, Hoffa wanted to hear about it personally. And he pledged to practice union democracy in its fullest form.

A month later, my second sister, Linda, was born on November 9, 1957—six years to the day after Dad had been consigned to Angola. He basked in the glory of almost four years of continuous employment in his first permanent and meaningful job. He had moved to the top and become a professional over-the-road driver for one of the best trucking firms in Minneapolis. He was a member of the greatest labor union in the world, which Jimmy Hoffa would lead to new heights of respectability and bigger paychecks. For my father, the federal government and the rest of Hoffa's union-busting critics had become nothing more than the enemies of progress for the working man. Judging by all that he could see, Hoffa was his man and might someday become the mentor for whom he had longed.

But his picture of Hoffa was both incomplete and distorted. It was

incomplete because no one at the time knew all that could be known about Hoffa's character and activities in the late 1950s. It was distorted by the special prism of personal experience through which he viewed the Teamsters leader. Perhaps the next message was emerging from my father's box: if what we don't know can hurt us, what we think we know—but don't—can hurt even more.

11

The Insurgency That Would Not Go Away

Hoffa's election euphoria was short-lived because the New York rank-and-file insurgents' lawsuit resurfaced to cast a giant shadow over his presidency. On October 23, 1957, Judge Letts issued a new injunction that precluded Hoffa and the other newly elected Teamsters leaders from assuming their posts or spending union monies. Further hearings would determine whether the ban should become permanent.

Almost simultaneously, the AFL-CIO threatened to expel the Teamsters from that organization unless Hoffa was barred from taking his new office. The AFL-CIO's criticisms included Sid Brennan's continuing presence in Minneapolis, even after losing all appeals of his extortion conviction. Hoffa's loyal warrior John English urgently pled to the AFL-CIO's executive council the Teamsters' case for remaining in the organization with which it had been affiliated since 1903. He relied upon the results of the recent election to argue his point. "We ask for one year, after giving you fifty years. We ask for one year to clean up our house," he said. "Beck is gone . . . Brennan is gone."

English was partially correct. Beck was certainly gone, and Sid Brennan had lost his bid to remain on the general executive board. But Gordon Conklin could not replace Brennan until the New York insurgents' litigation was resolved. More importantly, Brennan was still secretary-treasurer of Local 544 and would retain that position until someone displaced him. He would not face another Minneapolis Teamsters election until December 1958. English's words were fruitless, and, to Hoffa's chagrin, the AFL-CIO expelled the Teamsters.

Meanwhile, Hoffa could see that the insurgents' court case was going poorly for him. The time had come to settle the lawsuit that had stymied his presidency. On January 31, 1958, Judge Letts entered a negotiated consent decree that resolved the litigation by establishing a three-person Board of Monitors. The rank-and-file members who had initiated the litigation would choose one member; the International Teamsters would choose a second. If the parties could not agree

on a third, the court would choose that person, who would also serve as chairman. When former president Truman refused the offer to become the first chairman, the job went to a retired Washington, DC, municipal judge who held it for only six months before resigning. In his place, Martin O'Donoghue, a lawyer who had initially participated on Hoffa's side of the insurgents' litigation, became chairman. Hoffa must have assumed that he could control the former Teamsters' lawyer, but he was wrong in ways that he could not have predicted.

Most important to Hoffa at the time, the decree allowed him and his new general executive board to assume office immediately, even though they would hold their positions only provisionally until a new election occurred. The Monitors could recommend holding a new election a year later, but they could wait longer if Hoffa failed to clean up the union by then. The Monitors had additional powers that included protecting members' rights to free speech at meetings and to vote periodically for elected officers. They would also draft a model code of local union bylaws, establish meaningful financial accounting controls, seek an end to International control through trusteeships at locals throughout the country, and determine proper methods for selecting delegates to the next International convention. The Monitors could hear individual union member complaints and pursue legal actions accordingly. In short, the decree imposed a level of personal and financial accountability on the International Teamsters leadership that Hoffa and the organization had never before known.

With the lawsuit now resolved, Hoffa was able for the first time to author the "President's Page" for *International Teamster*. He wrote that he took pride in the fact that he'd always known and understood the problems of the union's members. He said he'd never forgotten that he was once a rank-and-file member himself, and he never would. Hoffa also described the Monitors as "a practical solution to a highly complex situation."

The magazine printed a lengthy "Statement of Board of Monitors to Members of the International Brotherhood of Teamsters." The part most important to Dad said the Monitors would consult with the general executive board to "insure the enforcement and protection of all rights of individual members." When my father read the union magazine, he would have concluded that Hoffa was actually pleased with the new board and its announced mission: a photograph adjacent to

the statement showed Hoffa grinning widely as he "greeted Monitors" and announced his full cooperation.

The Monitors themselves soon became Hoffa's newest headache. They required that all locals subject to International Teamsters trusteeship be returned to local control before the next national election could be scheduled; that edict saddled Hoffa with a "provisional presidency" indefinitely. The Monitors also required the International to issue a prompt and full report concerning any member's complaint. No longer could local controversies be swept under a rug or thrown into a river.

Through it all, Minneapolis became a deepening thorn for Hoffa. When he appeared before the Senate's McClellan committee on August 5, 1958, Hoffa faced pointed questions that took him back, once again, to Minnesota. Robert Kennedy wanted to know why Sid Brennan, a convicted extortionist, still led Local 544. How could Hoffa square that with his public condemnation of union corruption? Hoffa had to admit that Brennan hadn't been removed from the leadership of the local; he'd have to remedy that situation.

12

Hoffa's Biggest Minneapolis Problem

My research kept taking me back to Minnesota. I learned that my home state actually held the origins of what would become Hoffa's worst legal problems, but prior books about the Teamsters' leader had not focused on the Minnesota connection. Any such link to Hoffa's downfall was critical to me because it might help answer one of my central questions: why would Jimmy Hoffa care about my father's relatively insignificant Minneapolis Local 544 insurgency in early 1960? I now think I have the answer: although Hoffa had much more important Minnesota problems than Jim Harper, he wanted none of the media attention that Harper would focus on the Twin Cities.

At about the same time that Hoffa was secretly supporting Clark Mollenhoff's investigation of Sid Brennan in early 1953, Hoffa was developing another relationship that would produce an even more daunting Minneapolis difficulty for him a few years later. The central figure in that part of the story was Ben Dranow, who operated several small fur stores in New York City, Philadelphia, Wilmington, and Baltimore before going to work for one of his customers in Minneapolis. In 1952, Dranow accepted a job managing the fur department at the John W. Thomas Department Store.

A year later, the Retail Clerks International Association struck the store; four years of labor strife followed. Dranow befriended Minneapolis's notorious Teamster Jerry Connelly and eventually obtained control of the store. As the strike continued in June 1956, Hoffa's Michigan Teamsters made a loan of $200,000 to the store. Six months later one of Hoffa's friends intervened to settle the strike.

Despite the infusion of the Teamsters' loan money, Dranow's store remained in financial trouble. Sam Romer's personal files reveal that when the *Tribune* reporter asked Hoffa about the $200,000 loan in late October 1956, Hoffa insisted that it was sound. Those files also show that on April 16, 1957, Romer received information about a Teamsters' Central States Pension Fund meeting held the previous

day. Romer's longtime friend Gordon Conklin served with Hoffa as a charter member of the Fund's board of trustees. Someone, probably Conklin, told the reporter about a trustees' subcommittee meeting scheduled to discuss a second loan—projected at $900,000—to Dranow's store. A million-dollar loan was eventually made as the store careened toward bankruptcy while Dranow removed over $100,000 from its coffers. In short, Teamsters pension fund money was being channeled into a dying company owned by one of Hoffa's friends.

The McClellan committee scheduled Dranow for an appearance in September 1957. The government investigators wanted to ask about loans that the Michigan Teamsters had made to his store. With the New York insurgents' lawsuit under way, Hoffa didn't need publicity about Dranow's activities on the eve of his certain election. Claiming he was too ill to attend the hearings, Dranow entered a hospital. For more than a year afterward, he managed to avoid a McClellan committee subpoena. But the Teamsters pension fund loans to Dranow's company were less important than the problem Hoffa developed a year later. The scheme that Dranow devised to deal with that difficulty would eventually send Hoffa to jail. It was related to a Florida real estate project called Sun Valley.

Beginning in 1956, Sun Valley had been marketed to rank-and-file Teamsters as a place where they could retire. To finance the construction of streets, sewers, and homes, the developer needed cash, but the Florida National Bank at Orlando was reluctant to make the necessary loans. To help overcome the bank's fears relating to what it regarded as a risky real estate venture, Hoffa offered cash collateral. Unfortunately, the money he offered was not his; it belonged to the Detroit local over which he still presided. He transferred $400,000 from that Detroit Teamsters account to the Florida bank, where it would earn no interest. Ironically, fifteen years later, Hoffa criticized his successor for similar actions in a different context, saying bluntly, "You don't just let that money sit there. It's loaned out at the going rate of interest." Hoffa let the Detroit money "just sit there" in the Florida bank.

The profits from the sale of Sun Valley retirement homes were supposed to pay off the Florida bank loans. The $400,000 that Hoffa had put up as collateral would then be released and returned to Detroit. Once that happened, no one would know that the Detroit local's

money had been used as collateral for those loans in the first place. But that outcome required the Sun Valley development to prosper, and it didn't.

As Sun Valley failed, Hoffa's problems multiplied, and his earlier transfer of Detroit Teamsters' funds risked being revealed. Because the developer had diverted most of the Florida bank's loans for his own use, Hoffa had to come up with some other way to pay off Sun Valley's debt. Otherwise the bank would keep the $400,000 that Hoffa had sent from Detroit. If that happened, his use of the Detroit Teamsters' money as collateral for the Sun Valley loans would be discovered, and Hoffa would be open to the charge that he had misused union funds.

Hoffa's old friend from Minneapolis, Ben Dranow, came up with a plan. Dranow went to several promoters of high-risk construction projects and said he could arrange for the Teamsters Central States Pension Fund to make them loans. In return for this personal attention to their loan applications, the promoters were required to pay large cash commissions to Dranow. Witnesses would later testify that Hoffa performed his role, which was to make sure that the fund's trustees approved the risky loans. In addition to Hoffa, those trustees were Gordon Conklin, other International Teamsters leaders, and representatives from the trucking industry; all deferred to Hoffa. Dranow and Hoffa then used the cash commissions from the developers to pay off Sun Valley's debt. Only when those debts were finally paid would the Florida bank release the $400,000 of Detroit Teamsters money it was holding. The scam continued from early 1958 through early 1960, as Hoffa and Dranow scrambled to cover their tracks and one lie led to the next. Always, it seemed, Hoffa's story returned to Minneapolis.

As 1958 ended, Hoffa returned again to another Minneapolis problem: Sid Brennan. English had told the AFL-CIO a year earlier that "Brennan was gone." It had become time for Hoffa to make those words true. His loyalty to fellow Teamsters didn't extend to men like Brennan, who had been Tobin's man and then Beck's but never Hoffa's. In a conversation that Clark Mollenhoff first revealed in his 1965 book, one of Hoffa's lawyers, Ed Cheyfitz, told Mollenhoff in January 1958 that Brennan's days even as a local Teamsters leader were numbered: "Jimmy Hoffa has really learned his lesson, and intends to try to make the Teamsters a clean union. He's changed a lot. The hear-

ings have been a real shock to him. You'll be interested in one thing he is going to do out in Minneapolis. He's going to get rid of Sid Brennan and Gene Williams."

Only Hoffa and his closest confidants knew the magnitude of the manpower and money that he planned to pour into the December 1958 election at Minneapolis Local 544. If Hoffa had his way, Brennan would be out by January 1959 and his newly selected replacement, Fritz Snyder, would be in. Once that happened, Brennan would no longer draw investigative attention to Minnesota. With Brennan gone and only Gordon Conklin and Fritz Snyder around, Hoffa would gain greater influence in a state where he needed all the help he could get. Above all, he needed soldiers of unquestioning loyalty. Conklin owed his very survival as a local Teamsters leader and his new national office in the union to Hoffa; Snyder, too, would be far more loyal than Brennan.

When Fritz Snyder celebrated his forty-eighth birthday in October 1958, he was still adding inches to his waistline as the hair on his head disappeared. He lived alone. If he'd ever married, many of those closest to him had never heard about it. The truth was that no one was really close to him. When it suited his ambitions, Snyder had contented himself to be Sid Brennan's number-two man at Local 544, but now Snyder had the opportunity to become number one himself.

In the last Local 544 election four years earlier, secretary-treasurer Brennan had won by an overwhelming majority and vice president Snyder had run without opposition. But the November 16, 1958, session of Local 544 stewards and shop committeemen revealed a new and dramatic schism. In a remarkable turn of events, Snyder announced his intention to challenge Brennan for the top job in the local. The *Tribune* reported the story the next morning. In sharp contrast to the private remarks that Hoffa's lawyer had previously made to Clark Mollenhoff about Hoffa's true desires for the local, the newspaper quoted Hoffa's hands-off attitude in the election because "the local membership must sit in judgment" in deciding between Brennan and Snyder. As my father read the article over a cup of coffee and two Camels, he had no reason to doubt what labor reporter Sam Romer wrote in the area's largest and most respected news source. He also paid no attention to the short item buried on page 13B in the prior day's edition, where Clark Mollenhoff wrote about the McClellan com-

mittee's unsuccessful yearlong efforts to find and subpoena Minneapolis businessman Ben Dranow.

The voter turnout in the contest between Snyder and Brennan was unprecedented. Over 1,800 members cast ballots. The campaign was ferocious to the end, but the result was not as close as many had expected. Brennan lost by a margin of almost three to one—1,349 to 515—and the Snyder regime began on January 1, 1959.

At the International Teamsters headquarters where Hoffa sat at a large oak desk from which he could view the U.S. Capitol dome, he had to be pleased with the outcome. Bobby Kennedy could no longer harass him with the Brennan embarrassment in Minneapolis. Hoffa must have concluded that he had reduced the risk that his much larger Minneapolis problem relating to Dranow, Sun Valley, and the Teamsters Central States Pension Fund would become public. Brennan looked for opportunities to turn on Hoffa; Snyder would remain a good soldier. But Hoffa would soon discover that events were spinning beyond even his formidable ability to control them.

13

Hoffa Feels the Heat and Looks for Help

As my research took me ever closer to the earliest days of my father's insurgency in late 1959, I understood what Dad never knew: the location and timing of his effort could not have been worse. Seven months after Snyder's election, former Minneapolis resident Ben Dranow was again in the news. Clark Mollenhoff's front-page *Tribune* article on July 1, 1959, described a McClellan committee investigator's testimony about Dranow's fourteen bank accounts that had accumulated almost $3 million in commissions from Dranow-arranged loans of Teamsters pension funds. A week later, Dranow pled the Fifth and refused to answer questions about his Teamsters dealings.

The pressure on Hoffa intensified throughout the fall and winter of 1959. Despite Teamsters' opposition, President Eisenhower signed in September what became known as the Landrum-Griffin Act. Hoffa hated the new law, a direct result of the McClellan committee investigations, which imposed comprehensive new requirements of fairness and accountability on the leaders of organized labor. It codified the restrictive handicaps that the Board of Monitors had imposed on the Teamsters, and it added new ones. It required democratic union elections and regular financial audits. It prohibited convicted felons from holding union office, and the secretary of labor immediately directed Hoffa to remove all of them. Hoffa responded that only five such persons had been identified and removed but that no others would be touched.

The Monitors ordered the suspension of various Hoffa colleagues, including Tony Provenzano in New Jersey, and filed a court petition seeking Hoffa's indefinite suspension from the Teamsters leadership. Federal grand juries in Pittsburgh and Washington returned indictments implicating Hoffa in an extortion scheme. In early December the Department of Justice indicted two telephone operators at the Washington hotel where Hoffa lived. They were charged with destroying Hoffa's telephone records that the McClellan committee had sub-

poenaed. In short, Clark Mollenhoff's 1953 Minneapolis trip had mushroomed into a disaster for Hoffa by the end of 1959.

For Hoffa, Clark Mollenhoff had grown from a minor nuisance to a major problem. Hoffa's defense attorney, Edward Bennett Williams, blamed Mollenhoff's articles in the *Tribune* for the hostile public atmosphere that had helped convict Sid Brennan a few years earlier. From 1953 through 1957, Hoffa had personally sparred with Mollenhoff, who attended all of Hoffa's trials and most of his congressional appearances. Hoffa had given Mollenhoff extensive private interviews during that period, probably in the egomaniacal belief that he could win the reporter over to his cause. By the time of his 1957 bribery trial, Hoffa had given up on that effort, telling him, "The trouble with you, Clark, is you're anti-labor." But Mollenhoff never relented.

Perhaps a media counterpoint to Mollenhoff in Minneapolis seemed attractive to Hoffa. Perhaps another reporter in that city could provide an antidote to the poison that had been flowing from Mollenhoff's pen. Perhaps that is why, despite many competing demands, Hoffa still found time to grant numerous unpublished personal interviews to *Tribune* labor reporter Sam Romer.

Here is where my discovery of Romer's own personal papers in the Minnesota Historical Society archives revealed a dimension of the story that my father had never known. He would go to his death more than forty years later without ever learning the truth about the newsman who was, he had believed, his loyal friend and a supporter of the Local 544 insurgency that was nearly my dad's undoing.

Two years before my father launched his challenge, a professor at the University of California at Berkeley had asked Romer to write one in a series of book-length monographs relating to labor issues in the United States. Romer's subject would be the Teamsters. For his part-time effort, he would receive $2,000 annually plus expenses for two years—this at a time when intercity truck drivers earned about $2.50 an hour. He eagerly accepted.

After reviewing the existing literature, Romer decided that his best angle would be to draw upon new personal interviews with the International Teamsters' leadership. He would start with recently elected International vice president Gordon Conklin, a longtime friend. In addition to Hoffa himself, Romer's other acquaintances on the general executive board included Hoffa's closest confidant, International vice

president Harold Gibbons; Romer called him Hal. For the approach he planned, Romer needed Hoffa to grant unprecedented access to himself and the union leadership. For that, Romer had to convince Hoffa that he was a friend.

In his first correspondence to Hoffa on the subject, Romer obsequiously reaffirmed his support. He sent his January 27, 1958, letter as Judge Letts entered the consent decree allowing Hoffa to assume the general presidency. He wrote:

Dear President Hoffa:
The formal title is my form of congratulations to you on your taking the office to which you were elected.

I am also writing to tell you that (in a mild way) I have turned towards academic as well as journalistic pursuits. That is, I have agreed to participate in a trade union project sponsored by the Fund for the Republic which proposes to examine the problems of union government. I have been asked to serve the project as the author of a study of the Teamsters.

I agreed, of course, principally because of my long-standing interest in the Teamsters and yourself—I regard both the union and your own leadership as keys to the future development and accomplishments of the entire American labor movement. I should add, in all frankness, that the fact that there is a comfortable chunk of dough involved didn't deter me . . .

In any case, I think I should say that I do not intend to use this project for journalistic purposes, that is, although I will continue to work on the *Tribune*, I expect to limit my work on the project to a straight academic approach to the issues.

I shall, of course, be asking persons like yourself and Harold Gibbons for help before I am through; I am sure that you will.

Hoffa would have gladly assisted Romer's book-writing exercise. Romer and Conklin had come through for him in January 1953, when their work in Minneapolis had started Sid Brennan's descent from the Teamsters leadership. Mollenhoff had become an irritant since then, but that was not Romer's fault. As one of Conklin's best friends, Romer would have presented only limited risks to Hoffa and the Teamsters leadership. Conklin could monitor the situation, and Hoffa could end Romer's special access whenever it became necessary.

In July 1958, Romer told Hal Gibbons that he looked forward to the extended visit planned at the International Teamsters headquar-

ters in Washington. In August, he thanked Gibbons for the courtesies the Teamsters had extended during the two weeks he had just spent there and wrote of his desire for follow-up interviews with Hoffa, John English, Dave Beck, Lawrence Steinberg, and others. Gibbons responded that such interviews should be scheduled after the Teamsters' ongoing work with the McClellan committee was concluded. Hoffa made sure Romer got the interviews he wanted.

On May 21, 1959, Hoffa met personally with Romer in Minneapolis. On July 7, 1959, as Dranow was refusing to discuss Sun Valley and loans from the Teamsters, Romer again visited with Hoffa. Romer met with the Teamsters' former general president, Dave Beck, the next day. In August 1959, Romer wrote in gratitude to Gibbons—the man closest to Hoffa—thanking him for the "unstinted help and cooperation" during his stay in Washington. He commented that he "especially enjoyed the weekend with you and Mrs. Gibbons."

Romer also asked for Gibbons's help in gathering information about the Teamsters' Central States Pension Fund. He renewed his request two months later when that help was not forthcoming—even though Gibbons had confirmed that "President Hoffa is cooperating with your study" and had authorized the fund's executive secretary, Frank Murtha, to provide the materials that Romer sought. In sharp contrast to Hoffa's speedy arranging of the high-level interviews during the summers of 1958 and 1959, Romer's pension fund inquiries would go unanswered well into 1960. During that critical period in the Local 544 insurgency, Romer was becoming ever closer to his sources—the men who led the union he was covering for his newspaper.

Regardless of whether Romer realized it, it seems to me he was becoming Hoffa's newsman in Minneapolis.

Meanwhile, Hoffa's biggest Minneapolis problem continued to mushroom. On December 7, 1959, federal prosecutor James Dowd filed a letter authorizing a grand jury inquiry into Sun Valley. That process would transform the matter from a civil nuisance into a criminal problem of the highest order. The Florida loans for which Hoffa had transferred funds from his Detroit local as collateral had not been repaid, so the bank was still holding that money as security. Hoffa's exploding difficulties, especially in Minneapolis, were so large as 1959

drew to a close that even with the best lawyers that money could buy, he needed help from someone inside the federal government.

On December 13, Hoffa secretly met in a Miami hotel room with former Republican congressman Allen Oakley Hunter. Hunter had a direct line to a fellow Californian of national prominence and influence, vice president Richard Nixon. Hunter had served in the House of Representatives from 1951 to 1955. Among his jobs during a distinguished career, he had been a special agent for the FBI before serving in England and Germany as a counterintelligence agent for the Office of Strategic Services during World War II. He was a delegate to the Republican National Convention that nominated Eisenhower and Nixon in 1952. After losing his congressional reelection bid in 1955, he became general counsel for the Housing and Home Finance Agency. By 1959, he had resigned from his government post and was maintaining a private law practice in California.

"Dear Dick," began Hunter's eight-page letter to Nixon shortly after his private session with Hoffa. Nixon's presidential aspirations were no secret, and Hoffa was now offering a plan that might help both of them. Hoffa's worst nightmares would come true if Senator John Kennedy—the brother of his nemesis on the McClellan committee—became president of the United States. Hoffa suggested a way for Nixon to make Republican inroads into the traditionally Democratic organized labor vote. According to Hunter's letter, Hoffa preferred Nixon over the other presidential contenders, but he recognized his own controversial baggage. Hoffa's outright endorsement of Nixon could do more harm than good, but Teamsters' endorsements coming from the local level might well benefit any presidential candidate. Hoffa could help deliver support at that level.

The subsequent secret meeting marked the beginning of a symbiotic relationship between Hoffa and Nixon that would serve both men well in the coming years. For Hoffa, it had all begun in Minneapolis with the Teamsters' Central States Pension Fund. The last thing Hoffa needed in December 1959 was another problem in the City of Lakes. If only my father had known.

THREE

IMPACT

14

Harper Helps Hoffa—Or So He Thinks

In retrospect, things in our home seemed much calmer to me than they actually were at the time. As if the challenge of four pregnancies in as many years was not enough, my mother had to handle her father's sudden death in June 1958. I was four years old when I sat next to Dad in the backseat of a large black Cadillac that was part of an evening funeral procession. My grandfather Gervasius Fischer, whom I barely knew, had died of a heart attack as he walked up the stairs during a Wednesday night function at his Mankato church. While I attended the funeral service with my parents, a neighbor took care of my sisters, three-year-old Susan and infant Linda. I would have had a younger brother then, too, but he had died a few days after his birth two years earlier.

I remember only the ride to the cemetery. I can still picture the eerie sight of headlights forging a path through the darkness along the bumpy unpaved road in the graveyard. At our destination, people I didn't know had gathered around the hole in the earth. My minister grandfather had requested that his funeral be held at night so members of his congregation could pay their last respects without missing work. I'm still not sure what that directive says about him.

His death created a new series of challenges for our family. No longer able to reside in the parsonage reserved for the family of the church's pastor, my grandmother and her eleven-year-old daughter needed a place to live. My mother came to the rescue—none of her siblings was willing—and the two moved into our house for an indefinite period. In light of what I now know about Mom's difficult childhood relationship with her own mother, it was a remarkable offer.

My father left to Mom the job of sorting out our domestic situation so he could focus on his own career and how Hoffa might help it. Bobby Kennedy had started his attack in 1956, and, as far as my father could tell three years later, it had gone nowhere. Hoffa won case after case

that the government had brought against him. After a jury acquitted him in 1957 of bribing a McClellan committee staff lawyer, Hoffa prevailed in June 1958 on charges that he had wiretapped telephones and conference rooms in the Teamsters' Detroit headquarters. My father concluded that if the government was correct in its claims about Hoffa's links to organized crime, then he'd be in prison and certainly not living the Spartan life for which he had become famous. The Teamsters' general president still lived in the Detroit home that he and his wife had bought in 1939 for $6,800.

My father viewed with approval Hoffa's twin goals of ridding the Teamsters of corruption and enhancing its economic power. He believed Hoffa's testimony in response to Bobby Kennedy and the McClellan committee: solving all the union's problems was a tremendous job that couldn't be completed overnight. The September 1958 *International Teamster* reported Hoffa's acknowledgment that the union faced many problems; he said he'd resolve them under the due process of its constitution.

The magazine reported Hoffa's similar remarks the following month. He told his congressional interrogators that he'd already done more to rid the union of corruption than the combined efforts of his predecessors. He also reaffirmed that he was handling such matters in the only effective way: by calling individuals and helping them recognize that the Teamsters union was bigger than Jimmy Hoffa or any single member.

Hoffa had brought a new vitality to the Teamsters. Of course, he wasn't perfect, but that didn't matter to Dad. *Time* magazine's August 1959 cover story included a Harvard Business School professor's conclusion that Hoffa may "emerge as one of the outstanding labor leaders of all time." The author dismissed attacks on Hoffa with comments that resonated with my father: "Some of the greatest saints had their schooling in sin."

The accompanying economic progress made every Teamster want to believe whatever Hoffa said. He'd made a real difference in workers' lives; weekly paychecks increased steadily under his dynamic leadership. After he took over, the 1.5 million-man union was adding more than 50,000 workers yearly—a thousand a week—to its membership rolls. Hoffa had given new meaning to the concept of organizing labor, as he collected and combined individual locals into regional and national bargaining forces with which management feared

to reckon. Where Hoffa's negotiating presence had been longest and strongest, his men had fared best. In Minnesota and the eleven other states of the Central States Drivers Council, which Hoffa had dominated since vanquishing Farrell Dobbs, Teamsters over-the-road drivers had seen their average hourly wages increase by 40 percent between 1953 and 1959—an era of little inflation.

Our family had grown to four children with the birth of my brother, Michael, in March 1959, and Hoffa's beneficial impact on our lives was palpable. As Dad had risen through the ranks at Werner, we moved to a nicer home, ate better meals, and rode in fancier used cars. There must have been a million other similar Teamsters families, and the breadwinner of each household gave Hoffa the credit. In the final analysis, Hoffa empowered the "little guy." He had charted the union's path toward the nationwide over-the-road drivers' contract that would someday allow the Teamsters alone to shut down the entire country, if Hoffa decided it was best. No union worker—not even Dad—could have asked for anything more than Jimmy Hoffa embodied in a leader.

As much as anything, my father respected Hoffa's vigor in repelling the assaults on him: Hoffa repeatedly told his detractors to "go to hell." By the end of 1959, my dad was certainly aware of accusations reported in *Time* and *Life* about Hoffa's supposed underworld ties. But as far as he was concerned, the sinister qualities that some ascribed to Hoffa were not the complete story of the man; after all, Dad had many of those qualities himself.

Ultimately, Hoffa's overriding appeal was his clear and unambiguous public agenda: to clean up the Teamsters while strengthening it economically for its members. Hoffa's hands might get dirty as he proceeded, but so what? For Dad, Hoffa was a perfect fit—all the more so for his enigmatic qualities.

My father's mission to help Hoffa clean up the union began when trusted colleagues told him that Local 544's new secretary-treasurer, Fritz Snyder, was misusing union funds. Snyder was supposedly abusing union gasoline credit cards, taking an excessive salary, and being reimbursed for trips he'd never taken. Dad concluded that it was Sid Brennan all over again.

He was also told that Hoffa had handpicked St. Paul's Gordon Conklin to replace Sid Brennan on the general executive board in the 1957

election. Conklin was supposed to be a straight shooter, knew Hoffa personally, and would assist in any cleanup effort. After a personal call to Conklin, my father was convinced that his sources were correct.

"It's the kids and widows of Teamsters who require the most protection," he told my mother after his telephone conversation with Conklin during the late fall of 1959. "If crooked Teamsters officials are skimming union dues to line their own pockets, they're taking money right out of those helpless kids' and widows' mouths. The Teamsters' health and welfare funds and pension funds don't belong to corrupt Teamsters leaders who steal from them. They belong to the rank and file. They belong to the Teamsters' families who'll need that money for food and a place to live if they lose the man of the house."

My father had always identified with the unprotected, whose cause he would now pursue. This was his opportunity to demonstrate courage and conviction. Strength of character and willingness to do the right thing would be rewarded, just as his experience as an army instructor had taught him.

Conklin persuaded my father that a cleanup at Local 544 would appeal to Hoffa, my mother told me later. Conklin had confirmed Hoffa's concern about the same innocent people and the same corruption problems. Conklin said Hoffa wanted the Teamsters to be clean; that was why Conklin had taken Brennan's place on the International's executive board. He said Hoffa would support any member who helped make the union better, but Hoffa himself wouldn't weigh in until all the evidence had been gathered and all charges proven.

Conklin also gave him the name of a *Tribune* labor reporter who could help: "Sam Romer can be trusted to print the truth. Call Sam and tell him I told you to call him. Tell him what you find as you go along. He won't reveal you as his source, but he'll make sure the matter gets the public's attention."

Conklin's words were music to my father's ears. He knew from his Angola days that media attention could boost his reform effort. Immediately after his conversation with Conklin, he dialed Sam Romer's telephone number.

"Hello, Mr. Romer, my name is Jim Harper. Gordon Conklin said I should contact you about a situation involving corruption at Teamsters Local 544."

15

Let the Games Begin

My father was sure enough of his suspicions, but finding the necessary evidence to expose Snyder was something else. He needed someone with access to the Local 544 financial records who was willing to reveal the truth. He knew of no such person.

Snyder controlled the local's governing board, consisting of himself, three other officers, and three trustees. Theoretically, the trustees served to check and balance the otherwise unrestrained power of the secretary-treasurer, but that was only theory. As my father saw it, the incumbent trustees approved whatever Snyder wanted. Snyder and his fellow officers had been elected only a year earlier in the acrimonious contest that had deposed Sid Brennan, but the trustees faced reelection in December 1959. That race offered Dad's best chance to gain an insider for his cause.

With Conklin's assurances that the International leadership was already backing him, my father lined up grassroots support and formed what he called the Rank-and-File Group. He didn't focus on the fact that a similarly labeled group in New York had launched an insurgency whose aftermath continued to haunt Hoffa's presidency with the Board of Monitors. Rather, he thought Hoffa would like the name. The group's letterhead bore it as an acronym embedded in a slogan: "*R*etain your *A*uthority in our u*N*ion with *K*nowledge, *F*earless effort, *I*nterest, *L*eadership, and *E*nthusiasm." His initial group consisted of workers from all branches of Local 544, including over-the-road, grocery, and local cartage drivers. This would be participatory democracy at its best.

He walked into his local's November 1959 membership meeting with the confidence of a man on a just mission. The main purpose of the gathering was to nominate trustees for the December election. He was going to stand up for what was right and make Local 544 a better place—honest, fair, respectful of its members, and free of corruption. He was certain that he was on his way to his finest hour

with the Rank-and-File Group on his side and Hoffa silently in his corner.

About three hundred workers were in attendance. Ed Blixt was the local's nominal president, but Snyder was the boss. As the crowd settled in, my father asked to be recognized. He rose to address the group.

"Brother Teamsters. I'm just an ordinary Teamster, like all of you. I work hard for a living, just like you do. I want a good, clean union that will stand up for all of us to make our lives better. I know all of you do, too."

He seemed nervous as he began to speak—probably an adrenaline surge together with an unfortunate gag reflex that affected him, at least briefly, in stressful public situations. But after a few seconds the reflex subsided, and he was as eloquent as any man who ever faced a crowd. As Grandpa Harper had told me, my father was persuasive. In the middle of a driving thunderstorm, he could convince you—even as the rain pelted your head—that the sun was shining. On this particular night, he had one additional obstacle to effective public address: no upper teeth. A few months earlier, he had returned from a road trip with an excruciating toothache. Resolving never to experience that kind of pain again, he had told a dentist to pull every one of his top teeth. Remarkably, the dentist obliged. Dad hoped that he had killed two birds with the dentist's pliers. Unaware of the new problems that dentures could cause, he assumed he had eliminated oral pain from his life. As an added benefit, he thought he had finally eradicated the unsightly quarter-inch gap between his two front teeth that had bothered him since childhood. Once he got his dentures, his front teeth would look perfect and he'd have new teeth to match his new life.

"I'm standing up now, at this meeting, at this time, because the way the leadership of Local 544 plans to conduct the trustees' election is wrong," he continued. "I'm standing up because if we ourselves don't stand up and speak out, no one else will do it for us. And the price we'll pay is the loss of our union. Our wives and kids will pay the biggest part of that price."

The crowd became silent and still. Although my father was only thirty-one, they all knew he was smart and well liked and certainly would not speak out unless he had something to say; so they all listened.

"Just like our country, we Teamsters have a constitution. It gives us

rights—like the right to vote in union elections. President Hoffa has sent around special rules for those elections."

He then detailed for the members how he thought Snyder was running roughshod over them. As citizens and as Teamsters, every man's vote was supposed to count, which meant casting a ballot in a meaningful election. He believed Snyder was frustrating that right by running his three incumbents in three separate races for reelection. If there were multiple challengers in each election—as there certainly would be once his insurgency gathered steam—any opposition to Snyder would be divided and conquered.

He asserted that Snyder's procedure violated the union's constitution and the rules set forth in the prior month's *International Teamster*. He argued that Snyder's approach of separate elections for each trustee position would entrench the incumbents. My father wanted the entire field of candidates to run simultaneously, with the three highest overall vote-getters declared winners. He knew that his proposal created a greater likelihood of at least one Rank-and-File Group challenger displacing an incumbent. When that happened, he thought, the mere revelation of Local 544's finances to the new trustee should start a process that would overwhelm and discredit Snyder.

"What's happening here, at this meeting, at this time, is a violation of the laws of the United States."

The crowd began to murmur.

"What's happening here, at this meeting, at this time, is wrong. President Hoffa has urged each and every one of us, as the rank-and-file of this union, to do what we can to make our union better. If we follow what President Hoffa wants, the result will be that the Teamsters, all of us, will be stronger. In the end, we—the members—*are* this union. And if we, the individual members of Local 544, don't stand up for ourselves and protect our union, no one else will. And once the union is lost, we'll never get it back.

"You know, this local's leadership failed to follow the Teamsters constitution in 1957," he said, facing Snyder directly. "That's why this local was singled out at the last International convention. That's why this local's delegates to that convention weren't allowed to be seated. We lost our right to vote at the convention that elected President Hoffa because this local's leadership failed to protect it."

Audience members began shouting support; some broke into periodic applause.

"Each person in this room is entitled to have his vote count. But only you can make that happen. All the speeches in the world don't mean a goddamned thing—not unless each of us cares enough to stand up and fight for our union, our wives, our kids, and what's right. This union is not just for us. It's for our kids and our grandchildren. What we do will affect all of them for a lot longer than any of us will be around to see it. That makes it even more important that we do the right thing. So let's do it!" Telling me the story years later, my father roared his final four words, undoubtedly with the same enthusiasm as when he had first uttered them.

The room exploded with applause. Snyder squirmed in his chair, and Blixt looked terrified. My father was certain that neither of them had seen anything like this at a local membership meeting. He hadn't called Snyder a crook; he had simply implied that the local leader was seeking improperly to entrench himself. But both men knew the plot line for the play-within-the-play that had now begun with Jim Harper's opening scene.

He next asked for a secret ballot on his motion to change the voting process. He urged that the new federal Landrum-Griffin Act seemed to require it, as did principles of fairness and democracy. This move placed Snyder in a dilemma: any opposition to a secret ballot would seem un-American, but he'd lose his ability to intimidate if he couldn't see how individual members voted.

My father's secret ballot request was denied, but it didn't really matter. The more important initiative to upset Snyder's plan for conducting the election was put to a voice vote. The question was called and, based upon what Dad heard, his motion passed overwhelmingly.

Snyder was undeterred. This was a frontal assault on his power, and he'd do anything to retain it. Blixt quickly announced, "The chair concludes that it can't determine the result of the voice vote."

The union members became restless; a few shouted, "Boo!"

"So we'll now take a second vote of members rising," Blixt ordered.

"Members rising" meant that when the chair called the question again, all in favor would so indicate by standing up. After they sat, all opposing the motion would be asked to stand. The chair would then announce its observed result.

"All those in favor of Brother Harper's motion, please rise," Blixt said.

A majority of the men in the room stood.

"All right. Sit down. Now all those opposed to Brother Harper's motion, please rise."

Less than half of the audience rose from their seats. Blixt and Snyder pressed ahead: "The chair concludes it can't determine the result of the vote taken by members rising. So we'll proceed to vote by a house divided."

The members groaned in disgust. "House divided" was the most intimidating of all voting methods. It required all members to vote with their feet by walking to one side of the union hall. After Snyder spoke for more than twenty minutes in favor of his incumbent trustees, the entire Local 544 executive board walked to one side of the hall. Blixt then announced, "All those in favor of the motion, go stand over on the other side of the room with Brother Harper."

The vote had become closer. Snyder glared across the room at my father, who reciprocated with equal intensity, his icy stare and flaming red birthmark fully displayed.

Blixt announced that my father's motion had failed by a mere six votes. The hall exploded in a cacophony of shouts. Snyder had won, but he had overplayed his hand badly. Although the December election would proceed as Snyder desired, Jim Harper had gained respect in the eyes of his fellow union members. Brennan had ruled Local 544 with an iron hand for almost twenty years when Snyder took him on a year earlier. My father was now taking on Snyder; no one else in the room had ever been willing to do that.

But he still was not finished. My father wanted Snyder to understand that he knew the ugly truth and wasn't giving up. He had received a tip that Snyder was using union gasoline cards to pay for personal trips unrelated to union business, so he offered a seemingly innocuous motion in support of the obvious: "Resolved, that Local 544 gasoline cards are to be used for union business purposes only."

Snyder was livid. He continued to glare at my dad, who met his gaze steadily. "I'm not afraid of this guy," my father thought. "Compared to Angola, this is a walk in the park. Fritz Snyder wouldn't last five minutes in that Louisiana hellhole." Snyder had managed to win the vote on Jim Harper's proposed resolution, but now the real struggle would begin.

16

Nothing Worthwhile Is Easy

My father thought he had secret weapons in his arsenal; it was time to use them. As soon as he returned home from the November membership meeting, he called *Tribune* reporter Sam Romer to fill him in on the evening's events. He also described his plans for the next phase of the battle: to contact the Board of Monitors. Immediately thereafter, he called Washington to advise the Monitors of the illegal method by which Snyder was planning to conduct the December election. He also asked the Monitors to investigate Local 544's books. He told them that he believed Snyder was using union funds to support his incumbent trustees and to pay for excessive entertainment, travel, and personal expenditures.

When Romer's article on the membership meeting appeared in the newspaper's December 9 edition, my father became vaguely concerned that Sam was shading events oddly. He'd told Romer that hundreds of members supported his efforts, but the article said the "rank-and-file group . . . consisted of [only] 21 members." Romer also quoted Snyder as saying the union welcomed any decision by the Monitors on the elections issue. "We followed the rules as laid down by the [M]onitors and the International," Snyder reportedly said. "Our books are open." He noted that financial reports were posted in the union office and were regularly read at membership meetings. But given what Jim Harper had told him, Romer had to know that Snyder's words were suspect at best.

"I'm worried about Romer," Dad confided to my mother after he read the article. "How can he say that the Rank-and-File Group consists of only twenty-one members? And why would he let Snyder carry on like that?" She assured him that Sam Romer was a reputable reporter for the city's largest paper. He certainly could be trusted to report honestly. Besides, she said, the insurgents had no other allies in the media. If my father wanted to draw public attention to his cause, Romer was the only game in town.

. . . . .

After the November meeting, my father's real work began. Nine opposition candidates announced their intentions to run against Snyder's incumbents. My dad knew that such a large field was a prescription for disaster because the numerous challengers would divide the insurgent vote. They would all lose and Snyder's trustees would carry their respective individual elections with pathetic pluralities.

He assembled all of the challengers around our dining room table. "We can beat Fritz at his own game," he urged. "We can follow the incorrect rules Snyder has established for the elections and still win. But we have to agree on a limited group of candidates who'll challenge his trustees. We have to run only a single Rank-and-File Group candidate against each Snyder incumbent. All those opposing Fritz will then vote for our candidate because they'll have no other way to express their discontent with him and his cronies. There's no other way."

They agreed to cast secret ballots to determine the three Rank-and-File Group candidates. The result: Jack Velin would face one of Snyder's designated incumbents, Ed Zukaitis would run against the second, and Lloyd Harris would take on the third. Velin and his rival would eventually square off in a one-on-one contest, while two additional candidates also ran in the remaining two elections. All other challengers agreed to withdraw. It wasn't perfect, but it was the best my father could do with the diverse deck of Local 544 members he'd been dealt. He assumed that the three challengers running against Snyder's incumbents would be with him completely and without qualification. Velin, Zukaitis, and Harris would be the foundation for the Rank-and-File Group's future. Each man assured my father that he stood with him and the group on goals, philosophy, and allegiances. They were blood brothers in the cause—but two of the three nominees would eventually betray him.

He once again reported to Romer and Conklin on the latest developments. When the *Tribune* reported that the group had met and united behind a three-man slate, my father thought Romer was keeping the controversy in the public eye—which he was, as he disclosed in advance my father's every strategic move. Appearing without a byline, the same article reported that a "standing vote" had resulted in a six-vote margin in favor of Snyder's plan for the December election. The author had misstated the facts: the so-called "six-vote margin" was contrived, and it was not the result of a "standing vote." Snyder had lost the members rising vote, just as he had lost the voice vote preced-

ing it. His claim of victory on the third and final vote by the house divided method was dubious at best. "Why couldn't the newspaper get the story straight?" my father wondered.

Meanwhile, he had a month to take his message directly to the union membership. In his first flyer after the November meeting, he issued a "Statement from the Group United to Promote Rank and File Control of Local 544."

> The purpose and aim of this group is to promote truly democratic unionism within the local. By this we mean that we want men in office who will protect our rights at general meetings. That is, guarantee that any member can speak freely, without fear of reprisal or loss of job, regarding any aspect of union business . . . we want to protect "the dignity of the secret ballot . . . a complete financial report . . . we do not want to wreck our union; we want to strengthen it by placing honest men of principle in office . . . *honest representation, good public relations, the prestige of a member run union, and above all, freedom from fear for all members.*

My father was sure that he already had Hoffa's attention even before the publicity began because Conklin had told him so. He was equally certain that Hoffa would appreciate the Minneapolis media attention pouring like sunlight into the Local 544 infection of the Teamsters union. He was tragically mistaken.

As the election drew closer, Snyder reverted to survival mode. Only four days before the election, the local held its last membership meeting of the year on December 17. Snyder knew the stakes were high and intensely personal. Attempting to counteract the impression he had created in November, Snyder asserted that his financial affairs were an open book. He even brought up his salary and expense allowance. As he glared at my father, Snyder requested the membership's retroactive approval to January 1, 1959, of his $225-a-week salary and $50-a-week expense account. My father made a mental note of the episode. "Someday it might come back to bite the bastard in the ass," he thought.

My dad countered with a motion to correct the minutes of the November meeting so his proposed resolution prohibiting the personal

use of union gasoline cards would be shown as passed, rather than defeated. This was a traditional parliamentary tactic allowing new majorities to revisit prior votes they had lost. This time, his motion prevailed by the slimmest of margins, 47 to 46, but Blixt ruled that a two-thirds vote was required to change the minutes of the previous meeting. As Snyder clung to a tenuous and improperly gained victory, he could see the tide turning against him.

The trustees' election was held over two days, December 21 and 22. As it approached, Snyder pulled out all the stops. For the first time ever, local television ads ran in support of incumbent trustees for a Local 544 election. Every arm that could be twisted to support Snyder's slate was twisted. If members didn't feel comfortable voting for the incumbents, then the safer path was not to vote at all. Whereas 1,800 had voted in the Snyder-Brennan race a year earlier, this time only about 500 of the 3,300-member local turned out.

In the end, Snyder's trustees still lost. Despite the requirement that each challenger run separately against each incumbent, the Rank-and-File Group challengers won every contest. Romer reported in the December 23 *Tribune* that the turnout was small and the victory margins slim: Velin beat his incumbent by only 15 votes (245 to 230); Zukaitis prevailed over his closest opponent 203 to 157, with 134 votes going to others. Harris won by the greatest plurality margin: 205 to 122—but two additional candidates in that race captured another 155 votes.

The challengers' victories rendered moot my father's request that the Monitors act on the election procedures complaint he had initiated four weeks earlier. With all three of his trustees now in power, he concluded that his Rank-and-File Group now controlled Local 544. He was on an unstoppable roll—or so he thought.

17

On Top of the World

Jim Harper had won. His crusade had become front-page news in the *Tribune* and a local television reporter wanted to interview him. After a life of failures, he had finally succeeded at something that mattered when the triple win of his Rank-and-File Group exceeded his wildest hopes. The newly elected trustees gave his group meaningful influence over Local 544. Someone other than Snyder's people now had access to the financial records that he believed would prove Snyder's wrongdoing.

He mapped out his steps for the next Local 544 business meeting and kept his two silent partners, Gordon Conklin and Sam Romer, advised of his plans. In the January 1960 *International Teamster,* he was pleased to see Conklin pictured with Hoffa at a December testimonial dinner held in Conklin's honor. My father now had no doubt that he had chosen the right International general executive board member as a confidant.

In January, he returned to the union hall where two months earlier he had begun a revolution. He was greeted with handshakes and backslaps from his fellow Teamsters. It seemed as if he was now running the local, not Snyder. Shortly after the meeting opened, he offered a series of motions:

- ▸ Motion for detailed monthly financial reports of union dues and expenditures: Passed.
- ▸ Motion to authorize the trustees to hire independent auditors to review the books for 1959: Passed.
- ▸ Motion to create a bylaws committee to revise Local 544's governing charter so that power was transferred from the secretary-treasurer to the membership: Passed.

Snyder was in trouble. He watched my father's eyes twinkle as the cocky renegade tried to suppress a smile with every vote in his favor. But Snyder had dealt with adversity long before my father had walked

into his life. He'd survived the violent strikes of 1934, and he'd figure out a way to survive this ordeal as well. Every man has his price and his breaking point, he surely thought. Snyder just had to find a single weak link in Jim Harper's chain of support. Once that happened, the crusade would fall apart.

Sometime after the meeting, Snyder reported the results to Hoffa, who would have been extremely unhappy with the recent turn of events at Local 544. Hoffa could take no more risks in Minneapolis, a city that held some of his deepest secrets. If Snyder needed help to crush the insurgency, Hoffa would provide it.

The resounding successes of the trustee election and the subsequent membership meeting gave my father every reason to believe he was close to total victory in his quest to cleanse Local 544. Now more than ever, he wanted to make sure that the new Landrum-Griffin Act's prohibitions against convicted felons holding union office wouldn't interfere with his future career: he hoped Hoffa might someday offer him a job in the International as a reward for the Local 544 reform effort. Two weeks after the January membership meeting, he put the finishing touches on his "Petition for Full Pardon with Restoration of Citizenship" and submitted it to Louisiana governor Earl Long. He prepared himself for every opportunity that Hoffa might send his way.

He also sailed on his momentum, reinforcing his victories with written communications to the membership at large. In a flyer, he stated the group's aim in plain language that his fellow members easily understood. He wanted them to be proud of what they had already accomplished—but to avoid complacency, because their mission had only just begun.

"Say, what the hell is this 'rank and file group' trying to do?" read the flyer. "Part of the answer to the above question can be found in the full name of the 'Group United to Promote Rank & File Control of Local 544.'" It went on to describe the group's goals:

> ... to promote democracy in the management of local 544 ... a secret ballot, a more detailed accounting of union income and expenditures, a primary election which would select two men to run for each office in future elections, and finally, to support the right of any member to speak his mind without fear of reprisal.

Who could oppose such laudable goals for a labor union?

A few days later, my father got his answer when our home phone rang. The caller said he was a friend of Hoffa's from Detroit. He planned to be in Minneapolis later in the week and invited my parents to dinner—"to discuss things."

My father was sure this was his long-awaited signal from Hoffa himself. The Teamsters' general president certainly had heard about the Rank-and-File Group's successes in Minneapolis. Now, my dad thought, a man from Hoffa's hometown would personally confirm Conklin's initial encouragement of the cause from the very highest level. He was sure this emissary from Detroit would reaffirm Hoffa's support and maybe even offer him a job in the International.

They were to meet the Detroit visitor at one of the finest restaurants in Minneapolis, Charlie's Café Exceptionale. When my father asked how he would recognize their host, the voice on the line said softly, "Oh, Jimmy, don't worry about that. I know what you look like. I know what Mary looks like. Hell, Jimmy, I know what everybody looks like. Don't worry. I'll find you."

He was irked that the stranger called him Jimmy. Only his mother got away with that nickname for him, and she hadn't been his favorite person for a long time. But he thought nothing of the stranger's substantive remarks—or his awareness of Mary's name—because he was hearing what he wanted to hear and little else.

Later, both of my parents told me the same story of their memorable dinner at Charlie's. As they walked into the restaurant a few days after the phone call from Detroit, they immediately noticed the heady odor of a men's cologne. Accompanying it was a man who held out his hand and said, "Hello, Jimmy. Hello, Mary. Nice to finally meet you in person. I've learned a lot about both of you."

"He never told us his name," thought my mother.

"He's still calling me Jimmy," my dad bristled.

The stranger was about my father's height and build: six feet tall and trim, probably in his late thirties. He wore a perfectly tailored dark suit. Gold cufflinks that seemed to match his obviously expensive wristwatch secured his white French cuffs. He completed the ensemble with a dark tie and a large ring on the pinky finger of his right hand. With neatly trimmed black hair, he looked as though he had

just walked out of a barber shop—"or a beauty salon," my mother mused silently.

His teeth were straight but bore the permanent stains that accompanied years of smoking cigars and cigarettes. My mother thought that there was something frightening about his face, but she could not quite put the puzzle together. All of his individual features seemed in order; his skin was smooth and unblemished; yet something was amiss.

Then it hit her. It was his eyes. They were blue and ice cold. From time to time, his thin lips formed a smile or even a grin, but the look in his eyes never changed. His resulting facial expressions resembled a grimace more than a smile. Although those steely eyes were unsettling, she found herself magnetically drawn to them. It wasn't that they were attractive; she simply had never seen anything like them in her life.

Their host led them to a table in a quiet corner, and three facts became immediately apparent. First, although the restaurant was otherwise full, the tables next to theirs were unoccupied. Second, those tables were not very close; they had been moved several feet away to create a buffer zone around the area where the threesome would dine. Third, their table had been positioned so the Detroit visitor, sitting at the head with his back to the wall, could see the entire room and all its exits. Yet my parents somehow remained oblivious to whatever warning signs others might have seen in the strange configuration of furniture. Only when I reviewed the situation with her forty years later did my mother pause before admitting with a shudder, "I guess that was pretty weird, now that I think about it." The stranger held the back of my mother's chair as she sat. He invited my father to sit across from her and positioned himself between them. They ordered cocktails as my mother tried to make small talk.

"What's your job for Mr. Hoffa?" she asked. Only twenty-five and having spent most of the previous six years pregnant while attending to her young children, my mother was naïve to the danger that accompanied her as she dined.

"I go around the country to deal with hot spots—places where there's trouble," the stranger replied. "For example, I'm here because Mr. Hoffa wants me to make sure there ain't no more commotion in Minneapolis Local 544. Mr. Hoffa don't like commotion."

"*Commotion* was an odd word," thought my mother. She always hated the use of "ain't."

My father was hearing the words but processing them in a way that directly opposed the stranger's intent. "I'm sure glad to hear that," he jumped in. "I'm working very hard to make sure we have a good, clean local that Mr. Hoffa can be proud of. We're really making good progress in cleaning things up. Brennan was a disaster, and I think Snyder is just as bad. We're on the right track with this. And we're certainly having great success."

"Jimmy, don't you think you've gone far enough on this thing," the stranger replied. "You don't really need the audit, do you?"

My father was surprised at this question. If this stranger knew about the outside audit that the local membership had authorized, then he also must have known that it was the linchpin of the entire reform effort. He believed it would provide the documentary proof leading to Snyder's downfall.

"Well," he responded, "I don't know. It seems to me that Mr. Hoffa needs to see the audit so he can see what's going on around here. Otherwise, it's just a bunch of speeches and words."

"Jimmy, let me say this another way. What I'm telling you is that you've taken this far enough. It's time to let others take over from here."

My father was not sure what their host meant. He remained silent as the waiter delivered the chateaubriand that the stranger had previously ordered for the table. When the meal had been served, my mother decided to resume her earlier series of questions: "Is your work dangerous?"

"Well, it can be dangerous work, Mary, you're right about that." The stranger smiled with his lips but not with his eyes. The resulting countenance sent an involuntary chill down her spine, but there was more. "So I always carry my 'equalizer' everywhere I go." He spoke matter-of-factly as he opened the breast of his suit coat to display a gun holstered underneath. "I never go anywhere without my equalizer. My equalizer keeps me safe and keeps trouble away. You have to get rid of trouble, or trouble will get rid of you."

The table went silent until the stranger began to speak again: "You see, Jimmy and Mary, Mr. Hoffa don't want any more trouble in Minneapolis. I'm sure you can understand that. No more trouble. No more commotion. That's the message I'm here to deliver to you. And it comes from Mr. Hoffa personally."

My father still heard what he wanted to hear. He thought that this

stranger and the man he claimed to represent were on his side of the Local 544 controversy. If there was a threat in the stranger's remarks, he refused to perceive it.

"I certainly understand that. I know that Mr. Hoffa wants what all good Teamsters want: a good union, a strong union. Trouble certainly won't lead to a strong union," my dad said, meaning that his reform movement would continue. But the stranger heard my father's statement as accepting the warning that the insurgency should end. With the dinner concluded, my parents returned home. The ships had passed in the night—over steak, wine, and Dad's bottle of Bud.

18

Things Fall Apart

My father hadn't taken the Detroit stranger's comments about the audit seriously until Snyder and his supporters began to circulate petitions seeking a vote of confidence in all Local 544 officers. Accompanying those petitions were rumors of a move to quash the previously authorized special audit. Shortly before the February membership meeting, my dad sat down at his black Royal typewriter and composed another communication to his constituents:

> Our special audit may be in jeopardy . . . Any attempt to kill this audit or to kill possible necessary prosecution must be defeated . . . Such an attempt would indicate that facts may be revealed that the membership should know . . . The truth and facts should not be suppressed . . . Truth will not harm our union, it will strengthen it . . . It is your duty as a member to attend meetings and vote on these issues . . . in a member controlled union there is strength . . . Protect your rights.

At about the same time, he read in the February issue of *International Teamster* a "Statement of the Board of Monitors." It told members they could file complaints against local officers who deprived them of rights guaranteed under the International's constitution. He had turned to the Monitors once before, but his election victories over Snyder's incumbent trustees had made that complaint moot. He would go to them again if necessary. But first he wanted to give Hoffa the benefit of every doubt. The facts were the facts; the truth was the truth. Hoffa had repeatedly said that nothing else mattered. My father continued to believe him—for now.

At eight o'clock on the evening of February 18, Local 544 president Ed Blixt called the local membership meeting to order. One of Snyder's supporters moved to revise the minutes of the January meeting to eliminate the prior authorization of the special audit. When the mo-

tion failed by a vote of 173 to 103, my father sighed in relief. But as he looked at Snyder, he was surprised to see a man who was remarkably calm in the face of this latest defeat. In fact, he thought he detected a slight smile on Snyder's face when the vote totals were announced. That was odd.

Watching Snyder's eyes survey the crowd, my father also noticed a peculiar expression on the face of Jack Velin, one of the Rank-and-File Group trustees. Like the other two candidates on the slate, Velin had promised adherence to the goals and ideals of the group. With its support, he had been swept into office. Dad watched quizzically as Velin started to speak. He became concerned when his fellow Rank-and-File Group member refused to make eye contact. He had no idea what the man was about to say, but he had an uneasy feeling about it.

"I move that, when it is completed, the special audit be sent directly to President Hoffa before anything else is done with it," Velin stated, according to my father's contemporaneous written summary of the meeting.

"What the hell?" said my dad as he turned to Masteller, sitting beside him. He couldn't believe his ears. Someone must have gotten to Velin. The whole point of the Rank-and-File Group's effort was to put power in the hands of the members. Following the success of the trustees' election, the independent audit was the essential next step in that process. It would provide details about Snyder's misuse of Teamsters funds, begin the local's transformation, and eventually end Snyder's reign. It would continue the process of returning control of the local to the membership. My father had made that very point to the Detroit visitor only days earlier.

At that moment, the words of his dinner host echoed in his mind: "Jimmy, you don't really need the audit, do you?"

He speculated that Velin had been taken to dinner, too. Perhaps he had planted the seeds of the strategy himself by suggesting to his Detroit visitor that Hoffa should see the audit to confirm what was happening in Minneapolis. He surmised that his own remarks might have sparked an idea contributing to Velin's about-face.

"You can be a hero to your union, as well as to Mr. Hoffa," someone must have told Velin. "No one can accuse you of trying to cover up anything. You would just be acting in the best interests of the union in assuring that Mr. Hoffa himself reviewed the audit. That way, out-

siders couldn't use the audit against the Teamsters." That would make sense to Velin, Dad thought.

"Son-of-a-bitch," my father muttered to Masteller. "With guys like this on our side, we're screwed."

As cries from the audience went out for a secret ballot, Blixt called the question and ordered a voice vote on Velin's motion. The union hall was bedlam as shouts came from every corner of the room. Snyder smirked. Chaos would have served his purposes just fine that night. Chaos would have helped to dissolve the results of my father's hard-fought efforts. And chaos he was getting. Velin, one of my father's own chosen trustees, had turned on him. Snyder probably knew that more would follow, even though my dad did not. Others would betray the cause of the Rank-and-File Group; it was only a matter of time.

Blixt announced that the motion to send the audit to Hoffa had carried in the voice vote. From the back of the hall, a new figure emerged to address the membership. He introduced himself as Larry Steinberg.

"He's Hoffa's right-hand man," someone in the crowd whispered. Although Steinberg's home was in Ohio, he held the title "personal representative to the president" and regularly traveled to Washington, where he ran the International Teamsters headquarters office when both Hoffa and his chief aide, International vice president Harold Gibbons, were away. Steinberg was also on the list of influential Teamsters leaders Sam Romer wanted to interview for his book.

Steinberg spoke directly to the assembly. "I'm here to assure you that Mr. Hoffa will give the financial audit of Local 544 his closest personal consideration." Shooting a glance in Snyder's direction, he continued, "Mr. Hoffa will review the audit himself and take actions he believes will be in the best interests of the union."

Snyder nodded in agreement, as if he had nothing to hide.

"Bullshit," my father muttered loudly enough for Steinberg to hear.

Steinberg turned and looked directly at my father. "But let me also tell you that the continued existence of what some of you call the 'Rank-and-File Group' poses a very real danger. It must be dissolved. It's a threat to the Teamsters union itself and will serve only the purposes of those who seek to destroy our union. I urge all of you connected with the Group to disavow your involvement with it. The so-

called 'Rank-and-File Group of Teamsters Local 544' won't advance Mr. Hoffa's goals for this union. I'm also here to tell you that if it turns out that the audit reveals no discrepancies or misuse of funds, then those who are part of this 'rump faction' will find themselves on the receiving end of charges that will be brought against them. This is very serious business, and the risks to everyone involved are very, very real."

As Masteller threatened to throw Hoffa's emissary out the window, Dad returned Steinberg's gaze with his own icy stare and the flaming red birthmark on his forehead. "This pipsqueak is not about to tell Jim Harper what to do," he thought.

A hush fell over the crowd. This was higher drama than anyone in the union hall had expected. "Consider yourselves warned," Steinberg continued. "I'm here as Mr. Hoffa's personal representative. The Rank-and-File Group is not the way to pursue the best interests of the Teamsters. Stop now before further damage is done."

Damage to what or to whom? Steinberg did not elaborate. My father concluded that maybe Snyder wasn't yet finished after all. But Jim Harper was not going to give up either. He would confront Hoffa with facts that could not be ignored because, if they were, his failure to remove Snyder would reflect poorly on his leadership and undermine Hoffa's own public commitment to the eradication of corruption in the Teamsters. Dad was still on track—the course had just been altered a bit. His destination was the same: he would expose Fritz Snyder and gain Hoffa's respect. He would continue to speak truth to power.

19

Federal Visitors

At Hoffa's direction, Larry Steinberg had attended the February 1960 membership meeting of Local 544 to assist Snyder. Or was it really that simple? At this point in the story, my research led me to connect a series of seemingly unrelated events preceding the meeting. In their totality, I think they show the strength of the forces gathering against my father.

Only days after the tumultuous January session at Local 544—the one that authorized the audit—Hoffa chartered a small plane to make his first trip to Wisconsin since becoming the Teamsters general president. After more than two years, Wisconsin had earned a midwinter visit from the union leader at the precise time that Dad's insurgency was at its zenith. Moreover, Hoffa would stop in Toledo to pick up Steinberg. When they arrived at their destination, an airstrip near Lake Delton, Wisconsin, Gordon Conklin of St. Paul was waiting to greet them. The three men then headed for Mauston—my dad's turn-around point for Werner—to address a group of Teamsters. Shortly thereafter "Hoffa's friend from Detroit" took my parents to dinner. Two weeks after that, at the February meeting, Steinberg personally addressed the Local 544 membership in an effort to end the rebellion.

Although unaware of the Hoffa-Steinberg-Conklin rendezvous in Mauston, my father had still sensed an iceberg ahead; he would soon get two more clues as to its size. The first came when he read Sam Romer's newspaper coverage following Steinberg's appearance at the Local 544 February membership meeting. The second was a surprisingly brief telephone conversation immediately thereafter with his most powerful secret supporter, Gordon Conklin.

Believing he still had key media support in Sam Romer, my father had informed the *Tribune* reporter that he would turn to the Monitors in Washington for help. He wanted member access to the audit, but the vote at the February meeting now blocked it. The Monitors acted

quickly on his request and demanded to see the audit as soon as it was completed. Meanwhile, Snyder turned to the media and took full advantage of Velin's about-face. Romer's February 22 *Tribune* article reported that the motion to send the audit directly and exclusively to Hoffa had come from "Jack Velin, a union Trustee elected on an anti-Snyder slate." It also repeated Snyder's strange suggestion that submitting the audit to Hoffa didn't prevent the members from seeing it.

"I'm clean as a whistle," Romer quoted Snyder. "And any audit will show this. I'm not opposed to any audit—make that clear."

Romer also summarized Snyder's other comments: the local had shown financial improvement in the thirteen months since he'd taken over from Sid Brennan; reports were submitted monthly to membership meetings; all transactions were subject to the scrutiny of the trustees, all three of whom were elected on an anti-Snyder slate. The article didn't mention that an increase in union dues and elimination of one office position probably accounted for the supposed financial improvement, or that the membership received no detailed accounting for Snyder's expenditures of those dues, or that the "anti-Snyder trustees" were turning out to be not so anti-Snyder after all. But Romer knew all of those facts, because my father had told him so privately.

Romer also allowed Snyder to lodge a misdirected jab at my father's ongoing push for a secret ballot in Local 544 voting matters. "The January meeting that authorized the audit had done so without a secret ballot," Romer quoted Snyder. He also let Snyder put his spin on Steinberg's presence: "Hoffa's personal representative who attended Local 544's membership meeting had come at my request to convince these people that the audit would be scrutinized." He even reported innuendo: "Snyder charged that the group opposing him is 'being misled by outside interests' but declined to elaborate or identify who he meant."

"Goddamnit, what the hell good are allies like Velin and Romer?" my father wondered aloud to my mother. He placed a call to his most important secret ally, International vice president Gordon Conklin. He wanted insight into Hoffa's true reaction to this abrupt turn of events.

"I can't talk to you about this anymore. Don't call me," were Conklin's only words, according to Dad. Conklin had to be irritated that he

now found himself in the position of protecting his old nemesis, Fritz Snyder. He had initially encouraged my father's efforts, perhaps because he thought they would help eliminate the last remnants of the Sid Brennan regime that tried to take over Conklin's local a decade earlier. But as with so many Teamsters, Conklin's personal allegiance to Hoffa and instinct for survival probably trumped everything else.

So much for his inside line into Hoffa. "Weak bastard," was my father's assessment. "Nobody has any goddamned guts," he told my mother. The anger and isolation that had been a recurring theme of Dad's life once again combined to create unpleasantly familiar feelings. Although he could not account for Conklin's new reticence, he remained convinced that overwhelming proof of Snyder's deeds would nevertheless propel Hoffa to his side of the struggle—even if Hoffa might prefer otherwise for reasons my father could not understand.

A few days later, a Board of Monitors investigator visited our home to review my father's detailed written summary of the recent events at Local 544. He seemed interested, said he'd look at the materials, and promised to get back to my dad soon. He also said he'd already met with Snyder, who had shown him a "green sheet" listing my father's criminal conviction from 1951. Dad was livid at Snyder's dirty tactics, designed to divert the Monitors' investigation in Minneapolis down an irrelevant path. Only the facts concerning Snyder's wrongdoing should matter now—at least that was how he saw it.

Shortly thereafter, two federal agents contacted my father and Masteller. The agents—who were not Monitors' representatives— invited the men to meet with them.

"Sure," my father said over the phone. "You can come to my house."

"No," said the voice of the federal government. "We'll meet at a coffee shop. Just the two of you. Make sure no one follows you. You're in more danger than you realize."

The four met at a Minneapolis diner. My father assumed the agents were from the FBI, but he didn't know for sure. To his surprise, they listened but did not seem to hear his words. Rather than discuss a plan to help clean up Local 544, the agents instead began to outline a totally different program. They were talking about the complete destruction of Hoffa as a labor leader. He and Masteller were astonished because that was not their goal at all. The Rank-and-File Group was

supposed to protect, strengthen, and ultimately save the Teamsters from internal corruption; that was Hoffa's goal, too. Masteller told the federal agents to stop talking.

"See the goddamned door over there?" Masteller said. "You can put on your coats and walk your goddamned asses right through it. We want no part of what you're talking about." My dad was always amused at his mentor's rhetorical flourishes. He and Masteller were loyal Teamsters and loyal union men. They would take no aid from a federal government in pursuit of objectives that were anathema to them. My father had stopped trusting law enforcement officers years earlier when two Baton Rouge cops beat him.

As they rose from the table, one of the agents turned to the two Teamsters and said ominously, "Look, you guys don't have to accept our help in this. That's your decision. But you're in way over your heads in ways you don't understand. There are things happening out there you don't know about. Do yourselves a favor. If you continue with this craziness on your own, carry a gun. It might save you from a serious beating—maybe even death—down the road."

My dad decided then and there to acquire two items for his family's protection. The first was a snub-nosed .38 caliber handgun he would wear at all times, either under his coat or in an ankle holster on his left leg. The second was a German shepherd. He named the dog Fritzie as a living reminder of his principal antagonist and his mission. He had watched Hoffa emasculate Robert Kennedy with his consistent mis-spelling of the young McClellan committee lawyer's name as "Bobbie" in *International Teamster*. He would likewise emasculate Snyder. He loved dogs, but this female would wear the name of his nemesis.

Masteller got himself a shotgun. Neither man had any desire to pursue the federal government's approach to this mission. Now they could rely only on the Board of Monitors, which in fact meant they were alone—they just did not know it yet.

20

Hoffa's Minneapolis Travails

More than forty years later, I sat in the reading room of the Center for Research Libraries in Chicago and carefully reviewed the March 1960 issue of *International Teamster*. It reported Hoffa's visit to Mauston, Wisconsin, in late January—his first trip to the state since becoming the union's general president—for the stated purpose of dissuading area Teamsters from forming their own local. He wanted them to retain their respective affiliations with Snyder's Minneapolis Local 544, Conklin's St. Paul Local 120, and Chicago Local 710. While he was there, Hoffa also endorsed a Teamster from Conklin's local for mayor of Mauston. "We like to see our membership take an active part in politics," the magazine reported Hoffa telling his candidate.

Involving Teamsters in politics would have made sense to my father as he first read that article, although Hoffa's secret political dealings to that time would have stunned him. As for the Mauston trip itself, it would not have occurred to my father that Hoffa, Conklin, and Steinberg might have discussed the Local 544 controversy when they gathered at his Werner turnaround point. Even decades later, I can't be sure that they did. But given what I now know about subsequent events, I cannot imagine how they avoided the topic of Jim Harper's insurgency. By then, his crusade had reached Hoffa's radar screen; that doomed it. Hoffa's wish to keep all public attention away from his burgeoning problems in Minneapolis meant squelching my father's mission, even if someday he had to meet personally with my father to achieve it.

Hoffa's big Minneapolis-rooted problem had nothing to do with my dad's complaints about Snyder, but it kept getting bigger. Between the January and February meetings in the Local 544 union hall, a court ordered Hoffa to trial on the Monitors' civil complaint that he had misused Teamsters funds in connection with the Minneapolis-born Sun Valley venture. At the time, the Florida bank was still hold-

ing Detroit Teamsters' money as security for loans it had made to the developer—at Hoffa's direction.

Now Hoffa took the offensive. Only three days before Larry Steinberg's February visit to Local 544, several union locals throughout the country filed a lawsuit challenging the Monitors' fundamental authority. Just as my father was hoping the Board of Monitors' tentacles might eventually reach Local 544, Hoffa's plan was under way to cut off its head.

The Monitors found themselves increasingly under personal attack. Chairman O'Donoghue received threatening phone calls. Another member, originally anti-Hoffa, now suddenly and inexplicably began siding with the International Teamsters' appointed representative on the panel. Hoffa had achieved paralysis, if not functional control, of the body that was supposed to be scrutinizing his activities under the 1958 consent decree. Any aid the Monitors might have offered Jim Harper's reform effort in Minneapolis Local 544 was illusory because they were not even in a position to save themselves.

Congress had not left Hoffa's life, either. On February 26, 1960, the McClellan committee issued the first part of its final report, which included a scathing attack on Hoffa. My father knew, from the visiting federal agents, that the nation's leaders were out to get Hoffa and destroy the union. Those men had simply confirmed what he had concluded long ago: whatever the government said about Hoffa had to be dismissed as simply part of a larger union-busting agenda.

In the midst of this, Snyder had to tell Hoffa about the continuing insurgency at Local 544. Hoffa would have to deal with the situation personally. As a pretext, he would preside over the upcoming regular membership meeting of Local 544. Once there, he would end this newest Minneapolis problem once and for all.

My father continued to view his efforts to clean up Local 544 as following Hoffa's announced goal of union reform. He also knew, but could not understand why, Hoffa wanted the insurgency against Snyder to end; Conklin's abandonment, the mysterious visitor from Detroit, and Steinberg's warnings had made that clear. But Hoffa always said he wanted to hear directly from union members about problems, and my dad continued to take that offer at face value. In a personal letter to Hoffa dated March 11, my father expressed his admiration, explained his actions as in the union's best interests, and politely said

that Hoffa had no proper role in the upcoming meeting. "It has been announced that you have been invited by Fred V. Snyder to speak at a regular membership meeting of Local 544," he wrote.

> The members appreciate the opportunity to hear you speak, but we feel that a special meeting should have been called for that purpose. Mr. Snyder has postponed our regularly scheduled meeting of the 17th, and we do not feel that our regular membership meeting should be delayed. We want our regular membership meeting, and, in addition, a special meeting to hear you speak.
>
> We cannot understand why Mr. Snyder is trying so hard to keep the special audit from the members of this local. If, as he claims, there is nothing to hide, he should be anxious for the membership to see this audit. His continuing efforts to block the audit make us all the more keen to find out how the finances of this union were handled in 1959. The members want this audit to be made available to any Local 544 Teamster who wants it.

"We are struggling for a democratically run local, not a one man dictatorship," he suggested, with an irony he didn't comprehend and Hoffa would not have appreciated.

> We realized when we started this campaign for a member-run union that many of us were laying our jobs and futures on the line. We believe that the principles of democratic unionism are worth that risk . . . Many members who are now engaged in this struggle for a member-controlled union worked to elect Snyder when he ran against Brennan in December of 1958. Brennan was bad, and Snyder has proved to be no better . . . The only way to settle the conflict within Local 544 is to have the special audit made available to any member requesting it. We are speaking for the membership, and references indicating that we are only a group of 21 members are ridiculous. Our opposition group has had a majority at all of the membership meetings since we decided to act in defiance of the high-handed methods used to control this local. This fact must have been apparent to Mr. Larry Steinberg at our last membership meeting.

He closed by saying he would welcome an opportunity to meet with the Teamsters leader before the March 27 meeting, but unwittingly shoved a needle directly into Hoffa's eye with his concluding line: "We believe that the wishes of the members should rule, not the

dictates of one man." He signed the letter "Fraternally yours, Secretary, Rank and File Group of Local 544."

As one of Hoffa's closest aides, Larry Steinberg must have provided Hoffa with the insights he had gained from attending the Local 544 meeting a month earlier. Certainly among them would have been his observation that my father was not going away quietly. Hoffa did not respond in writing to my father's letter. But sixteen days later, he'd answer it—in person and in Minneapolis.

In fact, my father didn't really care if Hoffa came to the meeting because he held a secret ace: a copy of the Local 544 independent financial audit. He was certain it would end Snyder's career and force Hoffa to his side. He needed only to maintain the courage to see it through.

21

The Audit

It had become the Holy Grail of the cause. An independent financial audit of Local 544 was the last thing that Snyder wanted. Jim Harper knew it; Snyder knew it. Hoffa himself would soon know why Snyder had fought so hard to kill that audit.

Snyder probably thought he had managed to deflect outside scrutiny when one of the newly elected trustees, Jack Velin, proposed at the February membership meeting to send the audit to Hoffa alone, rather than make it available for any member's review. My father believed that Snyder or someone had gotten to Velin. That left the two other trustees on his Rank-and-File Group's winning slate of challengers: Lloyd Harris and Ed Zukaitis. He had harbored concerns about Harris from the beginning; by process of elimination, only Zukaitis, a friendly guy about Snyder's age, remained as a potentially reliable ally. When the audit was completed in March, Zukaitis would get a copy.

My father concocted a plan. On the day Zukaitis received his copy, he and Masteller would go drinking with him. Because Zukaitis was an honest and decent man, my father would not insult his integrity by asking him to share the report. But if Masteller could distract him long enough, my father could break into his locked car, grab the audit, drive to the Werner office, make a copy, and return it to the car. No one would know that it had ever been gone. So that's what he did.

A local bar provided the perfect setting. It had a front entrance and a back door—all that he needed. He knew when the audit was scheduled for delivery to the trustees. On that very day, he and Masteller asked Zukaitis to join them for a drink. Zukaitis accepted, and the enterprise commenced.

The two were already at the bar when Zukaitis walked in and flashed a grin. They sat for a while before my father announced that he needed to take a trip to the bathroom.

"Boy, I think I ate something that made me sick," he moaned as he placed his hand on his belly. "I've got to go to the can."

"Don't take too long," Masteller joked.

My dad headed for the bathroom, which was also the direction of the rear exit. He slipped through the door and paused in the cold winter night. Extracting a cigarette from his open pack, he pulled his silver Zippo lighter from his pocket. In a seamless motion, his thumb flipped open its top and spun the tiny black wheel to create fire. As he lit his Camel and took a deep drag, the cigarette's tip flared into a bright orange blemish on the darkness.

His mind raced as he walked deliberately to Zukaitis's car. The audit could be on the seat. It could be in the trunk. The seat would be easier because it was simpler to get through a door than a trunk, but his Louisiana jailhouse training had equipped him to cope with either circumstance. He peered through the car's windows. There it was: a manila envelope sitting on the front seat. He pulled a long wire from the waist of his trousers, bent the end, slipped it through the closed window, and pulled up the door lock. Within seconds, he was holding the audit.

He walked briskly to his own car, started the engine, and headed for the Werner office. The company ran a night operation, so it would be open and someone would be there. But at eight on a Friday night, he hoped to encounter no one as he walked up the concrete steps, through the main office door, and over to the photostatic copy machine. He carefully unstapled the document. In a procedure that would now seem tediously slow, he copied it one page at a time. After five minutes, he was done. He stapled the originals together, folded his copy, and stuffed it inside his Werner jacket.

The drive back seemed to last forever, but the entire heist had taken only about twenty minutes. After returning the audit to Zukaitis's car, he walked through the back door of the tavern and went into the men's room. He washed the ink from the copy machine off his hands before resuming his seat at the bar. My father gave Masteller a quick wink as his partner nodded acknowledgment. They spent another fifteen minutes with their guest, put him in his car, and watched him drive off.

He and Masteller then met with another Rank-and-File Group member in the basement of that member's home to review their prize. He believed it showed exactly what he'd been told: Snyder was misusing union funds. For example, it showed per diem reimbursement for a round-trip that Snyder claimed to have taken from Min-

neapolis to Detroit and Washington. But according to Dad, the audit listed union gas card receipts near Snyder's northern Minnesota cottage on the very days of that supposed journey. Another example was the secretary-treasurer's salary, which seemed especially ironic after Snyder's grandstand play on that issue at the December 1959 membership meeting. At that meeting, Snyder had specifically asked the members to vote retroactive approval for his $225-a-week compensation from January 1959, but my father believed the audit showed salary payments of $250 a week.

"How stupid could this son-of-a-bitch be?" my father wondered. The amounts involved were unimportant; my father had always viewed his crusade as a matter of principle from which he would not retreat.

He thought that he now had what he needed to make his case against Snyder airtight. So even if Hoffa accepted Snyder's plea to visit Minneapolis and preside over the Local 544 membership meeting in March, Dad would be ready for him. He would get his chance and he would make the most of it. He was sure of one thing: Hoffa could not ignore the black and white reality of a certified financial audit.

22

Hoffa Visits Minneapolis, Again

On March 27, 1960, Jimmy Hoffa returned to Minneapolis. The meeting was set for Hoffa's room at the downtown hotel then known as the Pick-Nicollet. My father had often described to me this momentous episode in his life. Hoffa had no bodyguards, but one of his men greeted Dad and Masteller in the lobby and escorted them to the elevator that stopped at Hoffa's floor. When they arrived at his suite, Hoffa himself opened the door. He initially blanched because my father still had no upper teeth. Hoffa had seen toothless truck drivers, but rarely were they so young.

My father apologized for his appearance, described how a mishandled toothache had deprived him of his permanent upper teeth, and explained that his new dentures weren't ready yet—although in truth he hadn't even ordered them. Hoffa just smiled and wished him the best. He maintained a firm handshake for an additional moment, as if the combination of his penetrating gaze and physical connection would extract some insight into this trucker who had caused so much trouble in a Teamsters local with a long and disquieting history. Hoffa probably thought there was something uniquely odd about Minnesotans, as he remembered his encounters with Farrell Dobbs twenty-five years earlier, Sid Brennan's attempt to take over Conklin's local in the late 1940s, unpleasant newspaper coverage by the *Tribune*'s Clark Mollenhoff, and Hoffa's more recent Central States Pension Fund dealings with former Minneapolis department store owner Ben Dranow. Maybe he thought there was something peculiar about the water that people drank in the "Land of Ten Thousand Lakes."

Except for Snyder and Hoffa, my father didn't know with certainty until he arrived who else might be present for this intimate gathering. Before the meeting, someone had suggested that maybe the *Tribune*'s Sam Romer should attend. But Dad knew that Hoffa alone would determine the composition of the group, and everyone understood Hoffa's negative view of reporters because the media rarely cast him

in a favorable light. He could think of no reason for Hoffa to include Romer or any other newsman in a small group of Teamsters meeting to resolve a purely internal matter.

But there he was. As my father walked into Hoffa's room, the guest list was now complete and consisted of only five men: Jim Harper, Jimmy Hoffa, Marvin Masteller, Fred Snyder, and the *Tribune*'s local labor reporter. Sam Romer was getting the exclusive of all exclusives: he would sit with Hoffa as the Teamsters' general president personally resolved corruption claims against the man leading one of the union's largest locals. Romer had even brought a photographer; he would remain in the hall outside Hoffa's room until they were finished.

My father's head was spinning. At Conklin's initial suggestion, he had confided in Romer from the beginning. Although he had developed a nagging concern about how the reporter described some of the events at Local 544, he didn't know how to process Romer's presence here. He was trying desperately to remember everything he had ever told the newsman as he and Romer exchanged pleasantries. The whole situation was confusing and began to make him physically ill.

Pick-Nicollet Hotel, where Harper confronted Hoffa in March 1960

For now, he had to act as if he was encountering Romer for the first time. He didn't want Snyder or Hoffa to suspect that he had secretly fed information about the Local 544 controversy to the media.

The complicated inside joke was on my father, who didn't know of the elaborate personal connections among Romer, Hoffa, and Gordon Conklin. He didn't know that Romer was writing a book about the union, or that Hoffa had been granting Romer special access to International Teamsters leaders since 1958. He was unaware that Romer had spent two weeks at Teamsters headquarters in Washington that summer, or that he had conducted several private interviews with Hoffa himself throughout 1959. He didn't realize that Romer was waiting for the International to provide information requested months earlier about the Teamsters Central States Pension Fund, or that Romer's book would ultimately provide a flattering account of Hoffa and his Teamsters at a time when the popular press was vilifying the union's general president and federal investigators were looking for ways to incarcerate him.

He forced his mind away from Romer and toward the task at hand. He was in the presence of the man who would listen to the facts, understand the truth, and do what was right for the union. He could ask for no more.

My father had never before seen the Teamsters' top man in person. He knew Hoffa was short, but not this small. Hoffa's image had always seemed larger than life, but at five foot five he was seven inches shorter than Dad and slightly smaller than Masteller, the human fireplug. He guessed that Hoffa weighed about 180 pounds: musclebound, without a trace of fat. He wore a dark suit, white dress shirt, and dark tie and had combed his slick, dark hair in the way it was always pictured: straight back from his forehead like a lion's mane. He was also wearing the white socks for which he had become famous because, in Hoffa's words, "colored socks make my feet sweat."

My father and Masteller took chairs opposite Snyder; Hoffa flanked them as if at the head of a table; Romer sat off to the side. Once seated, Hoffa's obviously inferior physical stature disappeared as even a potential subliminal issue in the upcoming discussions. His commanding voice and presence would dominate the meeting from this point forward. He was direct and wasted no time.

"All right, Fritz, you called me here," Hoffa snapped, according to my father's account. "What the hell is going on?" This was yet another

inside joke, of course, because Hoffa already knew much about what had been happening in one of his least favorite cities.

Snyder started rambling in an unfocused manner, describing his thirty years as a loyal Teamster. He'd fought for the union during the bloody and violent Minneapolis general strikes that claimed his brother's life in 1934. He'd been an officer in the local since 1941, after Hoffa himself had purged it of socialists. He'd done nothing wrong and didn't understand why Jim Harper was out to get him. He suggested that outside influences were at work here, Sid Brennan's supporters might be behind the insurgency, and one of the instigators even had a criminal record.

Snyder's innuendo enraged my father. He was attempting to play on Hoffa's well-known anticommunist views while impugning a fellow Teamster for adolescent mistakes made almost a decade earlier. My father didn't yet know that Louisiana governor Long had signed his pardon earlier in the month. For now, he and Masteller sat quietly, letting out the hangman's rope as Snyder continued to talk. Then it was my father's turn.

"Brother Harper," said Hoffa, turning to him. "I received your letter. What's your concern with respect to this audit and Brother Snyder?"

Slowly and deliberately, my father laid out his case against Snyder. He began by assuring Hoffa that no outsiders were involved: "This is an internal union problem with a Local 544 union officer and it should be dealt with under union procedures. No one involved in this dispute is connected in any way with any interests outside the Teamsters. We're all loyal Teamsters. Many of us supported Snyder's election over Brennan in 1958. We're all loyal to you. We all share your desire, Mr. Hoffa, to make our union as strong as it can be. We're here because we believe Snyder stands for what you've said is wrong with this union, and we're here to help you correct it."

He was rolling now. The gag reflex that momentarily stymied his efforts at public address never surfaced in small gatherings. He began to review each charge in as much detail as he had been able to gather.

"Brother Snyder shouldn't fear an independent audit of union funds. The membership of Local 544 is entitled to know where its dues are going," he continued. "In December of 1959, Snyder asked the entire membership to approve his salary for the year, retroactively. He told the membership his salary had been two twenty-five a week, plus a fifty-dollar expense account. We believe the truth may be different

and that he's been paying himself more. The local membership authorized an audit to find the truth. We should let that audit tell us what the truth is."

Hoffa's brow furrowed as Snyder bolted from his chair to interrupt. "Wait a minute—that's not true. This guy's just an ex-con who's out to wreck the union, Jimmy!"

Masteller leaped up and pointed a stern finger at Snyder. "Fritz, you just sit your damn self down," he bellowed. "You had your chance, and we sat quietly while you had that chance. Now it's your turn to be quiet, and you'll sit your ass in that goddamned chair, and you'll be goddamned still until we're done, you son-of-a-bitch!"

My father thought he saw Hoffa snicker at Masteller's colorful bravado. Although Hoffa had almost certainly chastised Snyder much more vehemently in recent weeks, he disingenuously asked Masteller, "Do you have to be so rough on him?"

Masteller was unapologetic: "Rough is the only language that bastard understands."

"Proceed, Brother Harper," Hoffa said as he refocused the participants. His smirk at their clash now resolved into intense concentration.

"Mr. Hoffa, we believe that from the first day that Snyder took over from Sid Brennan in January 1959, Snyder has been taking extra salary from the mouths of the Local 544 membership. If he is, it's wrong, and he knows it—" Dad had more, but it would have to wait.

"Hold it right there," Hoffa interrupted. "Brother Snyder, what's your salary?"

Snyder stammered, "Jimmy—"

"It's Mr. Hoffa to you," came Hoffa's rebuke. "I asked you a simple question. What's your salary?"

"It's kinda complicated, with expenses and some of the things I pay out of my own pocket for union expenses—"

"I don't give a good goddamned about any of your bullshit. What in the hell is your goddamned salary?" Hoffa persisted as his volume increased. It was all an act, but it convinced my father.

"I'm not sure of the exact amount," Snyder said softly as he squirmed in his seat.

"Shit," Hoffa muttered, rolling his eyes. Then he turned back to my father. "Brother Harper, proceed."

"Snyder went to the membership in January to say he wanted only what the membership authorized for him. But we believe he hasn't

been satisfied with that." My father was sure he was getting Hoffa's attention now. "We think there's more. For example, we think union funds may have reimbursed him for improper expenses, including gasoline purchases near his Grand Rapids cottage. The audit is absolutely essential to understanding the magnitude of the problem, if there is one," he said, as Hoffa glared at Snyder.

Hoffa now had a problem. He'd undoubtedly heard enough about the independent audit of Local 544 so that none of this particularly surprised him. The shock was that my father seemed to know as much about Snyder's problems as Hoffa did—maybe even a little more.

"Jimmy—" Snyder began.

"I am Mr. Hoffa to you!" he boomed so loudly his voice resounded down the hallway of the hotel. "Don't give me any bullshit excuses. What the hell do you think you've been doing here?"

Hoffa then turned to Snyder's articulate accuser. "Look, Jim, I'm not going to make any excuses for this bastard. If he's done something wrong, Fritz will have to defend himself. But this union is about contracts and making sure contracts are lived up to. Are your contracts being lived up to?"

My father actually didn't know the answer to Hoffa's question because he'd never read the contracts. It had never occurred to him that this meeting would somehow digress into a discussion on that topic, but he wasn't about to admit that to Hoffa. "As far as I know, I suppose so," he answered, caught off guard. He never really recovered his equilibrium for the balance of the meeting.

"Well, that's the really important point," Hoffa pressed ahead. "I'm certainly not pleased with what I'm hearing, and we're not done talking about it—not by a long shot." Dad took some satisfaction from the penetrating glare that Hoffa flashed in Snyder's direction. "We'll find out about that. But remember what I worry about. I gotta make sure this union is fulfilling its responsibilities to its members concerning our contracts," Hoffa continued.

For the next three hours, the four men went at it as Sam Romer watched and listened. By the time it was over, Hoffa had made two points clear, both of them disingenuous.

Hoffa's first point: he understood everything my father was saying. But Snyder had been elected by popular vote, and Hoffa had to back him. He couldn't defy the members' wishes and simply remove Snyder based upon Jim Harper's accusations. Hoffa was under pressure

from the court-imposed Board of Monitors to eliminate International trusteeships over local unions. He couldn't just step in and create a new one at Local 544, one of the Teamsters' largest and most prominent. Dad would be permitted to present his requests to the membership and, if the members wanted charges pursued, they'd be pursued. If they didn't, that would be the end of it.

Hoffa's second point: only the membership could wreck the union. The Teamsters could withstand any outside attack, as Hoffa was proving every day with Congress, the courts, and federal prosecutors. They were on the verge of a nationwide contract for all over-the-road truckers, and that was the main goal of the members' common struggle. Hoffa wanted my father to abide by the members' vote on the issue. Open disagreement within the membership would only hurt the Teamsters and help its enemies. The people and the government needed to see a united union. The membership had to emerge united in the brotherhood of the Teamsters.

My father wondered if Hitler's diatribes had sounded like this in 1945, as the Nazi leader lectured his generals on abstract subjects while Germany was losing World War II. He also harbored misgivings that he was about to receive less than a fair opportunity to state his case at the next membership meeting. Nevertheless, he had to accept Hoffa's deal because it was the only deal offered. He would live or die by the membership vote that was about to occur.

He and Masteller left Hoffa's suite and headed for the nearby Minneapolis Labor Temple. He'd play out the hand. Little did he know how carefully the deck had already been stacked against him.

23

Hoffa's Rules of Order

My father had first noticed the sinking sensation in his gut when he saw Sam Romer sitting in Hoffa's hotel suite. The feeling had left him as he made his case against Snyder, but now it was back. Hoffa had taken the discussion away from Snyder's wrongdoing and into the world of organized labor generally. He had pressured my father to accept the union membership vote about to be taken under Hoffa's direction. Dad had a very bad feeling about all of this.

He and Masteller entered the Floyd B. Olson Labor Temple and took their seats several rows from the slightly elevated auditorium stage. Named for the governor who had called out the National Guard to quell the Minneapolis Teamsters strikes of 1934, it was one of the few venues in the city that could hold the hundreds of members who had come to see Hoffa in person. The assembly greeted the Teamsters' general president with wild enthusiasm upon his entrance into the arena. Hoffa made his way past the handshakes to the front of the room. Local 544 president Ed Blixt introduced him, and Hoffa moved to the podium. Later, my father described to Mom and me the scene that followed.

"I have some remarks that I'll make at the conclusion of the meeting," Hoffa began. "But first, I want to open the meeting with a call for new business."

Someone spoke from the back of the hall, but the man was unfamiliar to my father. "I move for a vote of confidence on all of the current officers of Local 544," said the voice.

"Second," yelled another voice belonging to someone Dad strained unsuccessfully to see.

"Any discussion?" inquired Hoffa, the parliamentarian.

Dad and his supporters had previously agreed to divide the public criticisms of Snyder at the meeting, so Hoffa would see that he confronted more than a one-man crusade pursuing a personal vendetta. Now that the moment of truth had come, with Hoffa staring down at

the assemblage from his podium, the only point of agreement among my father's fellow insurgents seemed to be that he'd have to speak for all of them; otherwise, no one was going to speak at all.

Unfortunately, his involuntary gag reflex kicked in. With his colleagues urging him on, he fought the reflex, trying to swallow and cough at the same time. Dad rose from his chair, "Mr. President, I would like to—"

"Brother Harper, *sit down!* You have not been recognized by the chair!" Hoffa roared, extending his arm. Dad half-expected a lightning bolt to shoot from the finger that Hoffa pointed at him.

He stopped in mid-sentence and glared at Hoffa. This was betrayal. Hoffa had just promised him an opportunity to present the Rank-and-File Group's arguments to the entire Local 544 membership, but now he was cutting off that presentation before it had begun. The birthmark on his forehead turned bright red, and the two men glared, locked in ocular combat. Neither man blinked.

"Jimmy Hoffa is no tougher than the hell that I survived at Angola," my father thought. He had half a mind to tell him so on the spot.

Then Masteller grabbed the back of Dad's belt and yanked him down to his chair. Only moments earlier, he had been among those urging my father to speak. He now sized up the situation differently.

"Jim, shut up." he said. "Don't antagonize Hoffa in public. Take a look around the room. We're screwed. Do you recognize any of these people? No. And do you know why? Because goddamnit, there are hundreds of people here and most of these bastards aren't from 544. They've been shipped into this meeting from God knows where. They're here to make sure that Hoffa gets what Hoffa wants from this meeting and looks goddamned good getting it. Hoffa won't let you create a scene here. If you try to make your case in front of Hoffa and this crowd now, you'll get crucified! I ain't interested in that!"

My father surveyed his surroundings and saw immediately that Masteller was right. He didn't recognize most of the faces around him. About five hundred people had voted in the December election, but this gathering looked more like a thousand.

"All right," he replied. "We'll express ourselves with our vote on the confidence motion. Goddamnit, then Hoffa will see that he can't ram this through. He'll see that he's got a big problem here and the rank-and-file won't let him walk away from it."

He was certain that a resounding vote of no confidence in Snyder

would follow. Then Hoffa would have to act or risk embarrassment for his failure to do so. The hundreds of Local 544 Teamsters who had elected the anti-Snyder slate of trustees had promised to stand with my father at this very meeting and all the way to the end of this war. The moment of reckoning had come; the question was called.

"We'll vote by members rising. All those voting in favor of the membership's confidence in the current officers of Local 544, including Brothers Blixt and Snyder, will now stand at this time."

After a clear majority initially rose, one by one almost all the others joined them. Dad was shocked; his face turned white; his heart sank. He felt sick again.

"All those voting no on the question of the membership's confidence in the current 544 officers will now stand," Hoffa continued.

Snyder and Hoffa had done their jobs well. The stacked audience had produced the desired outcome even before the voting began. Only thirty members of Local 544 stood with Dad and Masteller.

"Motion passes. Any other new business?" Hoffa asked.

Again, a nameless voice shouted from the back. "I move that any charges against the current officers be dismissed and the special audit be rejected."

My father searched the audience to locate the speaker, but it was futile. He felt like he was in the nightmare where he tried to focus on an image but his eyes refused to process it. "How in the hell can the membership vote to reject an audit they've never seen!" he muttered to Masteller in disgust.

"Second," said another anonymous voice.

"All those in favor of the motion, please rise." Hoffa appeared to be enjoying himself.

The farce was starting to look like a game of Simon Says. This time, the entire crowd seemed to stand in unison.

"Opposed?" Hoffa requested.

In addition to my father and Masteller, only four other Teamsters stood to be counted. His hundreds of supposedly stalwart supporters, who had assured him shortly before the meeting that they would remain with him to the end, had dwindled to a measly five. It was over.

Hoffa then made the moment his, in words that would also appear in Sam Romer's later newspaper account of the day's events: "It's unfortunate that this internal crisis occurred. I believe it's the result of our union becoming soft and too many members failing to attend the

membership meetings that are vital to the life of the union. I'm pleased to see the fine turnout for this meeting. Perhaps the large turnout contributed to the wise decision that the membership of Local 544 has made today. You've decided to close ranks and put the past behind you. You've decided to start with a clean slate, all over again. Nobody's perfect. Everybody makes mistakes. The important question is not whether Snyder is right or wrong, or whether the Rank-and-File Group is right or wrong. The important question is whether union agreements are being lived up to. That is the way to a better life for all of us. We're approaching an important time in our union's history. We're approaching negotiations in which we must be strong. We're on the verge of a nationwide contract for over-the-road truckers. Stop the letter writing. Stop the committees. Only you can betray Local 544. And I know that none of you will."

The crowd roared its approval.

In a life filled with many sad days, my father thought this ranked right up there with the worst of them. His despair then turned to anger. Maybe Snyder had won this round, but Jim Harper wasn't done—not by a long shot.

He would not give up. He would make his case against Snyder so airtight that, if Hoffa ignored it, the resulting public embarrassment to the Teamsters' general president would be profound and personal. Hoffa would learn that Harper was as tough as any of his so-called tough guys. After all, how many of Hoffa's two-bit hoodlums had survived a year in Angola?

None.

24

The Calm Between the Storms

In a single day, Snyder had achieved a stunning victory and a complete reversal of my father's earlier successes. Adding insult to injury—but no longer surprisingly—my father's media confidant, Sam Romer, did not report accurately the prior day's private meeting in Hoffa's hotel suite. He didn't report the no-holds-barred exchange that had occurred, or Jim Harper's presentation to Hoffa of the indefensible Snyder record. He didn't depict a meeting in which the participants were literally screaming at each other.

Rather, Romer's article portrayed Hoffa as the ultimate diplomat; he had "acted as peace-maker" and "mediated" the dispute. Romer implied that the meeting involved more than just the five men who actually attended, and that the warring factions remained in separate rooms of "a four-room suite." He also suggested that Hoffa displayed Solomon-like wisdom in resolving what might seem to the uninformed reader a minor internal dispute. The overall effect of Romer's presentation now became clear: it made Hoffa look far better than he deserved. My father concluded that this was an unabashed attempt to push this entire problem under some enormous Teamsters rug. Even the article's large photograph was flattering: it showed Hoffa relaxed, dignified, and almost plaintive, gazing serenely upward from his hotel room chair with his hands folded neatly between his knees.

My dad had a much bigger problem than how all of this was reported in the newspaper. In the Minneapolis Labor Temple, he had watched his coalition of supporters evaporate before his eyes. Hoffa had come to town, crushed the rebellion, and muscled through a nearly unanimous vote, leaving Snyder firmly in control of Local 544.

Unwilling to accept his victory with grace, Snyder began the April 1960 membership meeting with the remarkable assertion that the union local had wasted its money on the special audit. "The audit failed to reveal one cent of misused funds," Snyder proclaimed.

My father had promised Hoffa that he'd abide by the membership

vote, which meant that he could not respond to Snyder's arrogant assertions. He wouldn't stoop to Snyder's level. He vowed to retain his honor and dignity as Snyder gloated that the insurgency had taken the membership on a wild goose chase leading nowhere. Snyder repeated his statements—that "the audit was a waste of the membership's money" and "failed to reveal one cent of misused funds"—whenever he had the opportunity, including several membership meetings and private discussions with individual Minneapolis Teamsters. My father remained quiet every time. Only the darkening mark on his forehead and his steely gaze revealed his reactions to what he was hearing. Otherwise, it was business as usual as he made his three or four weekly round trips to Mauston along the Great River Road.

Three months after the showdown in Hoffa's hotel suite, Sam Romer wrote Hoffa a letter. He was approaching the deadline for his manuscript about the Teamsters. "Dear Jimmy," he wrote on June 23, 1960, "I thought you might want to see a copy of a letter I have written Frank Murtha. I hope that the information will be available; it will be very valuable." Romer was renewing his earlier requests for information about the Teamsters' Central States Pension Fund. In an oblique reference to their March meeting in Hoffa's hotel room, he concluded, "It was good seeing you again the other week." Less than a week later, the International Teamsters' chief labor counsel directed Murtha, the executive secretary of the Central States Pension Fund, to provide Romer the information about the fund that the reporter had first sought in August and October of the prior year. Apparently, Hoffa had given Romer high marks for his *Tribune* coverage of Jim Harper's confrontation with the general president.

At about the same time, the Florida bank finally released the last of the $400,000 that Hoffa had transferred from his Detroit local. The bank had been holding the money as security for loans it had made to Sun Valley's developer, but by the summer of 1960 Dranow's "cash commissions" plan had produced enough to repay those loans. In fact, the Detroit Teamsters even received a little more: the interest their money would have earned if it had not remained in the Florida bank's non-interest-bearing account. No harm; no foul.

With his masterful stroke in Minneapolis, Hoffa was free to focus on much larger issues; events required him to do so. In fact, on the day

after Hoffa presided over the Local 544 membership meeting to save Snyder, the McClellan committee issued the second segment of its final report, stating, "Time and time again the Committee has found Hoffa to be faithless to the members of his own union. He has betrayed these members so frequently that it has become abundantly clear that Hoffa's chief interest is his own advancement and that of his friends and cronies—a great number of whom are racketeers. In addition, Hoffa has used union funds for his own benefit and that of his friends. Hoffa has consistently supported the interests of racketeer friends over those of his own members. Hoffa and his chief aides have consistently repressed democratic rights within the union."

Ominously, the report concluded, "This Committee is convinced that if Hoffa remains unchecked he will successfully destroy the decent labor movement in the United States. Further than that, because of the tremendous economic power of the Teamsters, it will place the underworld in a position to dominate American economic life in a period when the vitality of the American economy is necessary to this country's preservation in an era of world crisis. This Hoffa cannot be allowed to do."

But who would stop him? The committee's report answered that the new Landrum-Griffin Act was the end of the line for Congress; it would no longer take on Hoffa: "From this point on, the fate and the future of James R. Hoffa rest with the executive and judicial branches of the Government, the [M]onitors, and inevitably with his own members."

Hoffa surely knew he would have no problems with his own members; they would remain loyal to him and the Teamsters. Even rank-and-file members like Jim Harper, whose pursuits might otherwise reflect poorly on Hoffa and his leadership, always qualified their words and deeds with the caveat that they were "loyal to General President Hoffa and the Teamsters."

On the floor of the House of Representatives, eleven members denounced the Board of Monitors and the judge who still presided over the implementation of the 1958 consent decree. Hoffa followed with a flurry of his own punches and petitioned Judge Letts to allow a new International convention, after which Hoffa could jettison forever the "provisional" in his presidential title. In July 1960, the court of appeals reiterated the restrictions on the Monitors' power, and board chairman O'Donoghue resigned. He wrote that little or no progress had

been made in "cleaning up corrupt influences" within the Teamsters union. "The entire past year has been marked by unwarranted attacks on me," he said. "Such personal attacks on the Chairman and the Staff members of the Board have even become a disrupting influence on the deliberations of the Board at formal meetings."

My father read the official Teamsters' spin on O'Donoghue's parting valedictory in the August 1960 issue of *International Teamster*. It reported the resignation of a man "whose two years as chairman of the Board of Monitors were marked by rancor and inaction." The article explained that although the chairman's statement had sought falsely "to blame the prolonging of the Monitorship at the door of the union . . . the facts are that O'Donoghue willfully stalled the completion of Monitorial tasks in the vain hope of achieving success in his personal vendetta against James R. Hoffa."

Whatever the causes, it became clear to my father that the Monitors were on the verge of extinction. But it didn't matter to him. His mission had now been redirected to winning over Hoffa on his own; the Monitors were irrelevant to that effort. He would persevere as if his life depended upon it—because it did.

25

Hoffa Seeks an Oval Office Ally

With the Monitors dying and Congress removing itself from the continuing fray after passing the Landrum-Griffin Act, Hoffa still bore one enormous irritation: John Kennedy had defeated Minnesota's Hubert Humphrey in the Wisconsin presidential primary on April 15, 1960. Even though Hoffa had become even more active in the effort to defeat Kennedy, it did not seem to help. Kennedy continued to win every Democratic primary, systematically defeating Humphrey and all other challengers. Despite Hoffa's personal efforts in West Virginia, that state's election results became Humphrey's deathblow.

Notwithstanding his impressive showing in the primaries, Kennedy approached the Democratic National Convention without enough committed delegates to win the nomination on the first ballot. Hoffa now had one last gambit in the Democratic presidential race. Although the circumstances surrounding the encounter remain disputed, there is no doubt that Hoffa met with Lyndon Johnson's chief aide, John Connally. According to Connally, Hoffa told him that he would support Johnson's candidacy, but Connally responded that Johnson might not be a candidate. Johnson and Connally had concluded that Johnson's only realistic chance turned on Adlai Stevenson's fate. The Illinoisan had run against Eisenhower in 1952 and 1956, losing by a widening margin. Johnson's only hope was that Stevenson might garner sufficient delegate support to prevent Kennedy's nomination on the first ballot. If he did, then and only then would the prospect of a convention deadlock offer Johnson some possibility of emerging as a compromise nominee. The country and the Democratic party were otherwise unprepared for a president from the Deep South. In his heart, even Johnson knew that to be true.

Hoffa's version of the meeting was much different. He claimed that Connally had first come to Hoffa in search of support for Johnson, and Hoffa had refused. In the end, it didn't matter because

Stevenson's candidacy failed. Johnson's opportunity for the nomination in 1960 never materialized. On July 13, 1960, John Fitzgerald Kennedy received the Democratic presidential nomination on the first ballot.

Knowing that the head of the Democratic party's ticket was firmly against him, Hoffa wasted no time in turning to the Republicans. That party's national convention began in Chicago two weeks after the Democrats had finished their work in Los Angeles. Kennedy's victory had made Hoffa's promise of unqualified support for Richard Nixon easy, particularly since Nixon was on his way to winning the nomination without a contest. Hoffa campaigned vigorously, using *International Teamster* as a forum for his anti-Kennedy crusade. My father read Hoffa's comments on the upcoming election in the September issue, where the Teamsters' president wrote that the Democratic candidate couldn't be trusted to lead the country because he had been responsible for the "union-busting Kennedy-Landrum-Griffin labor law, the worst piece of labor legislation ever passed by Congress."

Starting with Hoffa's "Special Message to All Teamsters and Their Families," the tone of the October issue was even more strident. Hoffa accused the Kennedy brothers—"Jack and Bobbie"—of harboring a "police-state mentality." To support his assertion, Hoffa cited Kennedy's statement during the first nationally televised presidential debate that he was "not satisfied" when he saw "men like Jimmy Hoffa in charge of the largest union in the United States, still free." In the same issue, Hoffa told the membership that his general executive board had voted to endorse neither Nixon nor Kennedy, but that "the hatred Kennedy has displayed over the past few years against your union—the untiring efforts he has made to destroy this union—should be fair warning to you."

The scenario was unfolding exactly as Hoffa had predicted to former congressman Hunter in their secret Miami meeting the previous December. Hoffa's notoriety generated such strong public reaction that a formal endorsement of Nixon could backfire. But as Hoffa had also informed Hunter, local endorsements could benefit Nixon greatly. Hoffa made his position on the upcoming election clear to his Teamsters locals, as he traveled throughout the country with his anti-Kennedy campaign. He urged members to split their tickets and vote for Nixon at the top while supporting labor-friendly Democratic candidates for lesser office. It looked like Hoffa's help might even enable

Nixon to win the crucial state of Ohio, where Hoffa had important allies and secrets.

Hoffa's efforts on Nixon's behalf appeared to be reaping rewards for both of them, especially for Hoffa and his biggest Minneapolis problem: Sun Valley. In September 1960, as Hoffa worked hard to get Nixon elected, federal prosecutor James Dowd was working in Orlando on a criminal indictment of Hoffa. In the midst of his final presentation of the evidence to the grand jury—the last step before formal indictment—Dowd was interrupted to take an emergency call from his superior in Washington. Months earlier, that superior had specifically hired Dowd to identify matters that presented the best chance for successful criminal prosecution of Hoffa. Dowd had put Sun Valley at the top of that list. Now that Hoffa was on the brink of criminal indictment, the same man who had hired Dowd directed him to stop work and return immediately to Washington with all his files.

Hoffa had dodged a bullet. Someone at the highest levels of the executive branch of the U.S. government could take credit for the feat, but the reprieve was only temporary. Despite Hoffa's vigorous efforts to the contrary, Kennedy won the presidency in November. A few days later, Dowd received a new directive from his superior and returned to Orlando to proceed with his previously planned indictment of Hoffa. All roads seemed to lead back to Ben Dranow, the Teamsters' Central States Pension Fund, and Minneapolis.

Only a week after Kennedy prevailed over Nixon, Hoffa received a letter from my father, dated November 10. By then we had moved to a new house in the Minneapolis suburb of Bloomington, where I attended the third school of my young academic career. As I settled into first grade, my father's letter reopened wounds at Minneapolis Local 544—wounds Hoffa thought he had sewn shut more than six months earlier. Ostensibly, my dad sent it as a courtesy, advising Hoffa that he was soliciting help from members to defray the $146 debt still owed for Rank-and-File Group activities earlier in the year. He wanted Hoffa to understand that he was not seeking to fund a new offensive.

Dear Sir:
The statements and opinions expressed in the following letter are solely the responsibility of the undersigned. They do not represent the

views of any other particular individual or group; in fact, with the exception of my wife, no one else is aware that this letter is being written to you.

The accompanying letter is self-explanatory. I do not believe that its distribution is a violation of the agreement that was forced upon me by the vote of the membership of Local 544 on March 27, 1960. You may be certain that I have lived up to that agreement, without exception, since that meeting; and that I will continue to separate myself from any violation of it that may occur in the future. However, I consider it my duty to make this effort to satisfy our financial obligations, and further, to offer certain members of this union the opportunity to share this responsibility.

He then began the impossible task of trying to explain why Hoffa should not feel personally threatened by the words that followed, despite the ongoing reform efforts at Local 544.

These men, to whom the attached letter is being sent, are not agitators or "rebels," although numerous attempts have been made to brand them as such. They are men who are seriously interested in the good and welfare of the Teamsters; and have the determination to resist any attempt to harm or weaken this local, or the International Union. Truthfully, these men are the real backbone of the union, and I am proud to have been associated with them in their endeavor.

Even now, though giving the outward appearance of calm, a tempest is brewing within Local 544. My judgment is not clouded with hatred or desire for revenge against Fritz Snyder, for he has never done anything to me, personally, to cause such motives. The fact remains that I am more than ever convinced that he is a definite liability; not only to the local union, but to the International as well.

He was sure Hoffa could not ignore his next subject because the union's general president had made it central to the March 1960 discussion in his hotel room.

During the meeting in your room at the Nicollet Hotel on March 27th, you asked everyone present if our contracts were being lived up to. I am ashamed to admit, that at that time, I was ignorant of the text of the contract. Since then, I have studied its contents and I can now answer your question. The contract is so pitifully enforced that nearly

every company covered by Local 544 operates under a different set of rules. Some companies, with practically identical operations, have entirely opposite procedures to govern seniority and other similar union problems. Many members of this local wrongly believe that the final and absolute authority in these matters is the company-level majority. I recognize that contracts must often be enforced with consideration for company problems, but company-level majorities are as detrimental to the Teamsters as company-level contracts.

He then offered Hoffa some unsolicited advice on negotiation principles, describing Snyder's actions that he believed were undermining the union.

How can we ever hope to eventually enforce a coast to coast contract, when such practices are not only allowed, but encouraged by the top man in the local? The greatest unrest in this local is caused by the numerous "sweetheart deals" that were originated by Sidney Brennan, and have been allowed to continue under the leadership (?) of Fred Snyder. In the two years since his election to office, Snyder has made no attempt to correct this sick condition; and it is causing constant and growing discension [sic] among the members of Local 544.

He also reported his belief that Snyder was actually undermining Hoffa's authority—something Hoffa certainly would not tolerate: "Veiled attempts to undermine the International Union and some of its subordinates have been made, by questioning their authority in the settlement of grievances. I believe that such decisions should be made by the majority of the Teamsters, not the majority of employees in one single company."

His concluding paragraphs reaffirmed his allegiance to the union and his obedience to everything Hoffa had requested of him:

This communication is not intended as a request for action; nor, do I anticipate any as a result of it. I am learning that enthusiasm must be tempered with experience and foresight. It would be ridiculous for me to question your judgment in union matters, and I am not about to do so. Be assured that I will comply with the directive of the membership to "forgive and forget, for the good of the Teamsters," even though I do not agree with it. I do not want to deserve the tag, "rebel," and so, I have no choice. My devotion is *to* the union; not against it.

A final reminder that the foregoing contains only the viewpoints of the undersigned. I do not have the authority to speak for any other members of Local 544. I hope that this letter will thwart the rumors and misleading implications that will surely follow as a result of the letter to my former constituents.

The letter requested no response, and Hoffa would send none. But Hoffa must have recognized that this Minneapolis problem had to disappear. The last time he had to bail out Snyder, the Monitors were looking over his shoulder and controlled Hoffa's future. Hoffa had to be diplomatic; he had to be careful.

Times had changed. As a practical matter, the Monitors were gone. This time, if Jim Harper created controversy at Local 544, the nuances of due process needn't hamper Hoffa's reaction.

Greatly compounding the aggravation of Local 544, on December 7, 1960, the grand jury in Orlando indicted Hoffa for mail and wire fraud in connection with his alleged use of Teamsters money in the Sun Valley scheme. Nine days later, the new American president chose his brother to become the next U.S. attorney general, and Robert Kennedy began to assemble his "Get Hoffa" squad. It was an elite corps of investigators and attorneys whose single-minded mission was as unambiguous as its unofficial name.

On January 4, 1961, the *Washington Post* broke the story that vice president Nixon had engineered the delay in Hoffa's Orlando indictment over the Sun Valley affair. The story suggested that Hoffa's potential ability to give Nixon support from organized labor helped Nixon carry Ohio—another place where Teamsters leaders seemed to have special connections and dark secrets. Feeling indebted to Hoffa, the story continued, Nixon attempted to persuade attorney general William Rogers not to bring the Hoffa indictment. As proof, *Post* columnist Drew Pearson characterized former congressman Allan Oakley Hunter as "the secret intermediary between Nixon and Hoffa" and quoted from his letter to Hoffa:

I was sorry to hear of the indictment against you in the Orlando matter. I know for a fact that your side of the case was put before the Vice president and that he discussed the case with the Attorney General, Bill Rogers.

I do not know what was said by the Vice president to Rogers. I do know, however, that the Vice president has been sympathetic toward you and has felt that you were being subjected to undue harassment by certain parties. . . .

It would be my surmise that Bill Rogers acted as he did for reasons of his own. Mr. Nixon having lost the election, I doubt that he has since been in a position to exercise any decisive degree of influence. As Vice president, he has no authority to order the Attorney General to do anything.

My father did not read the *Washington Post,* but I'm not sure it would have mattered if he had.

26

Threats and a Wire

For Christmas 1960, my parents gave me a set of American Flyer S-gauge model railroad trains. In our basement, Dad constructed a large layout complete with mountains, bridges, roads, and a miniature town. Several plywood panels on sawhorses accommodated both the diesel passenger train and the smoking freight locomotive, running simultaneously. A pegboard master control panel was wired to hold power transformers, track switches, streetlights, and train whistles. It required both of us to run the operation—which was just as well because I was afraid to be alone in our basement.

In retrospect, I had little awareness of the facts that really should have terrified me at the time.

About two hours after Dad had left home on an evening trip to Mauston in early November 1960, the telephone rang. "Hi, Mary," said the voice at the other end. "This is one of Jim's friends."

"Who?" She struggled to recognize the voice. My father's only real friend at this point was Masteller, and this definitely was not Masteller.

"Oh, you know me. Jim and I are old friends. I know you have four kids, a dog, and a nice house in the suburbs."

"What can I do for you?" she asked as she lit a Salem.

"I'll tell you what you can do for me. Things can be very dangerous on the road and I want you to tell Jim that he needs to take very good care of himself, okay? Tell him that people get hurt on the road all the time. He needs to be very, very careful. Can you do that for me, Mary?"

She hung up and flipped on the outside floodlights her husband had mounted above the back door. He had said the lights were there so we children could play outdoors after sunset, but it seemed odd to me that ours was the only yard in the neighborhood with such dramatic backyard illumination. He returned the next evening and heard about the phone call.

"Those bastards," he railed. "Who do they think they are?"

He decided it might be time for Mary to learn how to use his .38 caliber pistol. Over her objections, they went to the basement, where he had set up a bale of hay with a paper bull's-eye target. He took out the pistol, demonstrated the proper stance, fired two shots, and hit the center of the bull's-eye. "See, it's easy."

Mary's right hand quivered as she wrapped it around the pistol's grip. She lifted the gun, aimed at the target, closed her eyes, and slowly squeezed the trigger. The bullet missed the target. It ricocheted off the cement block behind the hay bale, then off the side wall before passing two inches from her husband's right temple. That was enough of her firearms training for both of them. Concluding he needed something more to protect his family, my father took a trip to the drugstore, went directly to the pay telephone, picked up the receiver, and dialed the number of someone who could procure what he needed. To this day I do not know who it was, but I saw what resulted from that call.

As Christmas approached in 1960, he began building a fifteen-by-twenty-foot room in our basement. When he finished, it resembled what I thought a professional recording studio probably looked like. Equipping the room with two large reel-to-reel tape decks and a telephone receiver, he did the entire job—framing, electrical, wallboard—in two months. He did the work himself because he wanted no one outside our immediate family to know anything about the place that he called "Dad's den in the basement." From somewhere that he would never disclose he obtained two electronic devices to complete his setup.

The first connected his telephone receiver to a tape recorder that could capture every conversation on our line. The next time Mary received a threatening call, the voice of the coward on the other end would be recorded. He could then replay it and, perhaps, recognize it. Even if that were not possible, he'd keep the taped conversations for others to use if he met with foul play.

The second was a pocket-sized "Minifon" wire recorder of the type he remembered reading about in the February 1960 issue of *International Teamster*. He could wear one underneath his Werner jacket to tape his conversations. He had only one subject in mind: Fritz Snyder. He knew Snyder had a big mouth and would someday slip up. When that happened, he would have incontrovertible proof—sufficient to persuade Hoffa that Snyder had to be removed to avoid future embar-

rassment to Hoffa and the union. Surely the Teamsters' general president could not ignore the power of a human voice admitting its own misconduct.

He told only Mary that he had either of these devices, and he wouldn't even tell her how he had acquired them. He'd never share his recordings with any law enforcement agencies because, in addition to his own history with the police, he agreed with Hoffa's warnings that such outsiders were the Teamsters' enemies.

My father had a plan to reassure Hoffa that he remained a loyal Teamster as his assault on Snyder continued. He implemented the plan at the Local 544 membership meeting in November 1960, just a few days after his letter to Hoffa reignited an old Minneapolis fire. Seeking to neutralize any concerns that his correspondence might have created about his allegiance, he led an effort to pass a motion expressing the membership's approval and unwavering support for Hoffa. He wanted everyone to know that his attacks on Snyder had nothing to do with his continuing loyalty to Hoffa. The motion would confirm that Local 544 stood with Hoffa—no matter what. This ploy would create room for my father to maneuver as he assembled his evidence against Snyder in the upcoming phase of his battle.

Just as my father had predicted, Snyder began to make mistakes. At the same November meeting where my father offered his loyalty resolution, Snyder proposed new bylaws for Local 544 that would enhance his power. It appeared to my father that those bylaws would limit the membership's access to financial records and prevent meaningful officer oversight by the trustees, even if they were independent. The entire membership was supposed to vote on the new bylaws in December, so my father had just a month to investigate the matter and determine how best to exploit Snyder's power grab. Meanwhile, help came from an unlikely source: Hoffa sent model bylaws to all Teamsters locals for consideration and adoption. Local 544 created a special committee to compare them with Snyder's and report on the differences in January. My father was sure the comparison would hurt Snyder's standing with the membership.

He also thought that Snyder had damaged himself on another issue. Snyder was getting cocky and, therefore, sloppy, reporting to the membership that he had been serving on an over-the-road appeals

board charged with resolving deadlocked cases involving internal union disputes. My father attended that meeting, and his surreptitious wire recorder was running under his winter coat when Snyder said, "Now, we have another thing here. Like I said, we're trying to do what is right with you people. We're trying to guide you. We have in St. Paul, and I'm part of it, a twenty-four-man board on the over-the-road, which is headquartered in St. Paul, that hears our deadlocked cases on the over-the-road and the over-the-road local cartage. We have got some decisions out of this committee, of which we don't sit on our own, that are contrary and contradictory to our . . . our system, or our contracts, or our system of seniority. That's something that's going to have to be corrected in our negotiations."

Snyder seemed to be confirming exactly what my father had told Hoffa in his November 10 letter: company-level resolutions of member grievances were receiving priority and preference over Teamsters-wide solutions. Snyder's approach flew in the face of Hoffa's often expressed desire for a uniform nationwide contract. Snyder's remarks also seemed pertinent to Hoffa's specific question to my father in their private March meeting: "Are the contracts being enforced? If they are, that's the main point of the Teamsters union."

Snyder seemed to be providing my father with all the ammunition he needed. But in the larger game, my dad was the target.

27

Reopened Wounds Start to Bleed

For as long as I can remember, I loved cars. Dad told his friends that my first word was Buick. At the age of two, I had started cutting automobile ads from magazines and pasting them into scrapbooks. My neat lines of toy vehicles snaked throughout our house to create what I called "traffic." If I had failed to put them away before going to bed, I risked being awakened by Dad's cursing as he encountered pieces of my project while making his way from the front door to his bedroom. By the time I was three, he was proudly demonstrating to his Werner colleagues my ability to identify the make and model of every car on the road—just by viewing a small portion of its front, rear, or side. So when he got permission to take me out of first grade for a weeklong automobile voyage with him and his own dad to pick up my Grandma Fischer and her daughter in Gainesville, Florida, I was thrilled. They had moved there a year earlier after living with us for a few months following Grandpa Fischer's death. Now they were coming back.

He and Grandpa took turns driving as we went nonstop from Minneapolis to Florida. Our passage through impoverished areas of what Dad called Appalachia impressed me profoundly as I considered how fortunate my life had been in comparison. I think that was when he first told me about the boy who "cried because he had no shoes, until he saw a man who had no feet." At night, I slept in the backseat of our big 1950 Buick Roadmaster. I woke up once to see the needle on the speedometer pressing past 100 and decided I'd better go back to sleep.

The trip back home was a lot less fun. Even forty years later, Dad sneered that his mother-in-law had required the entourage to stop only at AAA-approved accommodations. He regarded that as an unnecessary extravagance. I now understand how the Great Depression and Angola had set his baseline for all comparisons, so almost everything seemed luxurious to him. What I didn't fully comprehend at the

time was how the return of his mother-in-law to our home added to his already considerable problems.

More trouble was on the way, but Dad thought the tide of events in his union was turning in his favor. When he visited the Teamsters' office on December 15 to pick up a copy of the proposed new Local 544 bylaws, Snyder accused him of tearing down the union. The two men soon were in a shouting match over whether the earlier audit had revealed any misuse of union funds. As the spindles of my father's wire recorder spun under his coat, Snyder said, "Now, you show me in that book where you can find one cent . . . Maybe some of the other business agents, but not me . . . But you bring in them charges, I'm telling you. I want you to bring in one charge, and I'll put you where you belong."

"Where's that?" Dad asked.

"Right back where you come from, down in prison. Goddamned check-writer."

When he received his *International Teamster* shortly before the January 1961 meeting, my dad knew he was on the right track in pursuing the bylaws question. The magazine reported how the prior year had ended with a big Hoffa victory on that issue. It said "major road-blocks" to the scheduling of a new International convention had been removed: the judge presiding over the earlier consent decree adopted a proposed set of model bylaws for all union locals. The magazine reprinted Hoffa's letter calling all locals to evaluate carefully the International's model. Dad reasoned that if the local bylaws were important enough to have been a convention "roadblock," Hoffa would not look kindly on Snyder's manipulation of them at Local 544. He concluded that the issues he was now pursuing were no longer simply matters of Snyder's petty wrongdoing; they went to the core of Hoffa's struggle to become the unconditional general president—no provisional status—through a new convention and election.

He prepared a flyer attacking Snyder's proposed bylaws, showing them to be dramatically at odds with what Hoffa and the International had recommended and well beyond the March 1960 vote of the Local 544 membership to "forgive and forget, for the good of the Teamsters." The flyer read:

The vote of this membership at the meeting held March 27, 1960, required that 11 charges against the officers of this local be forgiven. We have felt an obligation to abide by that mandate. However, we do not feel obligated to allow the membership of this local union to accept and approve bylaws which, in our opinion, transfer the authority of this union from the membership to the Secretary-Treasurer. We are duty bound to inform the membership of the hidden powers granted to this one officer by the proposed Snyder bylaws. We cannot understand why Snyder is so anxious to put through these bylaws, since we now have a set of good bylaws that were recommended by the International Union.

He then offered examples of how he thought Snyder's proposals sought to enhance his own power, concluding that he saw "traps and loopholes which we firmly believe are intended to smother the freedom and authority of the membership of this local union."

His flyer made the bylaws issue the number one agenda item at the January 1961 membership meeting. Fred Fournier, a member of the Local 544 bylaws committee, admitted that Snyder hadn't presented the International's model bylaws to that committee. That meant Snyder had disobeyed both the membership's vote in November and Hoffa's specific instructions. My father made sure the wire recorder under his jacket captured every word because Fournier was a Snyder loyalist who might someday deny or claim "memory loss" concerning his damning remarks.

"A tape recording doesn't forget," Dad thought as he tried to suppress a smile.

He didn't stop there. With his secret recorder running, he went to Snyder's office in February 1961 to see if he could get Snyder talking about his salary. Snyder admitted that he had told the membership at its December 1959 meeting his weekly salary was only $225—not the $250 he was actually taking. He acknowledged that the membership had approved only the lower salary but said he'd intended to take a cut in wages; that, he said, was why he'd sought approval only for the lower amount.

The salary cut never happened. Snyder knew it; my father knew it. Snyder knew that my father knew it. My father was becoming more than a nuisance. He had already embarrassed Snyder once in Hoffa's presence. Snyder would not want that to happen again.

. . . . .

On March 16, 1961, my father filed charges against Snyder, Blixt, and a third Teamster. The formal claims were: "Misappropriation, abuse of fellow members or officers by written or oral communication, and disobedience to the regulations, rules, mandates, and decrees of the local union, or of the officers of the International union." The third defendant had been included for the "abuse" charge. Dad alleged that the man had told a February 1960 meeting of Local 544 stewards that the dissidents were being led by a convicted felon—a clear reference to my father. Blixt had ruled the remark "out of order," but only after it had been uttered. The recording secretary had prepared two versions of that meeting's minutes: one noted the "convicted felon" reference; the other omitted it. Dad wanted someone to explain the discrepancy.

He could not have picked a worse time to file his grievances. After a three-year battle, Hoffa had finally prevailed against the Monitors. The International Teamsters would hold their national convention in July 1961. Until then, Hoffa would have wanted to maintain control and order at every level of the union to safeguard that election. What is now clear to me was less obvious to my father: Hoffa could not allow insurgents to disrupt his election as general president this time around. It was "déjà vu all over again," as Yogi Berra once said.

Nor could he have been in a worse place for his renewed assault. Hoffa's biggest concerns in Minneapolis would have been Ben Dranow and Sun Valley, not Dad's continuing skirmishes with Fritz Snyder. Dranow was already heading for trial on fraud charges relating to the bankruptcy of the department store that Teamsters pension fund loans had helped him to acquire and keep afloat. My father's new charges risked generating new media attention to Teamsters activities in a city where Hoffa's even deeper Sun Valley secrets dwelled. Once again, Hoffa had a problem in Minneapolis. He would have to deal with it swiftly and decisively.

Only three days later, Snyder struck back. Dad had complained to Hoffa about company-level majorities, but now he was going to experience them firsthand. At a Werner company-level meeting of Local 544 members on March 19, 1961, Snyder accepted a motion that severely impaired my father's seniority rights and, thereby, his livelihood.

The issue was simple. Drivers were paid by the trip and received jobs based upon their over-the-road seniority. The drivers with the longest tenure had the most assignments. Dad had somehow gained

his over-the-road position ahead of many city drivers who longed for that job. At the Werner drivers' meeting, Snyder now accepted a motion allowing city drivers who became new over-the-road truckers to jump ahead of Jim Harper on the seniority list. Although the motion passed, my father believed it violated a ruling from a superior Teamsters' governing body only six months earlier.

On March 22, 1961, he sent a telegram to International vice president Gordon Conklin, with a copy to Hoffa, complaining about Snyder's actions. A week later, he got his response:

> This matter was heard by the Minnesota State Committee and a unanimous decision rendered. This decision is final and binding, there is nothing that this office can do to assist you.

But it was not signed by Conklin, the addressee of Dad's letter. The signatory on the response was "James R. Hoffa, General President."

My father thought Hoffa's reply was pure subterfuge. The only decision of the Minnesota State Committee was precisely contrary to the Snyder-led action—the point Dad had made in his telegram. As he saw it, someone was refusing to apply that earlier ruling to him. He suspected that Snyder had told Hoffa that the Werner rules change would end the renewed Minneapolis insurgency. With this new seniority system in place, Snyder was threatening my dad economically, with Hoffa's blessing and Conklin's passive approval.

Snyder and his fellow defendants pressed for more detail and supporting evidence on the new charges. My father thought he had assembled the evidence needed to prove his claims, but he was concerned that revealing names and details would allow Snyder to intimidate witnesses. He believed that one of his three Rank-and-File Group trustees had turned on him a year earlier, when Velin had proposed sending the Local 544 financial audit to Hoffa rather than making it available to the membership at large. He was still worried about another trustee, Lloyd Harris. Snyder seemed able to manipulate people in ways my father could not understand.

So he responded that Snyder would have to look elsewhere for the additional information he sought. He told the Local 544 recording secretary that he could "find no provision in the International Consti-

tution that calls for specific details of charges in the manner that was requested by these charged members." He went on to state that "these accused brothers" could be informed that "some of the charges are based on evidence consisting of, but not limited to, findings resulting from the special audit of 544 financial records for the year 1959."

Snyder persevered and, with remarkable irony, invoked the new law that Hoffa hated. "We received the answer . . . to our request for specific charges," he said. "The answer does not make the charges specific. This is required under the Landrum-Griffin Law before a hearing can be held. The only reference made is to the audit and this audit is the one that has been submitted to the membership, passed on, and all matters in it approved by the membership."

My father thought Snyder's statement was ridiculous. The audit had never been "submitted to the membership" or "passed on." None of it had been "approved by the membership" because the membership could not approve what it had never seen. The whole point of Hoffa's March 1960 visit to Minneapolis had been to keep the audit under wraps. Although my father and a few Rank-and-File Group members had seen the copy that my father had surreptitiously made, it had remained a secret to the membership at large. Snyder's letter concluded, "We ask that you, as recording secretary, submit this letter together with our other requests to the International Union."

Snyder knew what he was doing in pushing the dispute up the chain of command. He was sure Hoffa would not like to see the continuing trouble that my father was creating in Minneapolis. My father followed up with another long letter to Hoffa, detailing how Snyder had "failed to heed the instructions that you gave him during the meeting in the Pick-Nicollet Hotel on March 27, 1960 . . . In view of the foregoing, it became our duty to prefer charges." He also enclosed a copy of the countercharges that Snyder had filed, which accused Jim Harper of "abuse" in pursuing his claims.

On the same day my father sent his letter, Hoffa's reaction to all of this came by registered mail. "I have assumed original jurisdiction over the charges," Hoffa wrote. "I have delegated a panel to hear these charges. The hearing will be held on Thursday, April 27, 1961 at 10:00 A.M. at the Hotel Radisson, Minneapolis, Minnesota. The panel will consist of Mr. Joseph Konowe, Chairman, Mr. Roy Williams, and Mr. Frank Fitzsimmons. The charges you have preferred against Brother

Snyder . . . should be made more specific, so that they may properly prepare their defense. Please send three copies of the specific charges so that I may present them to the panel members. Fraternally yours, James R. Hoffa, General President."

At Snyder's request, Hoffa had invoked Article 18 of the Teamsters constitution to take personal command of the situation. Dad pulled out his pocket copy of the union's governing document and read the provision. It authorized the general president to assume original jurisdiction and bypass the usual hearing process when charges involve or relate to a situation "dangerous to the welfare of the union."

"Maybe I've finally hit a raw nerve," he thought. "'Dangerous to the welfare of the union' sure sounds like it's something that matters a helluva a lot to Hoffa. Good."

My father understood the game. Hoffa and Snyder together were now giving him the bum's rush. They must have assumed that such short notice for a full hearing would not allow him sufficient time to develop and present a serious case. Dad immediately sent Hoffa a five-page single-spaced letter detailing his charges against Snyder and the others.

Dad didn't realize that the merits of his case would not matter. Without the Monitors, Hoffa could handle this internal matter as he chose; his invocation of Article 18 had made that clear. My father knew only that he had to move quickly in preparing for what came next. He had no idea what lay before him.

28

Lug Nuts

When my mother drove my father to the Werner yard for a trip to Mauston, sometimes the whole family went along. He'd pick up his paperwork from the office, then inspect his tractor-trailer combination while we waited by the exit. But on one particular trip that he told me about years later, he departed from his normal routine. He was thinking about Hoffa's recent letter setting an expedited hearing date for the newest charges against Snyder. He was planning his next moves. He was distracted. After walking out of the office, he skipped his pre-trip inspection of the rig, went directly to the truck, climbed into the cab, lit a cigarette, and pulled out of the yard. As always on these occasions, we followed him in our car for a few minutes to send him off.

His truck pulled a large trailer that blocked our view of him. As I stared at the WERNER letters on the back of the van, I couldn't see him behind the wheel, but I knew he was there. After a while, he waved at us with a sweeping arm motion out his side window and headed east for the River Road as we traveled southwest to our home. Having once accompanied him on the journey myself, I always wished we could follow him all the way to Mauston, but that wasn't going to happen. I watched the back of the trailer until it was completely out of sight. It never occurred to me that he might not return.

It was a beautiful spring evening as the setting sun flashed through barren trees. Dad motored toward the Wisconsin border, navigating through traffic and out of the city. Eventually, he gained enough speed to get beyond fourth gear. The road ahead was clear as he left the small industrial town of Red Wing and turned toward the Mississippi River. His favorite part of the voyage now began.

The Great Road narrowed and the trees overhead formed an archway through which his Autocar moved effortlessly in the darkness. He looked at the road sign—U.S. 61—the same highway that nine years

earlier and more than a thousand miles to the south had taken him from a Baton Rouge jail to the Louisiana State Penitentiary at Angola. At every turn, things that other people never noticed—like a simple highway road sign or the Mississippi River—forced him to acknowledge that he could never escape completely from the mistakes of his past. Alcohol could dull the memories, but nothing could erase them.

While the highway and the river itself were reminders of another time—another life—that he tried desperately to forget, these trips in his Autocar also gave him solace and reaffirmation that he was now in a different and better place. He moved progressively into higher gears to reach forty miles an hour, then fifty, and finally sixty before he stopped shifting. He lit another Camel and took a long drag.

The path ahead was winding before him. The dangling cigarette between his lips emitted vertical smoke, causing his left eye to squint in self-defense. He cruised up and down the hills, occasionally grabbing the round gearshift handle in the palm of his right hand as he maneuvered the stick in response to the terrain.

This is what he enjoyed most about driving: the solitude. There was solitude in a tavern, too. The existential experience of mastering a behemoth vehicle with its full load in tow was different from sitting in a cool, dark tavern with a cold Budweiser. But in the ways that mattered, the final effect was the same. In either place, a man was alone with his thoughts. In either place, he could in some sense disappear physically and emotionally from the rest of the world. In either place, no one could bother him; no bad news could be given or received. His truck didn't even have a radio, so there was no distraction of any kind

Jim Harper's Werner badge

from the outside world. He was trapped with his own thoughts and his own demons, but it was an isolation that he enjoyed.

My father always had a sixth sense for the road and his vehicles. It was as if the steering column and its connection to the axle were merely an extension of his hands on the pavement itself. He could feel when a front tire needed air pressure. He could feel a slight rumble in the steering column, which meant the wheels were out of balance. He could feel mechanical trouble before it surfaced. Masteller was more direct, calling it "knowing the truck in your ass."

As he drove, my dad was still preoccupied, trying to determine his next steps against Snyder. On another day, he would have noticed earlier that something was amiss, but these were extraordinary times. As he took one of the River Road's curves about thirty miles south of Red Wing, he felt an odd vibration in the steering wheel. Because there was no shoulder or rest area, he had to wait for an opportunity to pull over. Meanwhile, he slowed to thirty and drove cautiously to the outskirts of Wabasha, where he stopped the truck along the side of the road. Puffing on his sixth Camel since his trip had begun about an hour earlier, he jumped out of the cab and walked around the rig. Moving briskly to the tractor's passenger side, he saw the culprit.

A single lug nut held the right front wheel of his truck to its axle; the other five were missing. If he had maintained his mile-a-minute speed, that nut would have worked loose or snapped, the wheel would have flown off, and more than thirty tons of man, machinery, and payload would have careened toward disaster. Someone was trying to kill him and make it look like an accident.

He reacted with anger, not fear.

"Those bastards," he muttered as he flipped his half-smoked cigarette toward the river.

He went to the truck's toolbox, grabbed a wrench, unscrewed two lug nuts from the left front wheel, and moved them to the right one. He traveled slowly to Mauston, where he got replacement lug nuts and a few extras for his return trip. From that day on, he kept several additional lug nuts in his vehicle at all times. Never again would he fail to inspect every inch of his tractor, trailer, or even his personal car before taking a trip anywhere.

He now believed that his adversaries fell into the animal category in his Angola human classification system. These men happened to be

on the outside, but they were a different species from most of humanity. They had no boundaries and responded only to strength. His best approach would be to continue with life as usual and to act as if nothing had happened. He would simply add another layer of diligence to his daily routines. That would communicate his message to the instigator of this botched inside job: Jim Harper had no fear. Threats and even worse would not stop him.

"Do you know what those sons-of-bitches tried to do?" he said to Mary as he walked into our home and slammed the door.

"What?" she asked, having just received yet another frightening anonymous phone call warning her of the dangers that my father faced on the road.

"They took off all but one lug nut on one of the front wheels of my truck! Can you believe those bastards?"

He assured her that for every trip he took thereafter, six lug nuts would hold each front wheel of his Autocar conventional diesel tractor to its axle. But other vulnerable areas of a tractor-trailer rig did not lend themselves to his rigorous pre-trip inspections. And still other dangers lurked beyond the truck itself.

29

A Dangerous Game

When I was six, I never expected danger to walk with me when I went to school. It was an overcast day in early April 1961 when, as a civil defense exercise, all grades participated in an organized evacuation from the classrooms at the end of the day. Rather than take our regular school buses, we walked home in teacher-escorted groups. I guessed that the buses were expected to be the first casualties of nuclear war. My best friend, who lived across the street and whose father was a policeman, shared my view of the event as a grand adventure.

As we approached our homes, my friend and I left the group to make our own way for the final two blocks. Because of my special interest in cars, I noticed an unfamiliar vehicle parked a short distance from my house. Except for identifying the year, make, and model—a 1953 Chevrolet sedan—I paid no attention to it or to the man sitting behind the wheel. I did think it was odd that he was wearing sunglasses on such a cloudy day. From later events I've pieced together in understanding Dad's union fight, I think I've figured out what it was doing there.

A week after Dad's near-disaster involving the missing lug nuts, he left for another overnight round-trip to Mauston. The phone rang and Mom answered it.

"Hi, Mary," came the voice at the other end. She recognized the caller instantly. It was the same person who had repeatedly warned her about the unpredictable dangers facing over-the-road drivers. "You remember me, don't you?"

"What can I do for you?" She tried to remain calm.

"Well, I gave you a message last time—about Jim taking care of himself on the road. Mary, Mary, Mary, what good does he think that dog is going to do him?" Obviously, the caller knew that my father had been taking Fritzie with him since the last threatening phone call. Dad

was being watched. Was everyone being watched? Mom listened, terrified. The tar and nicotine she inhaled deeply didn't seem to help.

"Look, you need to tell Jim this is very serious stuff. He needs to be very careful. The road is a dangerous place. Lots of funny turns, you know. And that dog—well, no one likes to see a dog get hurt."

The caller hung up. She slowly placed the receiver back in its cradle. She was trembling and alone in a house with four children; I was the oldest—and only six. Again, she flipped the kitchen switch that turned on our outside floodlights.

When Dad returned two nights later, she told him about the call and one thing became clear to him: the dog would stay home to guard the family and he would take his chances on his own. He went to the basement and set up his telephone recorder. The next time an unfriendly voice came over the line, he would be ready for it. He did not wait long. A few days later, he was home alone with us kids when the phone rang.

"Hello," Dad snarled, waking from an afternoon nap on the couch in his den.

"Hi, Jim, you don't know me, but I know you."

My father sat up, walked over to one of his tape decks, and turned the switch to "record."

"I know all about you," the caller continued. "I know all about your family. In fact, I noticed your son walking home from school the other day—fine looking boy. I was wondering if he might want a car ride home once in a while. Anyway, a father is very important to a son growing up, right Jim?"

"What do you want?" Dad snapped. He had learned from Angola that the best way to deal with animals like this one was to communicate anger and determination; never reveal weakness through fear.

"Why, I don't want anything, Jim. I was just calling to tell you what a fine family you've got, and how important their father must be to all of them." Click. The call ended. My father reached over and stopped the recorder. He had something on tape, but he had no idea what to do with it or what he should do next. The next day, he and Mom sat down with the older of my sisters and me.

"Listen," he told us in words that I recall as if they had been spoken yesterday, "I've told you kids before that you're never to talk to strangers or accept anything from them, including a ride. That rule

goes for everyone, even someone you know. You're to speak with no adults—ever. You're never to accept a ride from anyone other than Mom, Grandpa, or me. Someone may tell you that Mom or I've sent them to pick you up. They may even tell you something has happened to me or Mom, and they're going to take you to us. That won't be true. Only Mom, Grandpa, or I will ever pick you up, no matter what. Anyone who tries to tell you anything else will be lying to you. And that person isn't your friend, even if you thought he was. If anyone tries to grab you, run away—and scream as loud as you can."

"What about—" I wanted to test a few names that might be added to Dad's approved list.

"No one else, period. Understood?"

Understood.

30

The Panel and the Charges

Threats and attempts to intimidate Jim Harper would not make a difference now. There was no turning back on his charges against Snyder. He would make the case against the union under-boss so compelling that Hoffa would have to throw Snyder out or risk personal embarrassment for failing to do so. Unfortunately for my father, Hoffa's invocation of original jurisdiction over the controversy had allowed Hoffa personally to appoint the three-man panel that would hear and decide the charges. Those selections were far from a random draw. None of the names was familiar to my father, but I have now learned quite a bit about them.

The chairman would be New Yorker Joseph Konowe, who had known Hoffa since 1939 and bore the official title of "administrative assistant to the president." His role was similar to Larry Steinberg's, who was still Hoffa's "personal representative." Konowe had unwavering loyalty to Hoffa and the power that went with access and influence. Like Steinberg of Ohio, Konowe traveled regularly to Washington, where he served as an emergency backup when Hoffa and his chief executive aide, Harold Gibbons, were both away from Teamsters headquarters. My father didn't know that the selection of Konowe as the panel chairman must have meant that Hoffa wanted the controversy in Minneapolis contained and eliminated.

The second panelist was Frank Fitzsimmons, who came from Hoffa's local in Detroit. Hoffa and Fitzsimmons had been friends and professional collaborators since 1936, although Fitzsimmons was five years older. He had started his Teamsters career on the loading docks and was an over-the-road driver when he became a shop steward. As Hoffa had moved up the Teamsters ranks, Fitzsimmons had ridden his coattails. By the time Hoffa appointed him to hear the Snyder charges in April 1961, Fitzsimmons was vice president of the Detroit local where Hoffa still held the title of president. It was the same local whose money Hoffa had transferred to the bank in Florida as secret

collateral for loans made to Sun Valley. As with Konowe, the selection of Fitzsimmons meant that Hoffa regarded the Minneapolis situation seriously, its outcome to be controlled.

The third panelist would be Roy Williams, another longtime Hoffa protégé and head of the Kansas City Teamsters. He served with Hoffa and Gordon Conklin as a trustee of the Teamsters Central States Pension Fund. Years later, a McClellan committee investigator would claim that Williams had once received a loan from one of Ben Dranow's companies. As Jim Harper was pressing his charges against Snyder, Dranow himself was heading for trial in Minneapolis on bankruptcy fraud charges.

My father didn't care about the panelists; he was preoccupied with his evidence. Hoffa's decree of a quick hearing date left him with little time to prepare. Two days after receiving Hoffa's directive to provide more information to Snyder about the charges, my father had complied. His submission was extensive, detailed, and complete. He even included a copy of a *Minneapolis Star* article carrying an Edward Schaefer byline. My father objected that it contained incorrect information someone had provided to the reporter. The nature of the report suggested that the source must have been a Snyder sympathizer, if not Snyder himself. In short, the newsman got the most important facts surrounding the controversy wrong.

The article said the dispute was similar to an "upheaval in local 544 about two years ago . . . Dissidents in the local at that time were given three positions on the Teamsters executive board." That was not true. The latest charges were new, and no one had "given" Jim Harper anything in this war. In fact, it was because the anti-Snyder slate prevailed in the December 1959 elections that Hoffa had come to town in March 1960 to quell the Local 544 rebellion. Schaefer also wrote, "The original dispute involved methods in which union meetings were conducted." That was not true. Far more than parliamentary procedure was involved in this crusade. "The dissidents also demanded an accounting of union finances," the article concluded. "An audit was made and reportedly showed nothing more than failure to account properly for some expense money expenditures." It was true that the Rank-and-File Group had demanded an audit of Local 544. But what source had provided the description of the audit's results? Certainly not anyone who was representing truthfully what was in that audit.

My father's formal submission to Hoffa cited the internal audit of 1959 books and records to prove his claims of Snyder's financial wrongdoing. These included

1. Snyder's overpayment of his own salary from the beginning of his tenure as secretary-treasurer of Local 544, followed by his wrongful actions in covering it up;
2. per diem reimbursement for a five-day trip to Detroit and Washington, but no supporting expense records for such a trip;
3. multiple charges to a union gasoline credit card on the same dates as the Detroit-Washington reimbursement dates, but from service stations near Snyder's Minnesota cottage;
4. per diem reimbursement for a Teamsters' Joint Council meeting that the local's executive council had voted unanimously not to attend.

Moreover, he described what he regarded as an assault on the bedrock principles comprising the foundation of the Teamsters, accusing Snyder of

1. flouting the International's recommended bylaws in favor of his own effort to entrench himself at Local 544;
2. orchestrating improper revisions to the seniority system at Werner and wreaking havoc on Dad's livelihood;
3. maligning and denigrating a superior governing body of the Teamsters, namely, the Minnesota Joint Council;
4. allowing members to defame fellow Teamsters.

Polished and professional, the submission was surely unlike anything that any truck driver had ever prepared for such a hearing. He'd done it himself—no outside advisors, no lawyers, nobody. The skills he had acquired as one of Angola's best jailhouse lawyers had come in handy. He was proud of his product and confident of his success. He'd labored hard to make certain he would have everything going his way in the hearing: witnesses, affidavits, financial records, and audiotapes. Unlike his earlier round against Snyder in Hoffa's hotel room, this time he would even have upper teeth when he argued his cause. Unfortunately, painful oral ulcers attested to the fact that his mouth was still adapting to his new dentures.

But as he prepared himself, he didn't know that the merits of his claims and the strength of his presentation would not matter at all.

With the CIA's botched Bay of Pigs operation to overthrow Fidel Castro in Cuba under way, my father walked into the Local 544 monthly membership meeting on Sunday night, April 16, 1961, to see that he, too, was on the brink of yet another failure. The main agenda item was to nominate candidates for election as Local 544 delegates to the International Teamsters' July convention in Miami—the one where Hoffa would formally jettison the "provisional" in his presidential title. In the eyes of the world, he had become the clear and unquestioned general president of the Teamsters. In the eyes of all Teamsters, he had already held that position for four years. The only open issue was how many Teamsters from locals nationwide would cast their votes in his favor.

Of the three Local 544 Rank-and-File Group trustees elected as part of the anti-Snyder slate in December 1959, Dad believed that Velin had already flipped to Snyder's side. Just two months after his election, he had proposed sending the internal financial audit of Local 544 directly to Hoffa and not disclosing it to the membership. Now it was Lloyd Harris's turn to show his true colors. Harris was nominated as a delegate to the Miami gathering, which was no surprise. But when Snyder himself seconded the nomination, my father knew that he and his best friend, Masteller, were now alone in this fight. Dad decided that he personally would run as a delegate to the International convention. No longer would he rely upon others to fulfill their empty promises to the Rank-and-File Group's cause.

He could not predict how the delegate election would end or where his increasingly futile effort might lead, but he could still work to support his family. He hit the road whenever he got the opportunity, which was becoming less frequent after the seniority revisions that Snyder had muscled through at Werner. His wife and kids needed to eat—and he still loved driving the Autocar along the Great Mississippi River Road.

31

Another Drive Down the River Road

"Master the truck or it'll kill you."

As had become his habit since the lug-nut incident, my father carefully inspected his rig before he began each trip from the Werner yard, whether in Minneapolis or at his turnaround point. This particular evening he was starting from Mauston, where Werner had a bunkhouse for its drivers. I'd been there; he had secretly taken me on one of his trips. I'd slept in one of several small rooms, each of which had a bunk bed. In retrospect, the fact that there were only two men to a room, and doors on the bathroom stalls, must have seemed to my dad like the lap of luxury compared to his Angola experience only nine years earlier.

But I was not present for the trip that began in April 1961, when the dispatcher awoke him from a sound sleep around eight in the evening. He showered, dressed, and headed out to his rig. All tires were properly inflated; all lug nuts were in place; lights, horn, and windshield wipers were operational. He checked everything he could—even under the hood for fluid levels. Confident that all was in order, he climbed into the truck and started his usual route toward the Great Mississippi River Road and home.

For some reason, old injuries were nagging him that night. His ankle ached from a mishap during his loading dock days: a coworker using a forklift mishandled a half-ton shipment and broke Dad's foot. His right index finger throbbed from an accident at home two years earlier: while fixing our furnace, he had caught the finger between the fan belt and a spinning pulley. In a novel five-hour procedure, surgeons reattached his severed digit and embedded a rod inside to hold it together while healing. The metal still protruded through his fingertip. Although the initial wounds had resolved, the wire rod inside the distorted finger made it stiff and slightly pointed. As a result, his hand resembled that of the Wicked Witch of the West in *The Wizard of Oz*. He viewed it as an external manifestation of his skewed inner life—always trying to straighten itself out, but never quite getting there.

As he drove for the first hour along the rough dirt roads leading to U.S. Highway 61, pain from a third source—his mouth—intensified with every bump in the journey. The oral sores from his new dentures were excruciating. Nothing about the ride in the Autocar was smooth; what felt like searing bolts of lightning surged through the roof of his mouth with every jolt.

"Stupid! Stupid! Stupid! I never should have told that dentist to pull all those teeth," he thought, grimacing. "Damn! This is hell."

After driving over the bridge at La Crosse and reaching full speed, he approached a curve where he always slowed slightly—not much, just enough to stay on his side of the road. "Time to throw out the anchor," he said to himself as he took his right foot off the accelerator and moved it to the truck's brake. He pushed gently on the pedal and prepared to downshift.

It went all the way to the floor. There was no resistance. Nothing. He released the pedal and tried again.

Still nothing. He pumped the brake pedal furiously. Nothing.

His Autocar sped around the curve and strayed into the opposite lane. He threw his half-smoked cigarette out the window, put both hands on the steering wheel, and wrestled the rig to its proper side of the highway. The pain in his mouth no longer mattered.

He tried the trailer brakes. Nothing there, either. He was traveling seventy miles an hour with a combined thirty-ton load of man, machine, and material—and no brakes. Now he knew how a bullet felt.

Masteller's words echoed in his head: "Master the truck or it'll kill you."

He had no time to think—only to try to save himself, his load, and any unsuspecting motorist he might encounter in the darkness on the two-lane road. In an instant, a routine trip home from a small Wisconsin town had become the drive of his life.

Engine braking was the only way out. But he'd never tried it at these high speeds or without the benefit of any brakes at all. He'd heard many truckers' stories of runaways down steep grades, but he'd never heard of anyone facing this predicament. It would require every bit of intelligence and ingenuity he could muster to save himself and his rig. He quickly concluded that if his truck endangered any oncoming vehicle, he would drive off the road—even if the act meant certain death.

Meanwhile, he grabbed the transmission stick in the palm of his

right hand. His three flexible fingers gripped the knob at the top of the shaft, his distorted index finger useless here. He visualized how he would rapidly move the stick out of tenth gear and into ninth while simultaneously engaging the clutch. Worst of all right now would be to get trapped in neutral—"idiot gear," meaning no gear at all. If that happened, the freewheeling truck would continue its downhill coast at ever accelerating speeds. Even in tenth gear, the engine had some braking effect, however minimal it seemed to him at the moment.

His left hand held the steering wheel. He could taste blood from the ulcers in his mouth. His right index finger continued to throb. His ankle ached. Mouth. Finger. Ankle. He had no time for pain.

"Master the truck or it'll kill you," he thought.

After a few seconds, he tried the maneuver that he'd rehearsed in his mind. He engaged the clutch, shifted out of tenth gear, and tried to slam it into ninth in a single swift motion. It wouldn't go.

"Shit!" he said softly.

The grinding sound of metal against metal was alarming, and he popped back into tenth. He could now attest personally to the fact that anyone who thought tenth gear afforded any serious engine-braking power was crazy. He was Casey Jones in a truck—the engineer of a runaway headed for disaster, unless he could forcibly downshift, and soon.

He tried the maneuver again. Again, it wouldn't go.

"Damn!" his voice rose. The juggernaut carrying him along the River Road seemed to be accelerating. He tried again, but still it wouldn't comply.

"Come on, you bastard," he coaxed. Finally, on the fourth try, he was in ninth gear.

"Whew," was his only thought. At least he now knew that he wasn't attempting the impossible. The truck slowed from seventy to sixty-five, but that was still too fast. There was no time to relax. In his mind, he retraced the Great River Road ahead. It had never seemed important to concentrate precisely on the road's topography. Now his ability to remember every rise and dip, every curve—that ability alone would determine his survival.

What he really needed was a steep hill for his rig to climb so that gravity would save him, but he wouldn't encounter one anytime soon. Still, a gentle rise in the road ahead promised to slow the truck a little. It was his only chance, and it had to work. After that rise came a steep

downgrade that could doom him if he couldn't get into a lower gear first. Ten miles beyond that was an even steeper decline, but it had the runaway truck lane he'd hoped he would never need. That lane became his new destination. He would have to make the most of every slight incline until he got there; he had nothing else.

His strategy was the same for each gentle rise in the road. Usually he could downshift on the second try; sometimes he got lucky the first time. With each downshift, the engine screamed as if in agony. But his perseverance worked. By the time he reached the top of what promised to be the sharpest drop of all, the runaway lane was in sight. He was still motoring along at fifty miles an hour.

"That's a lot faster than you might think, when you know you can't stop," he told me later. He barreled down the slope toward the runaway truck lane, where he forced his rig onto the gravel path that led slightly uphill to the right. His tractor and its load coasted to an involuntary stop at the end of the dead-end lane.

"Thank God for gravity," he thought. He killed the engine, lit a fresh Camel, and leaned back in his seat. He was spent. Every last inch of him had been consumed with his own survival. The tip of his right index finger was bleeding. His previously broken foot ached. He pulled out his upper dental plate and spat blood and saliva out the window.

"Those sons-of-bitches," he muttered.

As with the lug-nut incident, he was certain this was no accident. Someone was still trying to kill him in a way that would not arouse suspicion; someone who knew the particular tractor-trailer combination he would be taking and when he would be taking it. As with the lug nuts, only a person familiar with Werner's operations and equipment could have masterminded this murder attempt. And it was someone with clout outside Minneapolis because this sabotage had occurred in Mauston.

Not knowing whether those who had perpetrated the crime might be following him to assure their success, my father decided that he faced more danger waiting for help than if he kept moving. He backed his rig down the gravel and onto the River Road. He then drove in low gear and "clutch-braked" to the nearest diesel mechanic shop fifty-two miles away. At the low speeds he maintained, he had plenty of time to consider his next move. He would tell the mechanic that the brakes went out, as if it were no big deal. He resolved to say nothing about this incident to anyone else. He would say nothing to my mother; he'd

confided in her about the lug-nut incident but it had been too much for her. He knew he could trust her, but he had no idea whether he could trust anyone else. Even for his loyal friends—whoever they might be—revealing the incident would only subject them to danger as well. Masteller was certainly a loyal friend, but no one could control his reaction. For his own good, Dad would not endanger his fellow crusader by sharing this ordeal with him.

He had mastered the truck; it would not kill him. Neither would his fellow Teamsters.

32

The Hearing

The hearing on my father's newest charges against Snyder was set for April 27, two days after my seventh birthday. Dad had promised me a ride in a real passenger train as a present, but we never made it. I now understand far more important things were on his mind.

Gordon Conklin's hometown newspaper, the *St. Paul Dispatch*, previewed the hearing in an article reporter Harry Hite wrote after interviewing Fred Snyder as the "spokesman" for the defendants. "These charges are part of a harassment campaign that I have been subjected to since Blixt and I were able to take control of Local 544 from Brennan," Snyder reportedly said. According to Hite's article, Snyder described the charges as including "Raising my own salary. Brennan was getting $25 a week more than I was as a business agent and vice president and so I took his salary of $250 a week when I took office on January 1, 1959 . . . They claim that I took $75 expenses on a business trip when it should have been limited to $50." As for the charge arising from a fellow Teamsters' comment that the dissidents were being led by a convicted felon, Snyder said, "I can see no reason for . . . a charge of oral abuse of a fellow member because he was just stating a fact."

Snyder had not correctly characterized all of the charges against him, but my father would let the evidence speak for itself and let the panel make its own judgment. He had the facts and the proof; Hoffa always said that nothing else mattered. His plan, he later told me, was to "cram Hoffa's words down Snyder's throat."

Shortly after ten on the morning of April 27, 1961, the participants filed into a meeting room in the Radisson, one of several downtown hotels in which Grandpa Harper pursued his latest vocation—cleaning rugs. Coincidentally, eight years earlier it had also been the site of a testimonial dinner honoring Sid Brennan, with then-general president Dave Beck in attendance. Clark Mollenhoff had just begun his investigation

into the Teamsters when he arrived at that dinner after two days of interviews with disgruntled union members eager to speak out against Brennan—talks Sam Romer and Gordon Conklin had arranged with Hoffa's blessing.

Hoffa's administrative assistant, Joseph Konowe, was supposed to be the hearing's panel chairman, but the president of a Chicago Teamsters local, Dave Stark, came instead. Stark was just a placeholder; Fitzsimmons would now preside as chairman, while Roy Williams from Kansas City still served as the third panel member. Hoffa had all three votes and controlled the outcome of the contest before it began, but my father still knew nothing about any of them.

My dad set up his reel-to-reel tape recorder as the panel watched with a blend of fascination and concern. Then he opened his presentation by assuring the panel that he was not taping the hearing, but he had tapes that he would play later. He requested a copy of the written transcript to be made of the proceedings. Noting that Snyder had threatened to bring a civil suit against him, he wanted the documentation for his own defense. His request for a copy of the transcript was denied without explanation.

He began to read his typewritten remarks: "On March 27, 1960, the membership of Local No. 544, International Brotherhood of Teamsters, voted to dismiss the charges that had been filed against Fred V. Snyder on March 25, 1960. In our opinion, the vote indicated a determination, of the membership, to prevent the union from weakening its position in forthcoming negotiations, since existing contracts, in most cases, were due to expire on February 1, 1961. Fred V. Snyder, Secretary-Treasurer of Local No. 544, has failed to respond to the conditions and instructions that were given to him, at that time, by Teamsters General President Hoffa. Evidence will be presented, at this hearing, that clearly shows Mr. Snyder's indifference in the execution of mandates given to him, by both the local union membership and International Union officers, even since the meeting of March 27, 1960."

He paused to drink from a glass of ice water, his eyes scanning the room. Snyder looked unhappy, which couldn't have pleased Dad more. He then resumed his statement.

"Mr. Snyder, himself, reopened the subject of the special audit of Local 544 finances, for 1959, conducted by Wolkoff and Effress, Certified Public Accountants, Minneapolis, Minnesota. He did this by

stating, to individual members and to at least two meetings of the general membership, that the union's money had been wasted on this special audit; and further, that the audit had failed to reveal one cent of misused funds. From the March 27, 1960 meeting, until Mr. Snyder had made these statements belittling the audit, none of the members who had supported it revealed findings, or any other information relative to the charges. These charges, as we have previously stated, were dismissed by the 544 membership."

Fitzsimmons interrupted. "Was the information in the audit suppressed in 1960? Did anyone make any attempt to get that information before the membership at that time?"

"I tried to do just that at the general membership meeting after our private meeting with General President Hoffa on March 27, 1960," my father replied, "but Mr. Hoffa interrupted me and told me in no uncertain terms to '*sit down!*'"

Fitzsimmons had now confirmed with my father's own words exactly where Hoffa stood on all of this. But Fitzsimmons already knew he'd been sent to end this Minneapolis insurgency once and for all. My father saw Fitzsimmons's inquiry differently. He thought his answer had actually helped his own cause in two ways: first, it demonstrated that the membership had never seen the audit results; second, it revealed that Hoffa's handling of the situation to this point didn't match his public pronouncements about making the union cleaner. He thought the panel would have to take strong action against Snyder's wrongdoing to bail Hoffa himself out of this mess.

My father continued, "It is intended that the evidence which follows will prove, not only the specific accusations made but, also, that Fred V. Snyder has shown himself to be unable or, at least, unwilling to handle the affairs of this local union in a manner that supports the best interests of its membership or the best interests of the International Brotherhood of Teamsters."

He then proceeded through each charge and its supporting evidence in great detail. He examined Snyder and other witnesses on the particulars in the supporting affidavits he submitted to the panel. As Dad described it later, and as his contemporaneously prepared summary confirms, he asked Fournier about the bylaws issue: "The Local 544 membership had voted at its December 1960 meeting to require comparison between Snyder's proposed bylaws and the model bylaws provided by the International. These model bylaws were also men-

tioned in General President Hoffa's notice to all Teamsters in the January 1961 issue of *International Teamster* as crucial to the International's ability to hold a new convention and election of officers. Did you report to the membership of Local 544 at the regular meeting in January 1961 that Brother Snyder hadn't even provided your committee with a copy of the International's model bylaws so this comparison could be made?"

"I don't remember," Fournier replied.

"Well, a tape recording doesn't forget," my father snapped. He activated his reel-to-reel recorder and played the tape of Fournier's remarks at the December 1960 meeting. Fournier sat silently while Snyder glared, probably wondering what else had been taped. My father didn't notice the uneasy glances exchanged by the panel members as he played Fournier's recorded remarks. They all knew that Teamsters on tape rarely led to anything good for the leadership.

When the issue turned to Snyder's salary, Fritz reacted glibly. "When Brennan was in charge, he was paid 250 dollars a week. I was making 25 dollars less as vice president. So when I took over, I got the same salary Brennan had received. What's the big deal?"

"Well," my father persisted, "in December 1959 did you specifically ask the membership to authorize a lower salary—225 dollars a week?"

"I don't remember," Fritz replied.

"Take a look at the minutes of that meeting, which record that membership vote approving a 225-dollar-a-week salary for you. In March 1960, when we all met with General President Hoffa in his hotel room, and he asked you about your salary, did you tell him that you couldn't remember your salary?"

"I don't remember that," Fritz barked.

"Well, did you tell me and other brother Teamsters in February 1961 that you had requested authorization of the 225-dollar salary because you intended to cut your salary from the 250 dollars Brennan had received as secretary-treasurer, and then go on to tell us that, in fact, there was never any such salary cut?"

"I never said that," Snyder proclaimed indignantly.

"Would you like to hear it in your own voice?" my father asked, flipping the switch of his recorder once again. Snyder sank into his chair as he listened to his own words echo throughout the room. This time, my father observed that the panel members seemed concerned—not

over the substance of Snyder's damning remarks but over the fact that Dad had taped them.

He confronted Snyder directly on another subject: "How about the general membership meeting in which you derided the Minnesota State Committee and talked about actions contrary to Teamsters contracts and said, 'That's something that's going to have to be corrected in our negotiations.' Do you deny saying that?"

"Do you have it on tape?" Snyder asked nervously.

"No," Dad said, realizing that his taped conversations might be getting him into trouble with the panel. Even though he'd recorded Snyder's comments on this issue as well, he let the matter rest.

"Then I deny it," Snyder fumed.

As my father reported in his contemporaneous summary and in later conversations with me, Snyder had little to offer in his own defense. Snyder said that he'd attended all meetings for which he claimed a daily allowance. To the charges related to his union credit card purchases near his northern Minnesota cottage, he claimed an error by the gasoline company in recording the dates of his purchases.

Hour after hour, my father pressed on, sometimes referring to the financial records he had asked the local to provide for the hearing—to no avail. Continuing the charade, the panel now requested copies of those records from the Local 544 office; messengers shuttled back and forth to the Minneapolis Teamsters office. My father was sure that every record corroborated his every accusation. Believing his case to be as airtight as any could be, he still didn't realize that the strength of his evidence and the persuasiveness of his presentation did not matter. With this panel, Snyder needed nothing at all.

As the hearing ended at five-thirty, the man Hoffa would choose six years later to run the union during his jail-imposed absence—panel chairman Fitzsimmons—could see that Harper had made a strong case against Snyder. Surely Fitzsimmons, too, was concerned that the International Teamsters' executive board would not handle the matter in a flattering way for Hoffa or the union leadership. Hoffa had enough problems in Minneapolis, and this one was going away. Fitzsimmons therefore requested that all participants regard the proceedings as an internal and private Teamsters matter. He told them that their cases had been made in the hearing room; the panel would decide the outcome, not the people who read the newspapers. He told

them not to air these matters in the media because others who were out to destroy the Teamsters would use them against General President Hoffa and the union. He reminded them that nobody in attendance wanted that to happen.

Everyone agreed to Fitzsimmons's request, although my father had already decided that the panel chairman was weak. Especially compared to Hoffa, Dad said, "This guy was pathetic."

Notwithstanding Fitzsimmons's admonition, my father suspected that someone on Snyder's side had already planted the seeds of an article about the hearing. It appeared in that evening's paper. He believed that the *Minneapolis Star* had learned about events at the hearing before they occurred. Someone at the paper informed Dad that the April 27 edition went to press around one in the afternoon. At that time, the case against Snyder was still under way and the presentation against the other defendants had not yet begun. Nevertheless, and with remarkable clairvoyance, the *Star* reported, "One charge apparently is that Blixt was presiding at a union meeting when one member claimed one of the dissidents bringing the charges had a prison record. Blixt ruled the comment out of order and later said that under the Landrum-Griffin law he was required to give the member the floor at least long enough to determine what he wanted to talk about."

My father concluded that the newspaper reported this news before it even happened. Sometime after one o'clock, Blixt did defend his recognition of a fellow Teamster to speak at the membership meeting on the grounds that he didn't know what the member was going to say until it was too late to stop him. Blixt argued that the Landrum-Griffin Act gave him no other option because the law protected all members' free speech rights. But as Dad saw it, at the time the *Star* put the paper to bed with the article reporting this defense, Blixt had yet to assert it at the hearing.

In what seemed to be another violation of Fitzsimmons's directive to refrain from public comment on the proceedings, Snyder told his contact at the *St. Paul Pioneer Press* that "Harper was the leader of an insurgent group in the local that opposes the present leadership." The resulting article on April 28 also quoted Gordon Conklin's comment that the International Teamsters' general executive board, of which he was a member, would take up the hearing panel's recommendations in the matter at its next meeting, probably before the July convention.

The *Tribune* buried its coverage of the hearing on page 23: "The charges against the two local 544 officials, Fred Snyder, secretary-treasurer, and Edward A. Blixt, president, have not been made public, nor have the identities of the parties bringing the charges." This event should have produced a news story as prominent as the Local 544 controversy that had brought Hoffa to town a year earlier, but Sam Romer did little to associate himself with any media attention to this Teamsters mess.

Everyone assumed that a decision would not take long. After all, Hoffa had ordered the hearing to occur on only two weeks' notice. How much time was needed to render a decision where the evidence had been so clear and had generated no serious rebuttal? If Robert Kennedy had been asked, he probably would have volunteered to jump off the Capitol building if Snyder managed to slip away.

A better response would have been to offer Jim Harper a parachute.

33

The 1961 International Convention

Back at home, my father told my mother that he thought the hearing against Snyder had gone beautifully. He had watched Local 544's leader squirming at every turn. Every time Snyder had opened his mouth, he had put his foot deeper inside as the audiotapes impeached him with the sound of his own voice. My father was sure that Hoffa's panel would have to end Snyder's career once and for all, just to save Hoffa's reputation as a reformer.

As he waited for the final decision on his charges, my father turned to more important matters, especially the upcoming International Teamsters convention in July. Each local—including Local 544 in Minneapolis—would send delegates, and Hoffa had sent out the word that he wanted scrupulous adherence to all legal requirements in the selection process. He wanted no basis for anyone to challenge his inevitable election as general president. The problems with the last International election in 1957 had resulted in the Board of Monitors that had haunted him. There would be no room for criticism this time.

After realizing at the April membership meeting that he himself must run for one of the five delegate positions, my father had one month to campaign. He decided that his best approach was to declare unwavering support for Hoffa. So his campaign flyer headline read: "544 Teamsters . . . Send rank and file representatives to the International Teamsters' Convention on July 3rd." He then explained where he stood: "Contrary to popular belief, the forthcoming 544 election . . . is *not* a popularity contest or a test of strength between the different factions within Local 544. This election is being conducted solely to determine the members who will represent you at the Teamsters' Convention in July." The accompanying photograph showed my father with a broad smile revealing his new dentures.

On May 19 and 20, members of Local 544 voted on their choices for the Miami Convention. Dad lost. On May 21, page 1 of the *Tribune* reported that the federal government had sent four hundred U.S. mar-

shals to protect freedom riders who were being beaten in Montgomery, Alabama. Local 544 had ceded its place on the front page long ago. Now page 8 carried the results of the local's delegate election: "The Fred Snyder administration in Teamsters local 544 Saturday won a vote of confidence from the membership, electing all five candidates on the administration slate as delegates to the union's international convention in July. With 3,300 members eligible to vote, 462 cast ballots in the two-day election . . . Snyder, Local 544 secretary-treasurer, led the ticket with 322 votes. He was followed by Edward Blixt, president, 275; Emmett Brennan, vice president, 254; Clifford Meredith, recording secretary, 236; and Fred Fournier, 180."

My father could have suffered a far worse fate than merely losing that election. One of Hoffa's key East Coast supporters, International Teamsters vice president Tony Provenzano, took a much tougher approach to insurgents like my dad. The Monitors had ordered Hoffa to suspend Provenzano in late 1959 and recommended filing formal charges against him in early 1960, but Hoffa refused because "Tony Pro" had loyally supported his ascent to the Teamsters general presidency. Meanwhile, fellow Teamster Tony Castellito—who participated in Provenzano's long-term extortion of a New Jersey trucking company that began in 1952—grew in popularity among the local membership. On June 5, 1961, Castellito mysteriously disappeared; his body was never found. Almost twenty years later, Provenzano would be convicted of first-degree murder based upon his involvement in what was determined to be Castellito's killing.'

On June 28, three weeks after Castellito's still unsolved disappearance, the International Teamsters convention began in Miami with Tony Pro leading the cheers for Hoffa. Along with newly appointed International vice president Frank Fitzsimmons, Provenzano served on the convention's all-important "constitution committee" that Hoffa chaired. As he had in 1952 and 1957, Sam Romer attended and covered the convention for the *Tribune*.

On Monday, July 3, my father sat at our dining room table with a cup of black coffee, lit his third cigarette of the morning, and started to read the *Tribune*. The front page reported the previous day's death of Ernest Hemingway in Ketchum, Idaho. His demise was presumed to be accidental, but it seemed odd to my father that at the time of the

author's death, he was alone in a bedroom with the shotgun that killed him. On the same page, Sam Romer authored a long article on the Teamsters' International convention under way in Miami. He reported Hoffa's pledge that the union would maintain its fight against government prosecutors, even if it meant raising members' dues. When my father turned to the inside page on which Romer's article continued, he saw a small four-paragraph item with a Miami Beach dateline. As he read it, he became the last of the Snyder hearing participants to learn of its resolution.

Teamster Board Acquits 2 City Union Officials

Miami Beach, Fla.—The Teamsters general executive board has acquitted Edward Blixt, president, and Fred Snyder, secretary-treasurer of Minneapolis local 544 of charges of financial irregularities, it was learned Sunday.

The charges were preferred by local rank-and-file members. Such charges normally are tried first by the local union's executive board, but James R. Hoffa, Teamsters president, had intervened to set up a special non-Minneapolis trial board to hear the case.

The trial board reported Thursday to the union's general executive board, meeting here in preconvention sessions.

Informed sources said the board had directed acquittal because a local 544 membership meeting in 1959 had voted to withdraw the charges, thus "wiping the slate clean."

The charges against Blixt and Snyder involved the manner in which union meetings were conducted, convention allowance expenditures, and expense account and salary withdrawals.

The article had trivialized my father's entire battle. He wasn't surprised that the final installment in this sad story lacked Sam Romer's byline.

My father followed the events at the Miami convention as Romer reported them in the *Tribune*. On July 4, Romer explained Hoffa's plans to give himself greater power at the expense of the locals. On July 5, he wrote that the Teamsters had approved a pension plan for local officers and agents. On July 6, he described the delegates' vote to compel an increase in membership dues. On July 7, his front-page article included Hoffa's announcement of an eighteen-month ultimatum for the AFL-CIO to readmit the Teamsters into that organization. On July 8, he reported Hoffa's "sweep to predictable re-election." On

July 9, Romer analyzed the many ways in which Hoffa had enhanced his power at the convention. Even the Teamsters constitution had been revised to permit convicted criminals and racketeers to hold leadership positions; the grounds for internal charges against officers had been "narrowed."

As his death rattle, Dad sent a Western Union telegram to Hoffa himself, asking for a copy of the decision on his charges and firing one parting shot. "The *Minneapolis Morning Tribune* dated July 3, 1961, published a release stating that the accused had been acquitted by the General Executive Board," he wrote. "This article presented, as grounds for acquittal, the distortion that these charges had been previously forgiven by the 544 membership. Two-thirds of the charges that were filed on March 16, 1961 were the result of acts committed following this meeting which was held March 27, 1960 in your presence."

On July 19, he got his response.

The General Executive Board, at its meeting held in Miami, Florida, June 28, 1961, considered and discussed the report submitted by the panel in connection with the hearing of charges preferred against Fred Snyder, Secretary-Treasurer . . . General President Hoffa had assumed Original Jurisdiction over these charges. After such consideration and discussion, the General Executive Board voted unanimously to accept the recommendation made to the General President by the panel, that the evidence presented did not support the charges that had been preferred.

Hoffa was finished with this one. No longer would he respond personally to Jim Harper's communications; the International's general secretary-treasurer John English signed the letter.

He and Masteller followed one last avenue. They consulted a lawyer who reviewed the file of materials my father had amassed over the twenty-month struggle. After digesting the collection, the attorney met with them on a Saturday morning in his downtown office. "I've seen these things before," the lawyer said. "You have strong claims. But when you try to raise money for a legal case in pursuit of those claims, you'll go to people who'd supported you before. Now they'll avoid you. They'll say they can't afford to be involved in this. They'll say they need to keep their jobs. They'll say they don't want to rock the boat. You're right, but you're too poor to be right."

"What do you mean, 'too poor to be right'?" Masteller roared as he jumped from his chair and threatened to strangle the lawyer. "You son-of-a-bitch, what are you talkin' about?"

My father still owed Masteller for grabbing his belt and pulling him down to his chair when Hoffa had presided at the March 1960 membership meeting. Now it was his turn to hold Masteller back.

It was over. Jim Harper added yet another failure to his young life.

FOUR

AFTERMATH

34

Harper Starts Over, Again

Masteller eventually made peace with Snyder, but that option was not available to my father. As the ringleader of a two-year insurgency, he had traversed far beyond the point of no return with Snyder and Hoffa. Even if he'd wanted to reconcile—and he did not—it was out of the question.

In Minneapolis, Snyder's effort to displace Dad on Werner's seniority list was bearing serious fruit. There were no loads for him; no loads meant no money. Reluctantly, he realized he would have to abandon all that he had achieved at Werner and seek employment elsewhere. For a while, he sought work as a driver in the Twin Cities area. He then expanded his scope to include any kind of job, but no one would hire him. He was blacklisted through some process that was completely foreign to him but very real. By mid-afternoon of almost every day, he retreated to the solitude of a tavern where he could sit anonymously; where no one would know that he had failed yet again at something that he had thought would redeem and define him; where bottle after bottle of beer seemed to be his only friends in the world. A few prospective employers admitted the truth: "Look, Jim, you're qualified. I just can't afford to have any trouble with the Teamsters."

Summer gave way to fall in 1961, and money became so scarce that our family spent Halloween night in the dark: the electricity had been shut off, and we could not afford candy for the neighborhood trick-or-treaters. Not long thereafter, I watched from the bottom of our basement stairs as a grinning man carried up the plywood panels holding the elaborate train layout that my father had built for us. All of my trains were being sold. My main thought at the time was that Dad should have received more than the $150 the man was willing to pay.

It seemed that things could not get worse—but they did. My parents had taken my brother, the younger of my sisters, and our dog to Minneapolis for a visit with Grandpa and Grandma Harper on a cold Saturday afternoon in late 1961; my other sister and I were visiting

our cousins. On their way home, they passed a motorist who was having car problems. Dad parked his car on the highway's shoulder and walked back to help. While talking to the driver of the disabled vehicle, he saw another car approaching much too quickly for the slippery road.

The vehicle sped past him, slid out of control, and careened toward our car. My father watched helplessly as the world seemed to stop. "No!" he screamed.

The sound was deafening as the vehicle crashed into the rear of our car and both doors flew open. Dad sprinted to the car and looked inside; his family sat stunned. The steel car jack in the trunk had penetrated the back seat and pierced the passenger compartment like a spear, missing my sister by inches. The force of the collision had knocked off one of her red snow boots, while my baby brother had slid to the floor. Both children were crying, but miraculously neither had been injured. He looked to the front seat but did not see his wife.

"Mary?" he asked frantically.

"I'm right here," she said as she sat up in the front passenger seat. At the moment of impact, she had leaned down to look for a lost mitten. That position had saved her from potentially fatal neck and back injuries.

"Is everyone okay?" he asked, incredulous at his good fortune.

"Where's Fritzie?" my sister wondered. When the car doors had flown open on impact, the dog had jumped out.

"Fritzie!" Dad called. He spotted her standing nearby, dazed but unhurt. He ran to her and brought her back to the family. As the dog licked my sister's face, my father's eyes filled with tears. He didn't cry, but my mother and two youngest siblings were less stoic. My mom's neck and back were sore; she was otherwise unharmed. Somehow the driver of the other car had escaped injury as well.

The crash came with a silver lining. With the insurance money, Dad bought a replacement vehicle and had enough cash left over to get us out of town. To Mom's surprise, he bought a red two-door 1952 Buick convertible. He rationalized that he could buy a convertible during a chilly Minnesota autumn for a lower price than the vehicle would command in the warmer southern climate to which he had already decided we would go. With the profit from the sale of the car at the journey's end, he would replace it with cheaper transportation and have money left over to feed and house us until he lined up work in

our new town—wherever that might be. I knew the truth: he just liked red convertibles.

After splitting kindergarten between two schools, I had completed first grade and begun second in the same elementary school. The relative continuity of my education was about to end, as our family began a series of relocations that, for me, would mean two schools for second grade, three for third. For now, our departure was prompted by our inability to make our monthly house payment. Before Christmas 1961—like a scene from *The Grapes of Wrath*—we were on our way south in a sharp-looking red convertible towing a U-Haul trailer. With us kids in the back seat, the dog nestled herself into the boot area where the convertible top rested when it was down. The car was fully loaded with people, pillows, and my sisters' favorite dolls. Whatever the family could fit in the trailer made the trip; everything else remained behind. Our cover story was that we were leaving for Arizona because of my father's allergies. The truth was that we had no idea where we were going. Heading south, we would travel as far as the money in Dad's pockets would take us.

We got to Oklahoma City.

35

Hoffa's Failures

Hoffa's victory over Harper's crusade did not eliminate his more serious Minneapolis problems. A grand jury in Chicago began looking at Teamsters pension fund fraud generally in August 1962 and indicted Hoffa along with Ben Dranow and several others. Meanwhile, a prosecutor from Robert Kennedy's "Get Hoffa" squad persuaded a Minneapolis jury to convict Dranow of bankruptcy fraud and tax evasion in connection with Teamsters pension fund loans to his department store and related activities. At the same time, a federal grand jury supervised by another Kennedy protégé indicted Hoffa in Tennessee over dealings relating to the trucking company in which Hoffa's wife, Josephine, held an ownership interest—a subject on which congressional investigators had first confronted him a decade earlier. That case culminated in a jury tampering charge for which Hoffa was convicted in March 1964 and sentenced to eight years in prison. Three years of appeals followed.

Hoffa's string of courtroom victories was truly over. In late April 1964, Hoffa, Dranow, and six other codefendants went on trial in Chicago for defrauding the Teamsters Central States Pension Fund. The centerpiece of the case against Hoffa was, once again, his Minneapolis connection. Dranow's entire scheme to bail Hoffa out of his Sun Valley problem had finally reached the public eye. During the trial, several witnesses testified that Hoffa had transferred Detroit union funds to a Florida bank as collateral for loans the bank made to Sun Valley. Prosecutors also offered evidence on a subject relating to Hoffa's McClellan committee testimony. When Robert Kennedy had asked Hoffa in 1958 if he owned any interest in the Sun Valley project, Hoffa admitted that he and a Detroit colleague had an option to purchase part of the development company but asserted that he couldn't remember the details and hadn't exercised the option. At Hoffa's pension fund trial six years later, prosecutors pointed to a Sun Valley trust document bearing the signature "J. R. Hoffa." The developer's son had

found the paper after his father's death—tucked safely inside a cookbook in his father's home. It said Hoffa owned an actual interest in the project, not merely an option. Hoffa claimed an inability to recognize the signature as his, but his denial did not help. Both Hoffa and Dranow were convicted and sentenced to five-year prison terms. Hoffa's sentence was to run consecutively with the eight-year term the Tennessee court had previously imposed.

Hoffa's Tennessee appeals ended first. On March 7, 1967, he surrendered himself to U.S. marshals at the federal courthouse in Washington. It was reported that as Hoffa sat handcuffed in the backseat of the car that would take him two hundred miles to the Lewisburg penitentiary, he spat in Clark Mollenhoff's direction—against a closed window. If true, it was a metaphor for Hoffa's life: what he attempted to spew toward others eventually came back to haunt him. A few months later, the Chicago judge who had presided over his pension fund trial denied Hoffa's last motion for a new trial.

Hoffa appointed his longtime friend and Detroit colleague Frank Fitzsimmons as the caretaker to run the Teamsters, but only for as long as he was in jail. Hoffa retained the title of general president as a continuing reminder to all that he would someday return. Meanwhile, Fitzsimmons promised relentless efforts to free him from prison. With time credited for good behavior, Hoffa expected to be released sometime in 1973.

At the Lewisburg prison, another Hoffa comrade, International vice president Tony Provenzano, was already an inmate after his conviction for an extortion scheme during the 1950s. For awhile, Tony Pro supposedly helped Hoffa enjoy the privileges of VIP inmates, such as access to a special mess hall table where better food was served. But the two men had a falling-out. Their dispute centered on Provenzano's inability to collect his union pension while in prison. Tony Pro reportedly thought it unfair that Hoffa could continue to draw his pension but Provenzano could not. Apparently, the Teamsters' pension fund bylaws prohibited continued payments to Provenzano following his extortion conviction, but no such bar applied to Hoffa's jury tampering or pension fund fraud crimes. Hoffa refused to aid Tony Pro in his efforts to amend the bylaws.

According to one version of the events, the controversy came to a head when Hoffa and Provenzano reportedly exchanged harsh words at dinner. Presumably, Tony Pro was pressing Hoffa to exert influence

on the bylaws issue. Hoffa was said to have declined with his typical directness: "It's because of people like you that I got into trouble in the first place."

Tony Pro would have been understandably furious. "Old man," he allegedly screamed, "Yours is coming! You know, it's coming one of these days . . . You're going to belong to me!"

If so, it would take awhile. Hoffa hated prison and tried three times between 1969 and August 1971 to get released. Three times the U.S. Parole Board considered and unanimously rejected his petitions for freedom. In June 1971, shortly before his third request and on the eve of his union's International convention, Hoffa resigned from every Teamsters office he held in the hope that it would aid his quest for freedom. The move allowed Fitzsimmons to become his formally elected replacement at the July convention. The next election for the general presidency would not occur until 1976.

As Christmas approached in 1971, Hoffa filed yet another petition for commutation of his sentence. Usually, the petition review process took time, entailing consultation with the prosecuting attorneys and the sentencing courts, but no such discussions happened this time. Instead, his old friend Richard Nixon, now president, signed the petition within days of its filing. Hoffa was a free man. Unsubstantiated rumors circulated that in return for Hoffa's release, attorney general John Mitchell received large cash payments benefiting Nixon and his reelection campaign.

But there was an unprecedented catch, and Hoffa claimed to the end that he was not aware of it when he signed the document letting him out of prison. The commutation required Hoffa to refrain from direct or indirect management of any union organization until March 1980. Neither the sentences for which he was serving time nor the Landrum-Griffin Act had imposed that ban. Moreover, in only two years, he would have become an unconditionally free man. No one acting in Hoffa's interests would have accepted nine additional years of isolation from the Teamsters as a requirement of his early release. Hoffa believed that Fitzsimmons had double-crossed him because he had grown accustomed to the power and privileges that went with running the Teamsters. Once Fitzsimmons had been elected general president, Hoffa thought, he didn't relish the prospect of Hoffa's return for a 1976 contest over the union's highest office. Surely Fitzsimmons knew that Hoffa would easily win that election.

Even though Hoffa had hand-picked him to lead the union temporarily, he now believed that Fitzsimmons had worked with White House lawyers Charles Colson and John Dean—both of whom would later go to jail for Watergate-era crimes—to insert the union leadership prohibition as a condition of his release. Hoffa surmised that his old political ally Richard Nixon probably thought he was helping him when he signed the commutation, unaware of the restriction. Hoffa believed that payoffs had been made to embed that restriction in his release document. But whenever asked, he refused to elaborate.

Hoffa's lawsuit challenging the restriction was still pending on July 30, 1975, when he disappeared. By then, Tony Provenzano was out of prison after serving his time for extortion. Hoffa was last seen getting into a car near the Machus Red Fox restaurant in suburban Detroit, where he had told his wife he was going to meet others. Many have speculated that Hoffa's purpose in that contemplated session was to begin a reconciliation process with Tony Provenzano. Hoffa had made it clear that if he succeeded in his legal attack, he planned to seek the Teamsters' general presidency at the convention the next year. Tony Pro would have been a useful ally in Hoffa's reelection bid.

An eyewitness reported that Hoffa got into the vehicle with several men, one of whom was identified as Salvatore Briguglio. A few years later, Briguglio would be revealed as one of Tony Castellito's killers, who had acted at Provenzano's direction in 1961. Briguglio himself was gunned down outside a Little Italy restaurant in New York City on March 21, 1978, and his secrets died with him. Twenty-five years later, Hoffa's longtime friend Frank Sheeran claimed on his deathbed to have been the triggerman who ended Hoffa's life. He said Briguglio was with him in the car that picked up Hoffa in the Detroit restaurant's parking lot.

One Hoffa public position remained unchanged to the end. In a November 1963 interview published in *Playboy* magazine, Hoffa said: "After all this malarkey about a Mafia, what have they really got? A new name for it: the Cosa Nostra." Twelve years later, he reaffirmed the point in an interview published in the same magazine six months after his disappearance. The December 1975 issue of *Playboy* quoted him: "I don't believe there is any organized crime, period. Don't believe it. Never believed it."

Did Hoffa still believe it as he was taking his final ride on July 30, 1975?

36

Harper's Success

In 1952, after his unfortunate detour to Louisiana, Jim Harper had started life over. In late 1961, he started over again, except this time he had a wife, four kids, and a dog. At the time, my parents somehow made it seem like an adventure to us: we were all going on a trip to a new place. It would be fun and exciting, and we had each other—which mattered most to all of us. I was seven; my sisters were six and four; my brother was two. I remember most of our journey as if it had happened yesterday.

We ended our trip in Oklahoma City because the money was gone and we knew someone in that town: my mother's older half-sister. She was still married to Frank Kellert, a former professional baseball player who had backed up Gil Hodges at first base during the 1955 World Series between the Brooklyn Dodgers and the New York Yankees. My uncle Frank had taught me to play that position when their family had visited us in Minnesota a year earlier. He had also taken me to Shea Stadium, where I watched my first professional baseball game. That's when I learned that during one of my uncle's three at-bats for the Dodgers during the 1955 series, he'd been standing at the plate when Jackie Robinson stole home. A photograph taken of that play remains an iconic image of the sport. After the game, a radio broadcaster asked Frank about the close play and the umpire's controversial call that Yankee catcher Yogi Berra insisted was wrong. My uncle replied candidly: "Frankly, I thought he was out." The Dodgers' management apparently didn't appreciate his candor. After the series ended, they traded him to the hapless Chicago Cubs, and he finished his professional career without particular distinction. But I treasured the baseball he gave me in Oklahoma City: it had been hand-signed by his entire 1955 Brooklyn Dodgers World Championship team.

After working for only a few months at a nonunion trucking company in Oklahoma, Dad realized that he was being used as a "union

buster." Because he had no interest in such a turncoat role, we hit the road again. Having traded down from the snappy red convertible, we packed up our wood-trimmed 1949 Packard station wagon that consumed as much oil as gasoline. Whatever didn't fit in the car—including my autographed Dodgers baseball—remained behind in storage and would never be retrieved. It was a *Grapes of Wrath* reprise as the fall of 1962 began: we all headed north with Fritzie's feeding dish strapped to the back of the Packard, flapping in the wind.

My father drove our station wagon northward all day and into the night. The comfortable rest areas now dotting all interstate highways didn't exist in 1962, and we could not afford a hotel. So when he became too weary to continue, he pulled off the highway and found a park or secluded area. My siblings and I didn't care that we ate most of our meals cold, from bags of groceries, or that we slept in the car along the side of the road.

When we approached the outskirts of Minneapolis, Dad had less than a dollar in his pocket. He parked the car on the roadside and walked to an outdoor phone booth. He swallowed hard, took a deep breath, and used his last few coins to make a call to the home where he had grown up. To his pleasant surprise, his parents welcomed our family's return with open arms. Dad's relationship with his mother remained strained, but I think his children helped over time to bridge the divide between them.

For about two months, we all lived together in my father's childhood home. All of us kids slept in what had once been Dad's bedroom, and now it was our turn to listen through the metal grate in the floor to the alcohol-fueled arguments between our grandparents, or our parents, in the living room below. At least the disputes were not intergenerational. Mom got a job at the bank where she had been working when she and Dad first met in 1953. He walked the streets trying to find a job while she reviewed the classified sections of the newspaper for him. Eventually, she noticed a position for which he was initially reluctant to apply: an Iowa-based truck line was seeking a local manager to run its Minneapolis terminal. Except for a high school degree, he feared that he had none of the qualifications for the job. She convinced him he had nothing to lose in trying; trucking was still his life.

He got the job and entered the management side of the business. Fortunately, sufficient time had passed: his old Teamsters foes had

moved on to other issues, and Hoffa himself was preoccupied with the continuing criminal trials that would eventually land him in jail. My dad's new employer didn't care about his prior adventures as a Teamsters crusader. He could do the job; that was all that mattered.

His new position was similar to Dave Morris's at Werner: he matched drivers to their loads. His performance as a manager endeared him to customers and drivers alike while making him an independently valuable force in the competition for trucking business in Minneapolis. After five years, he acceded to a competitor's relentless pursuits and went to work as operations manager for a nonunion trucking company. He was amazed that for the first time in his life people actually *competed* for *him*. Along the way, he encountered Fritz Snyder one more time.

In the late 1960s, the Teamsters had set up a picket line outside the plant of one of Dad's shipping customers. His truckers were understandably reluctant to cross it: drivers simply didn't cross Teamsters picket lines—ever. As a result, the freight sat on the docks and the trailers outside remained empty. My father decided to set an example for his drivers and meet his customers' service needs. He went to the plant, where one of his company's rigs was parked on the street. Telling the driver to get out of the tractor, he climbed into the cab himself and grabbed the wheel. As my dad drove through the line, he saw Fritz Snyder standing there.

"I should've buried you when I had the chance," Snyder bellowed, raising his fist and scowling at him.

My father lifted his right hand from the transmission stick and silently pointed his middle finger skyward, unmistakably in Snyder's direction. His index finger on that hand was still crooked and stiff from his injury a decade earlier, but he took his left hand off the steering wheel just long enough to force that stubborn digit down and thereby remove any ambiguity in his nonverbal message to Fritz.

"He's still an asshole," Dad muttered.

EPILOGUE

For the last twenty years of his life, whenever Dad made periodic trips from his Chicago home to visit friends and relatives in Minneapolis, he always drove his own car. Rather than staying on the four-lane interstate through the middle of Wisconsin, he always took the "old route"—the Great Mississippi River Road—for part of his journey. I now understand why. The river and its road were unifying elements of his fractured life. As a child, he regularly walked across the Washington and Franklin Avenue bridges spanning the river in Minneapolis. In Louisiana, he rode the prison bus along U.S. Highway 61—the River Road—to Angola. Back at the northern end of the road ten years later, he almost met his end at the hands of hostile fellow Teamsters. But his trips along that thoroughfare in his final years reminded him that he had survived everything life had dealt him. It must have given him some sense of accomplishment.

He could have collapsed after losing his Teamsters battle, but he didn't. His life after Hoffa proves what he often told me: "Every person gets knocked to the ground. The true test of character is the speed with which you get back up again." My father passed that test over and over again, and he never failed to answer the bell when it rang to start the next round. In one sense, Hoffa did him a favor. After his picket line encounter with Snyder in the late 1960s, my father's career progressed on the management side of the trucking business. In the circular way his life seemed to run, he even managed to reacquire our suburban Minneapolis home that he had forfeited almost a decade earlier. I graduated from high school in the same public school system where I'd attended kindergarten, having moved through about a dozen other schools and communities in between. Meanwhile, my best friend from first grade still lived across the street, and his father had become Bloomington's chief of police. When people asked me why I had gone to so many different schools, I used to joke that my dad had thought it was harder to hit a moving target. In fact, I was serious.

What my father believed to be the ubiquitous jinx of his life reappeared when he lost his best job—as a vice president of operations—after his employer ran the company into bankruptcy. Unfortunately, he took personal responsibility for every failure anywhere near him, even those clearly the fault of others. With each new adversity, alcohol tightened its unfortunate grip on him. He continued in trucking until he was sixty, when he tried his hand at a longtime fantasy and became the proprietor of a bar and restaurant. I made him a loan to help that venture because, as I told him at the time without appreciating fully the ironic contrast to his relationship with Jim Sr., "How many sons have the joy of helping a father fulfill a dream?" He worked tirelessly, rising at five in the morning to open the establishment and staying past midnight, when he closed it. It kept him sober, but the business failed, and he added it to his lifetime list.

Still, he never gave up, and his perseverance eventually paid unexpected dividends. The Teamsters mementos were important to his treasure chest collection, but I now realize that other items in the box were even more significant and still are: his certificate of marriage to Mary Fischer, the birth certificates of their children, the small tokens of love and affection that he safeguarded to the end. Those items symbolized the things that truly mattered most to him. The Teamsters battle had been a piece of his life but ultimately not the most important piece.

That may be the most meaningful message of all.

My father eventually watched the sites of his early struggles disappear or transform. When he showed my mother the Angola prison for the first time in the late 1960s, she was horrified. But she saw a much better facility than where he'd lived for more than a year. The old buildings had been replaced with more modern structures, thanks to the statewide pressure for reform—pressure that had just begun while he was incarcerated.

His boyhood home near the University of Minnesota campus gave way to commercial development. And when I returned as an adult to the old Werner headquarters on Thirty-second Avenue South in Minneapolis, the building I'd known as a child was long gone. The company itself had disappeared when another truck line acquired it in the 1970s. Likewise, even Minneapolis Teamsters Local 544 is no more. Ironically, what was once Gordon Conklin's Local 120 in St. Paul swal-

lowed it, thereby closing the final chapter of a story that had begun in the late 1940s when Sid Brennan had tried to muscle in on Conklin's territory and Jimmy Hoffa had risen to Conklin's aid. By the time Local 544 disappeared altogether, Hoffa, Brennan, and Conklin were dead.

Dad watched those who had changed the course of his life from 1959 to 1961 leave, too. Even at the time of his death, he never knew about the network of people and relationships behind what he mistakenly perceived as a straightforward "union fight" forty years earlier. He'd done little to keep track of the key players, although he visited his old friend Marvin Masteller a few times after returning to the Twin Cities in 1962. But his fellow warrior from an earlier time was still "labor," and he regarded my father—who had become "management" by then—with a suspicion that made the resumption of their prior close relationship impossible.

The previously untold saga of conspiracy surrounding my father's crusade would have fascinated him. A web of intrigue underlay its outcome, and he never knew its complexity. Although he always enjoyed a good mystery novel, he didn't realize the leading role he himself had played in a real-life version of one. As for the other players, their journeys continued, too.

FRED V. SNYDER, secretary-treasurer of Local 544, remained in that position until he retired. After developing Parkinson's disease, he died of pneumonia in a suburban Minneapolis nursing home in 1989 at the age of seventy-eight. Patricia Snyder, who lived in Oregon, provided the scant information about his life appearing on his death certificate. It recorded the surname of his father as Schneider but included no first or middle name. Nothing was shown in the space for his mother's name. Even those who knew Snyder best were unaware of a fact that the small sheet of official paper also revealed: once upon a time he had been married. The certificate showed his marital status as "divorced."

GORDON CONKLIN, International Teamsters vice president, trustee of the Teamsters Central States Pension Fund, and president of St. Paul Teamsters Local 120, urged Jim Harper on and then refused to stand up to Hoffa when it mattered. When my father began his mission, he didn't know about Conklin's prior clash with Sid Brennan—a clash that had probably spawned Conklin's hatred of Brennan's fellow Local

544 officer Fritz Snyder. My father was also unaware of Conklin's private conversation with Clark Mollenhoff on the eve of Conklin's election as an International vice president in October 1957. The reporter asked him about Hoffa's increasingly sinister reputation, and Conklin supposedly responded that he preferred a leadership role in Hoffa's regime to no role at all.

Regardless of his real agenda in encouraging my father to pursue Snyder, Conklin's 1957 comments to Mollenhoff suggest his motives had little to do with helping to clean up the union. While he was using my father to stir up controversy over Snyder's misdeeds, Conklin served with Hoffa as a charter member and trustee of the Teamsters Central States Pension Fund, which held more than $150 million and was growing at the rate of $30 million annually. Simultaneously with my father's efforts, federal investigators were intensifying their inquiry into loans from the fund made at the behest of Hoffa's friend, Ben Dranow, years earlier. Those loans and Dranow's subsequent actions to help bail Hoffa out of his Sun Valley difficulties were bigger issues in Minneapolis than whatever Snyder was doing with Local 544 members' dues.

The truth eventually came out, but it took awhile. The Teamsters pension fund scandals continued into the 1970s and culminated in the resignation of all fund trustees. The fund remained under federal supervision for years. By then, Conklin would be dead; liver cancer ended his life on August 23, 1967—the same day Hoffa lost his request for a new trial on his pension fund conviction in Chicago. *St. Paul Dispatch* reporter Harry Hite, the man who had reported on my father's April 1961 hearing from a distinctly Snyder perspective, wrote Conklin's obituary, which ran on the newspaper's front page the day after his death. The extent of Conklin's actual knowledge of questionable Central States Pension Fund loans and practices will never be known. But even if he was an upright person who was otherwise well respected in his community, he clearly seemed to be in the wrong place at the wrong time.

SAM ROMER, *Minneapolis Tribune* labor reporter, made a mistake in keeping his work files for his 1962 book *The International Brotherhood of Teamsters: Its Government and Structure.* The error compounded itself when those papers wound up at the Minnesota Historical Society, where I reviewed them forty years later. Romer's

collection of notes and correspondence revealed what otherwise would have remained hidden forever. My father had no idea that Sam Romer was working on a book about the Teamsters while feigning loyalty as my father's confidant. Nor did he know of the remarkable access Hoffa and the International Teamsters leadership were providing to assist Romer's effort. In his book's preface, Romer expressed his gratitude to them: "Dave Beck and James Hoffa have been generous in giving me opportunities for interviews and informal chats . . . A special word of thanks is due to Gordon Conklin of St. Paul, the union's seventh vice president and an old and valued friend."

Romer's newspaper coverage of the Local 544 controversy declined dramatically after his meeting with Hoffa, Masteller, Snyder, and my father at the Pick-Nicollet Hotel on March 27, 1960. But his byline appeared in an April 18, 1961, *Tribune* article covering the hearing on my father's final round against Snyder. Although my father had thought the report "accurate and unbiased" at the time, I'm not sure he'd think so today, if he read it more closely. Noting that Hoffa had chosen the panel members to decide the charges, Romer concluded, "There has been no announcement as to the nature of the charges. However, they are believed to be linked to similar charges made in March 1960 against Snyder reportedly alleging excessive expense accounts and salary withdrawals. At the time, Snyder denied any wrongdoing and called Hoffa in to settle the dispute. At Hoffa's request, the membership voted not to accept a special audit upon which the charges were based. Hoffa told the membership its action did not constitute a vindication of Snyder but a determination to start with a clean slate." Romer's words were technically correct, but, in retrospect, his spin was remarkably similar to the panel's final decision that so enraged my father three months later and prompted his final and futile communication to Hoffa.

While his book was still in draft form, Romer received a letter from one of its sponsors, who wrote on July 31, 1961, "The other night, Jimmy Hoffa told me that you were unhappy with Walter Galenson's editing of your book . . . If you are, I'd like to know about it." A week later, he wrote Romer a follow-up letter expressing his relief that Hoffa was "just teasing when he told me your feelings about the book." It appears to me that Hoffa had viewed Romer's book about the Teamsters as a joint project—just as Romer had.

By early 1962, Romer's draft of the manuscript generated an in-

sightful comment from his editor: "It is a shame to have you cut out the chapters on racketeering, AFL-CIO relationships, and bargaining, particularly the first two. Could you not add back 50 to 75 pages on these?" The answer would be "No." Romer's transmittal with his final manuscript "expanded on the relationships between Hoffa and the Dorfmans [the Chicago family that won bids to handle Teamsters insurance business in the early 1950s], especially where it concerned the [McClellan] Committee probe of the health and welfare funds," but that was it.

Compared to every other publication about Hoffa at the time (except for the monthly *International Teamster*, of course), Romer's monograph reads as an apologetic tribute to the Teamsters and their charismatic general president. For example, Romer wrote: "The [McClellan] committee built a strong case against Hoffa for his failure to keep a promise to purge the Teamsters Union of underworld characters who have infiltrated its ranks, although it should be noted that this condition antedated Hoffa's rise to power." Romer must have forgotten about Tony Provenzano and a long list of other new and unsavory faces that became associated with the Teamsters during Hoffa's ascent to power and his subsequent reign.

Romer also tried to excuse Hoffa for the continuing presence of dark figures in the union: "Some of this failure to act can be explained away by the realization that even the extensive powers of the general president are restricted by the realities of union politics." Frankly, it's hard to fathom that the James Riddle Hoffa known to Sam Romer and the world ever regarded "union politics" as a constraint on his power or actions in any sphere of human endeavor.

Romer likewise dissected and rebutted other public criticisms of Hoffa. At the time Romer was writing his book, federal investigators had focused primarily on the Teamsters' health and welfare funds. The government had not turned its full attention to Hoffa's use of the Teamsters pension fund, although Sun Valley had certainly put them hot on his trail. Accordingly, Romer probably assumed he was helping his friends Hoffa and Conklin when he cautioned his readers not to confuse these various Teamsters funds. He noted that the pension fund was "administered by a committee of seven employer and seven union representatives, including Hoffa and Gordon Conklin of St. Paul, a Teamsters vice president" and that it "should be distinguished from the health and welfare (hospitalization and sick benefit) funds

which the Senate committee charged were milked by excessive commissions." Romer also said that Hoffa and the Teamsters actually controlled the pension fund: "Despite the theoretical bipartisan control, there is general agreement that the crucial power of deciding where the fund's reserves will be invested rests with Hoffa, subject to recommendations from the fund's financial consultants."

Over the subsequent decade and beyond, abuses associated with the pension fund would dwarf earlier criticisms relating to the health and welfare funds. But Romer could not have predicted that development. In 1962, he may have thought that his clarity in distinguishing among these funds would help both Hoffa and his "old and valued friend" Conklin. In fact, Romer's precision put both men at the center of an emerging storm: the Teamsters' pension fund scandals. In my view, Romer's careful and ultimately feeble distinctions seem to have worsened his friends' reputations.

When his book was completed, Romer sent autographed copies to all of the Teamsters leaders who had helped him write it. To Hoffa, he wrote:

Dear Jimmy:
I am enclosing a copy of my book, "The International Brotherhood of Teamsters."
Although I know that you must disagree with many of my interpretations, I hope nevertheless that you will enjoy reading it, and will find that, for the most part, it fulfills my goals of writing an objective, if candid, study of a great union under dynamic leadership.
With my most sincere thanks for your help,
And best wishes.

The Teamsters leaders loved Romer's book. International vice president Hal Gibbons wrote that it was "an objective study of our organization." His assistant, Jake McCarthy, wrote on Gibbons' stationery: "Congratulations. I think you did a magnificent job on the book." Dave Beck's autographed copy of Romer's book had to be delivered through his prison caseworker.

When a publisher approached Romer in August 1962 about authoring a book specifically on Hoffa, he replied, "I do not have much knowledge of the book-buying public, but I feel quite strongly that I don't want to write the kind of book about Hoffa which would sell well."

Romer's response was a colossal understatement; he remained a Hoffa cheerleader to the end. On April 8, 1963, Gibbons wrote to thank Romer for his note on Hoffa's recent appearance on David Brinkley's television program. "We, too, were pleased with the show," Gibbons said.

Sam Romer died of a heart attack on April 13, 1965, at the age of fifty-two.

CLARK MOLLENHOFF, investigative reporter for the publisher of the *Minneapolis Morning Tribune,* the *Minneapolis Star,* and the *Des Moines Register and Tribune,* owed his early career to Hoffa. Indeed, the union leader sowed the seeds of his own destruction when he gave the Washington reporter access to a story that otherwise might not have been told. Myopically focused on ending Sid Brennan's career, Hoffa sent word in January 1953 to Minnesota Teamsters, including Gordon Conklin, that the membership should cooperate with Mollenhoff's investigation of "Teamsters racketeering" in that state. The result was a story that continued for years. Without Hoffa's assistance, Mollenhoff would have been left with the nonstory he expected when he first arrived in Minneapolis. The broader saga of Teamsters corruption would not have been revealed—at least not as it unfolded through Mollenhoff's tireless efforts.

Instead, Mollenhoff's initial Minnesota interviews, coupled with Romer's and Conklin's aid in exposing Brennan's corruption, inspired the newsman to push harder. More than any other single person, he became responsible for the continuing series of congressional investigations culminating in the McClellan committee, Robert Kennedy's national profile, the Landrum-Griffin Act, and the criminal convictions of Hoffa and many other Teamsters leaders. It had all begun in Minnesota.

Mollenhoff's ten-year pursuit of Hoffa and the Teamsters was repeatedly rewarded. In 1958, only halfway into his investigation of possible Teamsters racketeering, he won the Pulitzer Prize in Journalism for National Reporting. He continued his distinguished journalism career and served in several presidential administrations, for both Democrats and Republicans. As special counsel to president Richard Nixon, he was charged with keeping the administration free of corruption, but he resigned in 1970 and became one of its loudest critics. He died of cancer in 1990 at age sixty-nine.

LLOYD HARRIS, Rank-and-File Group supported trustee, eventually confirmed my father's misgivings about him. Although he was an original member of the anti-Snyder slate of trustees elected in December 1959, Harris eventually gave himself away. In the April 1961 meeting that capped my father's futile struggle, Snyder had seconded Harris's nomination as a Local 544 delegate to the International convention. But the definitive proof of his true allegiance came from Harris's own mouth after our family returned to Minneapolis in 1962. When Masteller's first wife died, my mother felt obligated to attend her funeral. Dad had warned her to stay away from everyone associated with his Teamsters fight, but she went anyway. Harris didn't mince words when he saw her at the funeral reception in the Masteller home: "You know, Mary, we always knew where Jim was. We could've gotten him any time we wanted." Harris died in 1983.

MARVIN MASTELLER remained a loyal Teamster and Werner driver until he retired. When I told him I was writing the story of my father's life and he had been an important positive chapter in it, he said, "Well, get it right or I'll come after you with a club." I fully understand my father's admiration for the man who had once been his best friend—perhaps his only real friend.

THE INTERNATIONAL BROTHERHOOD OF TEAMSTERS remained in the news long after Jim Harper's battle ended, of course. Federal investigators continued to examine the union's possible links with organized crime. On March 11, 1989, another consent decree resolved a government lawsuit against the Teamsters and placed the union under federal supervision. "[T]here should be no criminal element or La Cosa Nostra corruption of any part of the IBT," the decree stated, "It is imperative that the IBT, as the largest trade union in the free world, be maintained democratically, with integrity and for the sole benefit of its members and without unlawful outside influence."

Perhaps the sins of the father are visited upon the son who seeks to walk in his old man's shoes. On December 7, 1998, newly elected Teamsters International general president James P. Hoffa, a graduate of the University of Michigan Law School, was quoted as saying, "The mob killed my father. They're never going to come back in this union. I'll see to that." A year later, on January 12, 2000, he unveiled his plan to keep the Teamsters clean, so the union could extricate itself from

the federal supervision that the 1989 consent decree had imposed. He announced the hiring of former U.S. attorney Edwin Stier to oversee the anticorruption project and told more than two hundred Teamsters leaders, "When I ran for office, I promised to run a clean union. I now call on you to be our partners in fulfilling the commitment."

Although we've never met, I have every reason to believe that the Teamsters' current general president is a decent and honorable man. I'm certain that we share many views about the importance of the progressive labor movement in America and the challenges facing all unions, especially in the current political and economic environment. I would not be surprised if he has achieved some level of objectivity about his own father, as I have about mine. I would also wager that his stated mission to achieve a clean union was and is genuine—but it may have become more difficult than he anticipated. I have no knowledge about or particular interest in the Teamsters' current internal situation, but I couldn't help but notice an April 30, 2004, *New York Times* article reporting that former prosecutor Stier had resigned on the grounds that, in his opinion, the younger Hoffa was blocking his investigation into corruption. It noted that the anticorruption program had been created five years earlier as part of Hoffa's effort to persuade the federal government to abandon its longtime oversight of the union. It continued, "Mr. Hoffa insisted yesterday that he remained committed to eliminating the union's ties to organized crime." In what can only be regarded as the ultimate circularity of history, the younger Jimmy Hoffa in late 2005 led his union out of the besieged AFL-CIO, which had expelled his father's Teamsters almost fifty years earlier.

The elder Hoffa had another child, a daughter. Like her younger brother, Barbara Hoffa Crancer also became a lawyer. After many years in private practice, she became a Missouri state court judge. In an odd generational symmetry, both of Hoffa's children and I eventually found ourselves in the legal profession.

JAMES R. HARPER, my grandfather, worked as an exterior housepainter throughout the 1950s and into the early 1960s until his concerns about climbing ladders required him to find a new vocation. His most regular employment after 1968 was cleaning carpets and rugs in downtown Minneapolis hotels and private residences throughout the city. He never stopped playing the violin, and he accepted the pleasure of giving his grandchildren lessons on the instrument, coupled with a

regular Sunday chess match against me. But apart from these satisfactions, his life remained an unfulfilled promise; he spent most of his final days in his favorite tavern on Franklin Avenue in the City of Lakes. At the moment of his fatal heart attack in December 1973, he was with the equally elderly widow of the man who had owned his rug cleaning equipment. Soon thereafter, my father had to make the difficult decision to cease heroic efforts by hospital workers to save him. When it was over, he hoped James R. Harper had finally gone to a place where he could be happy and his dreams fulfilled.

ALICE MAY HARPER, my grandmother, continued to work at the information desk at the University of Minnesota's Coffman Memorial Union until her retirement. I still wonder whether, as a girl in Blue Earth, she knew the Conklins, then the owners of that small city's feed-supply store—and particularly whether she'd met the son named Gordon. Among the papers in her albums was a copy of her July 1959 letter to Minnesota senator Hubert Humphrey in support of what would eventually become the Landrum-Griffin Act. As her health failed after her husband's death, she turned to her son for support, and he remained loyal to the end. She died on January 2, 1978. In one of her albums, the last several pages contain materials from the 1960s and 1970s, along with a number of newspaper clippings from 1925. I wonder what her life looked like to her by the time she had completed her final revisions to it.

A dozen books have been written about Hoffa over the past forty years. I've now read all of them and supplemented my understanding with the sources and references listed at the end of this book. It was never my goal to write the definitive biography of Jimmy Hoffa; Arthur A. Sloane already has. I was after something else, and it soon became clear to me that a Minneapolis theme ran through Hoffa's life in a way that no prior work had shown. The city had been integral to both his rise and his demise, but that particular story had not been fully told. When my research began to reveal the intricate story of personal betrayal by those who professed support for my father's cause, I was amazed.

In retrospect, I now realize that my father was especially vulnerable to the circumstances that later crushed him. In 1959, most Teamsters saw Hoffa as he did—as a powerful leader who inspired loyalty—

but Jim Harper thought he saw much more in him. As scandal and criminal convictions rocked Sid Brennan's leadership at Local 544, Dad concluded that he and Hoffa were a perfect fit: Hoffa was a father figure who coincidentally had the same initials as Jim Harper senior, JRH; he was the champion of a great and noble cause; he possessed a charismatic personality to match my father's. But there was more to Hoffa—more darkness—than even my father discerned. Hence, another message emerges from my father's safekeeping box: there is almost always some important truth about a situation that we can't fully know while we're still in the midst of it. In fact, what we *do not* know often matters more to our lives than what we *do.*

It was true for Hoffa himself. When he returned to Michigan after his Minneapolis successes against Farrell Dobbs in the early 1940s, he became associated with dark characters who would haunt him and his union for a long time. Likewise, Hoffa's vindictiveness toward Sid Brennan led him to assist Clark Mollenhoff's first Teamsters investigation. In both respects, Hoffa set in motion a series of events culminating in his own destruction, although it took more than a decade for the boomerang to return. His life and presumed death are object lessons in the unintended consequences of deliberate acts taken with incomplete information. In the end, no bad deed went unpunished.

My father's union fight, too, was an exercise in unknown truth. He was myopic in ways we all are: he viewed Hoffa from the perspective of his own life's experiences. Having survived Angola, he thought he knew a criminal when he saw one. But what is clear in retrospect is not always visible at the moment. When he had to make his own critical judgments about who Hoffa was and how he should approach him, the record on the Teamsters leader was far from complete. His hopes that Hoffa could become his mentor further skewed his vision. He had to assess the man based upon what he saw and, even more importantly, what he wanted to see.

. He had started his 1959 crusade believing he was following Hoffa's lead. Taking Hoffa's public pronouncements at face value, my father perceived him as an embattled reformer who would condemn ongoing corruption at Minneapolis Local 544. Although Hoffa's alleged connections to organized crime had begun to surface publicly by 1959, my father regarded such reports as part of a government union-busting agenda aimed at destroying organized labor. The key fact as

he saw it supported his conclusion: how could Hoffa be a criminal when he and his wife still lived in the Detroit home that he'd bought for $6,800 in 1939? My father pressed ahead—and men he trusted urged him on.

It was all a lie. But the truth is often hard to find, especially for one who stands at the center of the storm. Some part of the exercise requires keeping your eyes open; another part requires seeing something other than what you want to see; the final part requires knowing that certain critical determinants of your own life's story are beyond your knowledge or control—whether you call them fate, fortuity, or the hand of God.

In the end, the most important facts were unavailable to my father. He had no awareness of the complex and interrelated stories linking Hoffa, Sid Brennan, Gordon Conklin, Ben Dranow, and Sam Romer together in Minneapolis. He could not predict that Conklin's separate agenda would lead to abandonment. He didn't know that Romer had become too deeply allied with his regular sources—Hoffa, Conklin, and the International Teamsters leadership—to report my father's story of union corruption as it should have been told, all the way to the end. Even the mythology about Hoffa's seemingly humble lifestyle was misleading. During the 1970s, Clark Mollenhoff instructed his college students on a key technique of investigative reporting: "Follow the money." The December 1975 issue of *Playboy* magazine reported Hoffa's analogous insight in acknowledging his own status as a millionaire: "Power gives money. You got *both* if you got power."

Nevertheless, I'm not sure my father would have acted much differently even if he'd known the whole truth. In that respect, his box holds a message about the difference between courage and stupidity. Risk-taking was never a problem for my dad. One of his universal complaints throughout life was that most people were sheep. "No guts," I heard him say over and over again, noting one of the worst flaws that he thought a person could have. Through his experiences, I've learned that only a very thin line separates "guts" from "idiocy." Now, having assembled the story of his battle with Hoffa, it's clear to me that my father often didn't really know where that line was. Or even if he did, there were times when he simply didn't care. But it was not for want of intelligence that he did stupid things. Rather, other overriding psychological motivations swallowed his rational judgment.

Even with the knowledge that virtually all of his friends and sup-

porters had deserted him and his cause, and even after Hoffa himself had made clear that he wanted it all to end, Dad continued his quest. That perseverance makes sense only in the context of his prior string of failures. He saw his union fight as his defining moment. Once he had raised the internal stakes that high, walking away seemed equivalent to running. It would have entailed psychic loss beyond anything he could bear. For him, it would have been better to carry on to the end—whatever that might be. Until he'd done all he thought he could, he had to press onward. Someone else would have to stop him, because he could not stop himself.

But that's not a complete answer. What about his family? How could he knowingly put all of us in harm's way by treading where Hoffa had told him not to go? I think the answer lies in Angola. To survive his thirteen months there, my father had to deny himself all access to a critical emotion: fear. Whatever his mind had done to accomplish that feat remained with him long after he left prison. As a result, he rarely perceived the reality of physical danger surrounding him. When it appeared, he regarded it as a challenge to conquer rather than a warning sign. In Angola, the technique saved him: "Look a bully straight in the eye and make him look away first." Life was about nothing more than calling the other guy's bluff. The problem, of course, is that sometimes fear is healthy. Sometimes it is simply the manifestation of the human instinct for survival. But after Angola, my father never saw it that way and, as a result, he viewed Jimmy Hoffa through a distorted prism.

In his initial encounters with all men, my father applied two simplistic litmus tests. The first was the firmness of the handshake; the second was directness of eye contact. In formal settings where it was relevant, he also applied a third: the shine on a man's shoes. He told me that Hoffa passed all three tests. Even when he knew that Hoffa was not on his side because Hoffa personally had told him so, he still refused to give up. His greatest strength—his "line of bullshit"—became his greatest flaw, when he convinced *himself* that he could somehow win Hoffa's admiration against all odds. With a suicidal intensity, he continued to speak truth to power and meet force with force. He remained confident that once he passed the tests of strength that he thought Hoffa had placed before him, the union leader would have to acknowledge, accept, and reaffirm him in ways his own father hadn't. Ironically, at another time or place, Jim

Harper's approach to Hoffa might have succeeded. But from 1959 to 1961, Minneapolis was not a place where Jimmy Hoffa would risk anything on another local insurgency.

For all of his life, my father always regarded himself as an ordinary man who had made far too many terrible mistakes in his life, but his "union fight" was not among them. I am the only Harper offspring who was old enough at the time to remember many of the events in that two-year span. My hope when I started my research was to understand his origins so I could always retain my own focus on the right destinations. He was one of the youngest members of what many have called the Greatest Generation: the men and women who fought in World War II and saved freedom and democracy for the world. His story is dramatically different from theirs. His is the saga of a darker American experience during the second half of the twentieth century—from the Louisiana State Penitentiary at Angola to Jimmy Hoffa's Teamsters. But it is ultimately a success story of its own.

His journey was certainly unique, but some aspects of his life's messages seem to speak universally. As he did, we all engage in the human struggle without full awareness of the forces fighting against us; we suffer setbacks; we decide whether to continue or capitulate; we wrestle with our own personal demons; we succeed; we fail; we persevere. I now realize that sometimes a person's greatest achievements are the most difficult to measure. Sometimes, they become apparent only as the end nears or, for those less fortunate than my dad, after a person is no longer around to see them at all. But even death does not diminish their importance.

That takes me to the final message from my father's treasure chest. When I now sit in my favorite chair in my own living room, four photographs surround me. In the first, Grandpa Harper is shown playing his violin, but collaged into this scene is his smiling three-year old son: a photo that Grandma cut, pasted, and superimposed to suggest that he was happily sitting nearby. The composite photo is only an illusion: Grandma's wishful thinking.

The second is a 1946 portrait of my father at the age of eighteen as he entered the army. He looks tentative, vulnerable, and almost fearful. He can't smile for fear of revealing the unsightly quarter-inch gap between his two front teeth, but there's no suggestion that he wants to smile anyway. Ironically, the gap is still visible, between his slightly

parted lips. He's still a boy and he's handsome, but it's clear that he accepts neither as his personal reality.

The third portrait was taken about eighteen months later, showing Dad in his dress uniform complete with paratrooper wings. His expression is firm and determined. At least in his own mind, he has become a man.

The fourth photograph is the most important. It portrays Jim Harper at the age of sixty-five, grinning broadly with Mary as they celebrate their fortieth wedding anniversary. All of his kids, our spouses, and his nine grandchildren surround them. Although the scene is professionally posed, no photographer could coach the gleeful expressions on the faces; some are even laughing. The picture itself tells the story. Notwithstanding all of his many faults and failures, two generations of progeny were devoted to my father throughout his life, and beyond it, because of his finest accomplishment: he loved all of us unconditionally. As his final days neared, even he saw that this single success had more than offset what he otherwise regarded as a lifetime of failures. In the end, his life had been worthwhile because, armed with his special gift and the unique confidence it created for us, those he left behind were making the world a better place; nothing else really mattered.

The series of photographs and other mementos in Dad's treasure chest are reminders that dreams are important and life is fragile. Perhaps my father's most enduring message is that the lines separating hope from despair, success from failure, and victory from defeat are so thin that we often cannot see them. We all live closer to the edge of our own personal abyss than we imagine. Few of us comprehend the individual and collective vigilance required to remain on firm ground. Even with the most diligent efforts, failures will occur. But failure need not beget failure. Individual decisions matter; effort, encouragement, and hope matter; love matters most of all.

The photographs silently communicate one final message.

THERE IS NO SUCH THING AS AN ORDINARY MAN.

Notes

13   James H. Harper's collection of union materials and other personal papers are referenced as the "Harper Papers" in these notes.

18-21   The Harper family history is based upon my own conversations with my father, James H. Harper, and his parents, James R. Harper and Alice May Langguth Harper, whose albums also provided many details. So did genealogical research by my father's sister, Ruth V. McKee.

21   "They arrived in time for the 1934 Minneapolis Teamsters strikes . . ." For a complete description of these events, see Philip A. Korth, *The Minneapolis Teamsters Strike of 1934* (East Lansing: Michigan State University Press, 1995).

22   "Jimmy Hoffa was twenty-four when he walked the streets of Minneapolis . . ." For a complete description of Hoffa's early life and Minneapolis connections to his career, see Arthur A. Sloane, *Hoffa* (Cambridge, MA: MIT Press, 1992), 3–9, 13–18, 20–22, 25–34; James R. Hoffa, *Hoffa: The Real Story* (New York: Stein and Day, 1976); Thaddeus Russell, *Out of the Jungle: Jimmy Hoffa and the Remaking of the American Working Class* (New York: Alfred A. Knopf, 2001), 7, 11–15, 17–20, 23, 33–43, 79–83; and Ralph and Estelle James, *Hoffa and the Teamsters: A Study of Union Power* (Princeton, NJ: Van Nostrand & Co., Inc., 1965), 69–116.

23   "Hoffa thought socialists and 'commies' like Minneapolis's Dobbs were 'screwballs' . . ." Hoffa, *The Real Story*, 50.

24   "At that point, one of the Teamsters' competitor unions . . ." Sloane, *Hoffa*, 29; Russell, *Out of the Jungle*, 79.

24   "There was little doubt about Hoffa's success . . ." Sloane, *Hoffa*, 29–31.

24   "At a dinner honoring Tobin a few years later . . ." Sloane, *Hoffa*, 29.

25-30   This chapter is based upon the Harper Papers and my conversations with my father.

31-33   The description of the events that led to my father's criminal

conviction and incarceration is based upon my conversations with him.

34-37 The description of Angola prison and its conditions is based upon the following: Anne Butler and C. Murray Henderson, *Angola—The Louisiana State Penitentiary: A Half Century of Rage and Reform* (Lafayette: University of Southwestern Louisiana's Center for Louisiana Studies, 1990); Burk Foster, Wilbert Rideau, and Douglas Dennis, eds., *The Wall Is Strong: Corrections in Louisiana*, 3rd ed. (Lafayette: University of Southwestern Louisiana's Center for Louisiana Studies, 1995); Wilbert Rideau and Ron Wikberg, *Life Sentences: Rage and Survival Behind Bars* (New York: Three Rivers Press/Random House, 1992); and Daniel Bergner, *God of the Rodeo: The Quest for Redemption in Louisiana's Angola Prison* (New York: Ballantine, 1998).

35 "Because of the physical isolation that rendered unauthorized flight unthinkable . . ." Rideau and Wikberg, *Life Sentences*, 39.

35 "The segregated prison population of 2,700 . . ." Edward W. Stagg with John Lear, "America's Worst Prison," *Collier's*, Nov. 22, 1952, reprinted in Foster, Rideau, and Dennis, *The Wall Is Strong*, 46.

35 "Long had told taxpayers . . ." Stagg, "America's Worst Prison," reprinted in Foster, Rideau, and Dennis, *The Wall Is Strong*, 47.

36 "In the 1940s, the state constructed a prison hospital . . ." Ron Wikberg and Wilbert Rideau, "Prison Medical Care," *The Angolite*, Nov./Dec. 1991, reprinted in Foster, Rideau, and Dennis, *The Wall Is Strong*, 111; Rideau and Wikberg, *Life Sentences*, 39; Butler and Henderson, *Angola*, 19, 22–23.

36 "In 1948, Huey's brother Earl Long, now governor . . ." Stagg, "America's Worst Prison," reprinted in Foster, Rideau, and Dennis, *The Wall Is Strong*, 47.

36 "Twenty-five guard towers surrounded the perimeter of the compound." Rideau and Wikberg, *Life Sentences*, 39.

36 "That structure was built after an escape attempt in 1933 . . ." Rideau and Wikberg, *Life Sentences*, 38; Bergner, *God of the Rodeo*, 63.

36 "Twenty years after my father was there . . ." Rideau and Wikberg, *Life Sentences*, 41; Burk Foster, "Angola in the Seventies," *The Angolite*, Mar./Apr. 1988, reprinted in Foster, Rideau, and Dennis, *The Wall Is Strong*, 56–68; Sister Helen Prejean, *Dead Man Walking: An Eyewitness Account of the Death Penalty in the United States* (New York: Random House, 1993), 25.

40 "Angola utilized inmate trusty guards . . ." Butler and Henderson,

Angola, 9; Rideau and Wikberg, *Life Sentences*, 37; Bergner, *God of the Rodeo*, 62.

40 "My father had never told me about the warden's standing offer . . ." Bergner, *God of the Rodeo*, 62.

41 "About half of the prisoners were 'wide-stripers' serving life terms . . ." Prejean, *Dead Man Walking*, 24; Douglas Dennis, "The Living Dead," *The Angolite*, Sept./Oct. 1994, reprinted in Foster, Rideau, and Dennis, *The Wall Is Strong*, 243.

41 "The state itself acknowledged a number of prisoners who died of 'sunstroke' . . ." R. L. Krebs, "Blood Took Penitentiary 'Out of Red,'" *New Orleans Times-Picayune*, May 11, 1941, reprinted in Foster, Rideau, and Dennis, *The Wall Is Strong*, 33, 43–44.

41 "As a designated execution date approached . . ." Craig Brandon, *The Electric Chair: An Unnatural American History* (Jefferson, NC: McFarland and Company, Inc., 1999), 234–35.

41 "In addition to Louisiana's official executioner . . ." Rideau and Wikberg, *Life Sentences*, 312–13.

41 "Angola's portable electric chair performed about 4 percent of the executions . . ." *Statistical Abstract of Louisiana* [New Orleans: Louisiana State University College of Business Administration, Division of Business and Economic Research, 1967 (2nd ed.], 125; *Sourcebook of Criminal Justice Statistics, 2002*, Table 6.82, "Prisoners executed under civil authority," 539, citing U.S. Department of Justice, Bureau of Justice Statistics, *Correctional Populations in the United States, 1997* NCJ 177613 (Washington, DC: U.S. Department of Justice, 2000), Table 7.25 and data provided by the U.S. Department of Justice, Bureau of Justice Statistics.

41 "Every convict knew . . ." Rideau and Wikberg, *Life Sentences*, 313.

41 "Brutality was an institutional theme . . ." Rideau and Wikberg, *Life Sentences*, 39.

41 "Guards tied prisoners to posts . . ." Butler and Henderson, *Angola*, 24.

42 "Only nine months before his arrival, thirty-one protesting inmates . . ." Stagg, "America's Worst Prison," reprinted in Foster, Rideau, and Dennis, *The Wall Is Strong*, 47.

42 "One of the original cutters told an investigating commission . . ." Butler and Henderson, *Angola*, 18.

42 "The most recent of Angola's superintendents . . ." Rideau and Wikberg, *Life Sentences*, 39–40.

43 The depiction of my father's illicit sexual liaisons in prison is based upon my conversations with him.

43 "In my later research, I learned that Louisiana made July 11, 1952, memorable . . ." http://www.burkfoster.com/StruckbyLightning (accessed Apr. 6, 2004), reproducing the article "Struck By Lightning: Louisiana's Executions for Rape in the Forties and Fifties," originally published in *The Angolite*, Sept./Oct. 1996, 36–47.

44 "As my father arrived in November 1951 . . ." Stagg, "America's Worst Prison," in Foster, Rideau, and Dennis, *The Wall Is Strong*, 51–52; Rideau and Wikberg, *Life Sentences*, 40.

45 "His assessment in that regard was borne out by the prison's nurse . . ." Stagg, "America's Worst Prison," in Foster, Rideau, and Dennis, *The Wall Is Strong*, 46.

49-50 The description of my parents' courtship and early marriage years is based upon my conversations with them.

51 "After vanquishing the Minneapolis socialists from the Teamsters union . . ." Sloane, *Hoffa*, 31–34.

51-52 The description of the events at the 1952 International Teamsters convention is based upon the following: Sloane, *Hoffa*, 38–39; Walter Sheridan, *The Fall and Rise of Jimmy Hoffa* (New York: Saturday Review Press/Doubleday, 1972), 18–19.

52 Sidney Brennan's biographical information is based upon the following: *International Teamster*, Oct. 1957; Clark R. Mollenhoff, *Tentacles of Power: The Story of Jimmy Hoffa* (Cleveland, OH: New World Publishing Company, 1965), 19–21; Brennan's Death Certificate, Minnesota Historical Society (hereafter, MHS).

52 Fred Snyder's biographical information is based upon the following: photographs in various *Minneapolis Morning Tribune* and *Minneapolis Star* articles referenced in these notes; my father's descriptions of him; Snyder's Death Certificate, MHS.

53 Gordon Conklin's biographical information is based upon the following: *International Teamster*, Nov. 1957; Sam Romer's Oct. 4, 1957, article "Conklin Steers Way Into Union Hierarchy" in the *Minneapolis Morning Tribune;* photographs of Conklin in *International Teamster* magazine, 1957–61; Conklin's Death Certificate, MHS.

53-54 Clark Mollenhoff's biographical information is based upon Tom Longden, *Famous Iowans*, http://desmoinesregister.com/extras/iowans/mollenhoff.html (accessed Oct. 3, 2005).

55 Clark Mollenhoff's interactions with Sam Romer and Gordon Conklin during his first visit to Minneapolis in 1953 are described in Mollenhoff, *Tentacles of Power*, 13, 20, 224.

56 "In a February 14, 1953, letter to Romer . . ." letter from C. Mol-

lenhoff to S. Romer (included in the MHS collection of Sam Romer Papers, referenced in these notes as "Romer Papers").

56 "Mollenhoff covered the hearings in Detroit . . ." Mollenhoff, *Tentacles of Power*, 34–39.

56-57 "But Mollenhoff refused to let the congressional investigation . . . " Mollenhoff, *Tentacles of Power*, 44–49.

57 "Because of Mollenhoff's persistence, the House of Representatives was ready . . ." Mollenhoff, *Tentacles of Power*, 50.

57 "The testimony that guided the subcommittee's investigation toward Minnesota . . ." Mollenhoff, *Tentacles of Power*, 53–54; *Minneapolis Morning Tribune*, Nov. 5, 1953 and Nov. 26–29, 1953; *Detroit News*, Nov. 22–28, 1953.

57-58 "The *Detroit News* broke the story . . ." *Detroit News*, Nov. 29, 1953.

58 "A few months later, Ohio Republican congressman George Bender . . ." Mollenhoff, *Tentacles of Power*, 77–85; Sheridan, *Fall and Rise*, 84.

59 "After a break for the summer, Bender moved his committee to Cleveland . . ." Robert F. Kennedy, *The Enemy Within: The McClellan Committee's Crusade Against Jimmy Hoffa and Corrupt Labor Unions* (New York: Harper & Row, 1960), 49–52; Sheridan, *Fall and Rise*, 84; Sloane, *Hoffa*, 46–47.

59 "Although Bender was a member of the House . . ." Kennedy, *Enemy Within*, 49; Sheridan, *Fall and Rise*, 84; *Biographical Directory of the United States Congress*, http://bioguide.congress. gov/ (accessed Nov. 7, 2003).

59 "During the six-week break between the Cleveland and Washington hearings . . ." Kennedy, *Enemy Within*, 49–51; Sheridan, *Fall and Rise*, 84.

59 "Four days after his Washington appearance . . ." Kennedy, *Enemy Within*, 50.

59 " 'We found, especially during the latter portion of the hearings . . .' " Kennedy, *Enemy Within*, 50.

59-60 "An Ohio Teamsters leader would tell federal investigators several years later . . ." Kennedy, *Enemy Within*, 50–51; Sheridan, *Fall and Rise*, 85.

60 "When asked what the money was for . . ." Kennedy, *Enemy Within*, 51.

60 "In 1955, Senator Bender was the guest of honor . . ." Kennedy, *Enemy Within*, 52; Sheridan, *Fall and Rise*, 85–86.

60 "Inside an envelope marked 'Christmas list' was a December 8,

1955 invoice . . ." Sheridan, *Fall and Rise*, 86; Mollenhoff, *Tentacles of Power*, 323–24.

60-61 "While in private practice, Judge Connell had been an attorney for Teamsters locals . . ." Mollenhoff, *Tentacles of Power*, 321–22; *The Federal Judicial Center*, http://air.fjc.gov/ (accessed Dec. 16, 2003).

61 "'Now looka here, Clark. They don't pay newspaper reporters enough . . .'" Mollenhoff, *Tentacles of Power*, 108–9.

66 "In 1956, Teamster Jerry Connelly was again in the news . . ." *Minneapolis Morning Tribune*, Mar. 20, 1956.

66 "A day after Connelly's Minnesota state court conviction . . ." *United States v. Brennan, et al.*, 137 F. Supp. 888 (D. Minn. 1956), *aff'd*, 240 F. 2d 253 (8th Cir. 1957), *cert. denied*, 77 S. Ct. 718 (1957); *Minneapolis Morning Tribune*, Mar. 21, 1956.

66 "Clark Mollenhoff's 1965 book reported that shortly after his conviction . . ." Mollenhoff, *Tentacles of Power*, 134–35, 137.

67-68 The description of the Autocar is based upon Robert Gabrick, *Autocar Trucks: 1950–1987 Photo Archive* (Hudson, WI: Iconografix, 2002).

71-72 The description of my father's student driving experiences are based upon my conversations with my parents and Marvin Masteller.

73 "The result: the McClellan committee entered the scene." Mollenhoff, *Tentacles of Power*, 122–25, 144–46; Sheridan, *Fall and Rise*, 31–32.

73 "'If Hoffa isn't convicted, I'll jump off the Capitol.'" Mollenhoff, *Tentacles of Power*, 156, 184.

73 "'It proves once again that if you're honest and tell the truth . . .'" *International Teamster*, Aug. 1957.

74 "My father would have laughed if he'd known that Hoffa later claimed . . ." Hoffa, *The Real Story*, 86.

74 "Hoffa waited only ten days after his acquittal on bribery charges . . ." Sloane, *Hoffa*, 78–80.

74 "On September 17, 1957, thirteen rank-and-file Teamsters from a New York local . . ." Mollenhoff, *Tentacles of Power*, 220–21; *Cunningham v. English*, 175 F. Supp. 764 (D.D.C. 1958), modified, 269 F. 2d 517 (D.C. Cir. 1959).

74 "F. Dickinson Letts, an elderly judge who had been appointed . . ." Sheridan, *Fall and Rise*, 49; Sloane, *Hoffa*, 91; *The Federal Judicial Center*, http://air.fjc.gov/ (accessed Dec. 16, 2003).

75 "'The chair desires to announce at this time that Chief Justice Warren has . . .'" *International Teamster*, Nov. 1957.

75 "In that role, he had welcomed the Teamsters delegates to their last national convention . . ." Sloane, *Hoffa*, 323.

75 "International Teamsters general secretary-treasurer John F. English took the podium." *International Teamster*, Nov. 1957.

76 "In his 1960 book *The Enemy Within* . . ." Kennedy, *Enemy Within*, 119.

76 "'I've got one guy you'll approve of . . .'" Mollenhoff, *Tentacles of Power*, 224.

76 "Mollenhoff's 1965 book also revealed . . ." Mollenhoff, *Tentacles of Power*, 224–25.

77 "My father believed every word of Hoffa's inaugural speech . . ." *International Teamster*, Nov. 1957.

79 "On October 23, 1957, Judge Letts issued a new injunction . . ." Sheridan, *Fall and Rise*, 49.

79 "Almost simultaneously, the AFL-CIO threatened to expel the Teamsters . . ." Sheridan, *Fall and Rise*, 49; Sloane, *Hoffa*, 99.

79 "He relied upon the results of the recent election to argue his point." Sloane, *Hoffa*, 100–101.

79 "On January 31, 1958, Judge Letts entered a negotiated consent decree . . ." Mollenhoff, *Tentacles of Power*, 266–68; Sheridan, *Fall and Rise*, 53.

80 "With the lawsuit new resolved, Hoffa was able for the first time . . ." *International Teamster*, Mar. 1958.

81 "Through it all, Minneapolis became a deepening thorn . . ." Sheridan, *Fall and Rise*, 75, 104.

82 "The central figure in that part of the story was Ben Dranow . . ." Sheridan, *Fall and Rise*, 105–6.

82 "Sam Romer's personal files reveal . . ." Romer Papers.

83 "A million-dollar loan was eventually made . . ." Sheridan, *Fall and Rise*, 106.

83 "The McClellan committee scheduled Dranow for an appearance in September 1957." Sheridan, *Fall and Rise*, 106.

83 "Beginning in 1956, Sun Valley had been marketed . . ." Kennedy, *Enemy Within*, 110–14; Mollenhoff, *Tentacles of Power*, 333–34.

83 "Ironically, fifteen years later, Hoffa criticized . . ." Hoffa, *The Real Story*, 17.

84 "As Sun Valley failed . . ." Kennedy, *Enemy Within*, 113–14; Mollenhoff, *Tentacles of Power*, 387–98.

84 "Hoffa's old friend from Minneapolis, Ben Dranow . . ." Mollenhoff, *Tentacles of Power*, 333–34; Sheridan, *Fall and Rise*, 373–74.

84 "In a conversation that Clark Mollenhoff first revealed in his 1965 book . . ." Mollenhoff, *Tentacles of Power*, 267.

86 "In a remarkable turn of events, Snyder announced his intention . . ." *Minneapolis Morning Tribune*, Nov. 17, 1958.

86 "Brennan lost by a margin of almost three to one . . ." *Minneapolis Morning Tribune*, Dec. 9, 1958.

87 "A week later, Dranow pled the Fifth . . ." *Minneapolis Morning Tribune*, July 7, 1959.

87 "Despite Teamsters' opposition, President Eisenhower signed in September . . ." Sloane, *Hoffa*, 160–61; *Minneapolis Morning Tribune*, Sept. 3, 1959.

87 "The Monitors ordered the suspension of various Hoffa colleagues . . ." *Minneapolis Morning Tribune*, Sept. 3, Nov. 17–19, Nov. 22, 1959; Sheridan, *Fall and Rise*, 134–39.

88 "'The trouble with you, Clark . . .'" Mollenhoff, *Tentacles of Power*, 193.

89 "In his first correspondence to Hoffa on the subject, Romer obsequiously reaffirmed . . ." Jan. 27, 1958 letter from S. Romer to J. Hoffa, Romer Papers.

89 "In July 1958, Romer told Hal Gibbons . . ." Romer Papers.

90 "On May 21, 1959, Hoffa met personally with Romer . . ." Sam Romer, *The International Brotherhood of Teamsters: Its Government and Structure* (New York: John Wiley and Sons, Inc., 1962), 149, 155.

90 "On July 7, 1959, as Dranow was refusing to discuss Sun Valley . . ." Romer, *International Brotherhood*, 150.

90 "Romer met with the Teamsters' former general president, Dave Beck, the next day." Romer, *International Brotherhood*, 149.

90 "In August 1959, Romer wrote in gratitude . . ." Aug. 11, 1959 letter from S. Romer to H. Gibbons, Romer Papers.

90 "He renewed his request two months later . . ." Oct. 6, 1959 letter from S. Romer to H. Gibbons, Aug. 25, 1959 letter from H. Gibbons to S. Romer, Romer Papers.

90 "On December 7, 1959, federal prosecutor James Dowd . . ." Sheridan, *Fall and Rise*, 139.

91 "On December 13, Hoffa secretly met in a Miami hotel room . . ." Sheridan, *Fall and Rise*, 140.

91 "Hunter had served in the House of Representatives . . ." *Biographical Directory of the United States Congress*, http://bioguide.congress.gov/ (accessed Nov. 17, 2003).

91 "'Dear Dick,' began Hunter's eight-page letter to Nixon . . ." Sheridan, *Fall and Rise*, 140–42.

96 "After a jury acquitted him . . ." Sheridan, *Fall and Rise*, 60; Hoffa, *The Real Story*, 103–4; *International Teamster*, July 1958.

96 "The Teamsters' general president still lived . . ." *Time*, Sept. 9, 1957.

96 "*Time* magazine's August 1959 cover story . . ." *Time*, Aug. 31, 1959.

98 "Where Hoffa's negotiating presence had been longest and strongest . . ." James and James, *Hoffa and the Teamsters*, 321–45.

101-4 The description of the November 1959 membership meeting at Local 544 is based upon the Harper Papers.

105 "When Romer's article on the membership meeting appeared . . ." *Minneapolis Morning Tribune*, Dec. 9, 1959.

106 "When the *Tribune* reported that the group had met and united . . ." *Minneapolis Morning Tribune*, Dec. 14, 1959.

107 "In his first flyer . . ." Harper Papers.

107-8 The description of the December 1959 membership meeting at Local 544 is based upon the Harper Papers.

108 "In the end, Snyder's trustees still lost." *Minneapolis Morning Tribune*, Dec. 23, 1959.

109 The description of the January 1960 membership meeting is based upon the Harper Papers.

110 "He wanted them to be proud of what they had already accomplished . . ." Harper Papers.

111-14 The description of my parents' dinner with the "visitor from Detroit" is based upon my conversations with my father and mother.

115 "Shortly before the February membership meeting . . ." Harper Papers.

115 "At about the same time . . ." *International Teamster*, Feb. 1960.

115-18 The description of the February 1960 membership meeting is based upon the Harper Papers.

117 "Although Steinberg's home was in Ohio . . ." Sloane, *Hoffa*, 143–44; Sheridan, *Fall and Rise*, 134; Romer, *International Brotherhood*, 67. Steinberg is pictured in the Dec. 1961 issue of *International Teamster*.

119 "Only days after the tumultuous January session . . ." *International Teamster*, Feb. 1960.

120 The description of my father's telephone conversation with Gordon Conklin is based upon my conversations with my parents.

121 "A few days later, a Board of Monitors investigator . . ." Harper Papers.

121 "The four met . . ." The description of this episode is based upon my conversations with my father and Marvin Masteller.

123 "More than forty years later . . ." *International Teamster,* Mar. 1960.

123 "Between the January and February meetings in the Local 544 union hall . . ." Sheridan, *Fall and Rise,* 144.

124 "Only three days before Larry Steinberg's February visit . . ." Sheridan, *Fall and Rise,* 144.

124 "Chairman O'Donoghue received threatening phone calls." Sheridan, *Fall and Rise,* 148, 150–51.

124 "On February 26, 1960, the McClellan committee issued . . ." Sheridan, *Fall and Rise,* 146.

125 "'It has been announced that you have been invited by Fred V. Snyder . . .'" Mar. 11, 1960 letter from J. Harper to J. Hoffa, Harper Papers.

127-28 The description of my father's acquisition of the Local 544 audit is based upon my conversations with my father and Marvin Masteller about the event. The contents of the audit itself are described in the Harper Papers.

130-35 The description of the March 27, 1960, private meeting with Hoffa is based upon my conversations with my parents and Marvin Masteller.

132 "He was also wearing the white socks for which he had become famous . . ." *Time,* Sept. 9, 1957, 30.

137-140 The description of the March 1960 membership meeting is based upon the Harper Papers and my conversations with my parents and Marvin Masteller.

141 "Adding insult to injury . . ." *Minneapolis Morning Tribune,* Mar. 28, 1960.

141-42 The description of the April 1960 membership meeting is based upon the Harper Papers.

142 "'Dear Jimmy,' he wrote on June 23, 1960 . . ." letter from S. Romer to J. Hoffa, Romer Papers.

142 "At about the same time, the Florida bank . . ." Sheridan, *Fall and Rise,* 107–9, 373–74.

142-43 "In fact, on the day after Hoffa presided over the Local 544 membership meeting . . ." Sheridan, *Fall and Rise,* 149–50.

143 "On the floor of the House of Representatives, eleven members . . ." Sheridan, *Fall and Rise,* 151.

143 "Hoffa followed with a flurry of his own punches . . ." Sheridan, *Fall and Rise,* 150–51.

143 "In July 1960, the court of appeals reiterated the restrictions on the Monitors' power . . ." *Hoffa v. Letts,* 282 F. 2d 824 (D.C. Cir. 1960).

143-44 "He wrote that little or no progress had been made . . ." Sheridan, *Fall and Rise*, 155.

145 "Although the circumstances surrounding the encounter remain disputed . . ." Sheridan, *Fall and Rise*, 155–56.

145 "Hoffa's version of the meeting was much different." Hoffa, *The Real Story*, 107.

147 "In September 1960, as Hoffa worked hard to get Nixon elected . . ." Sheridan, *Fall and Rise*, 157–59.

147 "Only a week after Kennedy prevailed over Nixon, Hoffa received . . ." Nov. 10, 1960 letter from J. Harper to J. Hoffa, Harper Papers.

150 "Greatly compounding the aggravation of Local 544 . . ." Sheridan, *Fall and Rise*, 159.

153 My father transcribed many of his secret recordings and submitted them in support of his formal charges against Snyder, included in the Harper Papers. Additional information about these recordings came from my conversations with my parents.

154 The description of the November 1960 membership meeting is based upon the Harper Papers.

157 "When he visited the Teamsters' office on December 15 . . ." Harper Papers.

157 "He prepared a flyer attacking Snyder's proposed bylaws . . ." Harper Papers.

158 The description of the January 1961 membership meeting is based upon the Harper Papers.

159 "On March 16, 1961, my father filed charges against Snyder . . ." Harper Papers.

159 "At a Werner company-level meeting of Local 544 members . . ." Harper Papers.

160 "On March 22, 1961, he sent a telegram . . ." Harper Papers.

160 "Snyder and his fellow defendants . . ." Mar. 27, 1961 letter from F. Snyder to C. Meredith, Harper Papers.

160-61 "So he responded that Snyder . . ." Apr. 7, 1961 letter from J. Harper to C. Meredith, Harper Papers.

161 "Snyder persevered and, with remarkable irony . . ." Apr. 11, 1961 letter from F. Snyder to C. Meredith, Harper Papers.

161 "My father followed up with another long letter to Hoffa . . ." Apr. 13, 1961 letter from J. Harper to J. Hoffa, Harper Papers.

161 "On the same day my father sent his letter . . ." Apr. 13, 1961 letter from J. Hoffa to J. Harper, Harper Papers.

163-66 The description of the lug-nut incident is based upon my conversations with my father. In the process of writing this book, I

learned that his description to me was identical to my mother's recollection of the event, as he had first described it to her more than forty years earlier.

167-68 The descriptions of the hostile telephone calls to my parents are based upon my conversations with them and my brother, who later listened to the recorded threat that had been directed toward me. Apparently, my dad was not the only Teamster in Minneapolis who received such calls: Sheridan, *Fall and Rise*, 75.

170 Joseph Konowe's biographical information is based upon the following: Sloane, *Hoffa*, 143–44; Romer, *International Brotherhood*, 67; Sheridan, *Fall and Rise*, 134.

170 Frank Fitzsimmons's biographical information is based upon the following: Sloane, *Hoffa*, 62, 316–17; Steven Brill, *The Teamsters* (New York: Simon and Schuster, 1978), 80–81.

171 Roy Williams's biographical information is based upon Sheridan, *Fall and Rise*, 94, 109. Williams is pictured in the July 1961 issue of *International Teamster*.

171 "He even included a copy of a *Minneapolis Star* article . . ." *Minneapolis Star*, Apr. 15, 1961.

172 "My father's formal submission to Hoffa . . ." Harper Papers.

173 The description of the April 1961 membership meeting is based upon the Harper Papers.

174-78 The description of the brake-failure incident is based upon my conversations with my father. In the process of writing this book, I learned that he had similarly confided in my brother about the incident.

179 "Gordon Conklin's hometown newspaper, the *St. Paul Dispatch* . . ." *St. Paul Dispatch*, Apr. 27, 1961.

179-84 The description of the April 27, 1961, hearing is based upon the Harper Papers and my conversations with my parents.

184 "He believed that the *Minneapolis Star* had learned about events at the hearing . . ." Harper Papers.

184 "In what seemed to be another violation of Fitzsimmons's directive . . ." *St. Paul Pioneer Press*, Apr. 28, 1961.

185 "The *Tribune* buried its coverage . . ." *Minneapolis Morning Tribune*, Apr. 28, 1961.

186 "He decided that his best approach . . ." Harper Papers.

186 "On May 19 and 20, members of Local 544 voted on their choices . . ." *Minneapolis Sunday Tribune*, May 21, 1961.

187 "One of Hoffa's key East Coast supporters . . ." Sloane, *Hoffa*, 393; *People v. Provenzano*, 79 A.D. 2d 811 (N.Y. 1980); *People v. Konigsberg*, 137 A.D. 2d 142 (N.Y. 1988).

187 "On June 28, three weeks after Castellito's still unsolved disappearance..." *International Teamster*, July 1961.

187 "As he had in 1952 and 1957, Sam Romer attended..." Romer, *International Brotherhood*, ix.

187 "On Monday, July 3, my father sat at our dining room table..." *Minneapolis Morning Tribune*, July 3, 1961.

188 "My father followed the events . . ." *Minneapolis Morning Tribune*, July 4–8, 1961; *Minneapolis Sunday Tribune*, July 9, 1961.

189 "As his death rattle, Dad sent a Western Union telegram . . ." Harper Papers.

189 "On July 19, he got his response." Letter from J. English to J. Harper, Harper Papers.

193-95 The description of the Harper family's life after the final resolution of my father's charges against Snyder is based upon my own observations and memory of the events, as well as my conversations with my parents.

196 "A grand jury in Chicago began looking at Teamsters pension fund fraud..." Sheridan, *Fall and Rise*, 212; Mollenhoff, *Tentacles of Power*, 386–87.

196 "Meanwhile, a prosecutor from Robert Kennedy's 'Get Hoffa' squad..." Sheridan, *Fall and Rise*, 173–74, 185.

196 "At the same time, a federal grand jury supervised by another Kennedy protégé..." Sheridan, *Fall and Rise*, 206.

196 "That case culminated in a jury tampering charge..." Mollenhoff, *Tentacles of Power*, 368–85.

196 "In late April 1964, Hoffa, Dranow, and six other codefendants went on trial..." Mollenhoff, *Tentacles of Power*, 386–403; Sheridan, *Fall and Rise*, 363–77.

197 "On March 7, 1967, he surrendered himself to U.S. marshals..." Sloane, *Hoffa*, 329–31.

197 "Hoffa appointed his longtime friend..." Sloane, *Hoffa*, 335.

197 "At the Lewisburg prison, another Hoffa comrade . . ." Sloane, *Hoffa*, 342–43.

198 "'It's because of people like you that I got into trouble...'" Sloane, *Hoffa*, 343.

198 "'Old man,' he allegedly screamed, 'Yours is coming! ...'" Dan E. Moldea, *The Hoffa Wars: Teamsters, Rebels, Politicians, and the Mob* (New York: Paddington Press, 1978), 257.

198 "Three times the U.S. Parole Board considered..." Sloane, *Hoffa*, 344–49.

198 "As Christmas approached in 1971, Hoffa filed yet another petition..." Sloane, *Hoffa*, 350–51.

198 "Unsubstantiated rumors circulated that in return for Hoffa's release . . ." *Playboy,* Dec. 1975, 78.

198 "But there was an unprecedented catch, and Hoffa claimed to the end . . ." Sloane, *Hoffa,* 351–52.

199 "Hoffa was last seen getting into a car near the Machus Red Fox . . ." Sloane, *Hoffa,* 370–75, 389.

199 "An eyewitness reported that Hoffa got into the vehicle . . ." Sloane, *Hoffa,* 389.

199 "Briguglio himself was gunned down . . ." Sloane, *Hoffa,* 396.

199 "Twenty-five years later, Hoffa's longtime friend Frank Sheeran claimed . . ." Charles Brandt, *"I Heard You Paint Houses": Frank "The Irishman" Sheeran and the Inside Story of the Mafia, the Teamsters, and the Last Ride of Jimmy Hoffa* (Hanover, NH: Steerforth Press, 2004), 248–57.

199 "In a November 1963 interview . . ." *Playboy,* Nov. 1963, 38.

199 "The December 1975 issue of *Playboy* quoted him . . ." *Playboy,* Dec. 1975, 82.

203-4 This description of my father's life during the later 1960s and beyond is based upon my personal observations and memory of the events, including my frequent conversations with him.

205 "Fred V. Snyder, secretary-treasurer of Local 544 . . ." Snyder's Death Certificate, MHS.

206 "By then, Conklin would be dead . . ." *St. Paul Dispatch,* Aug. 24, 1967.

207 "In his book's preface . . ." Romer, *International Brotherhood,* ix.

207 "While his book was still in draft form . . ." July 31, 1961 letter from P. Jacobs to S. Romer, Romer Papers.

207 "A week later, he wrote Romer . . ." Aug. 7, 1961 letter from P. Jacobs to S. Romer, Romer Papers.

207-8 "By early 1962, Romer's draft of the manuscript . . ." Jan. 28, 1962 letter from W. Galenson to S. Romer, Romer Papers.

208 "Romer's transmittal with his final manuscript . . ." Feb. 23, 1962 letter from S. Romer to W. Galenson, Romer Papers.

208 "For example, Romer wrote . . ." Romer, *International Brotherhood,* 44.

208 "Romer also tried to excuse Hoffa . . ." Romer, *International Brotherhood,* 44.

208-9 "He noted that the pension fund was 'administered by a committee . . .'" Romer, *International Brotherhood,* 88.

209 "Romer also said that Hoffa and the Teamsters actually controlled the pension fund . . ." Romer, *International Brotherhood,* 88.

209 "To Hoffa, he wrote . . ." Dec. 26, 1962 letter from S. Romer to J. Hoffa, Romer Papers.

209 "International vice president Hal Gibbons wrote . . ." Jan. 31, 1963 letter from H. Gibbons to S. Romer, Romer Papers.

209 "His assistant, Jake McCarthy, wrote . . ." Jan. 15, 1963 letter from J. McCarthy to S. Romer, Romer Papers.

209 "When a publisher approached Romer in August 1962 . . ." Aug. 24, 1962 letter from S. Romer to A. Cameron, Romer Papers.

210 "Sam Romer died of a heart attack . . ." *Minneapolis Tribune,* Apr. 14, 1965.

210 "Mollenhoff's ten-year pursuit of Hoffa and the Teamsters . . ." Longden, *Famous Iowans.*

211 "Harris didn't mince words . . ." The description of Lloyd Harris's comments to my mother is based upon my conversation with her.

211 "On March 11, 1989, another consent decree resolved . . ." *International Teamster,* July 1989.

211 "On December 7, 1998, newly elected Teamsters International general president . . ." www.cnn.com/US/9812/07/teamsters.01/index.html (accessed May 17, 2004).

211-12 "A year later . . ." www.cnn.com/2000/us/01/12/teamsters.01/index.html (accessed May 17, 2004).

212 "I have no knowledge about or particular interest in the Teamsters' current internal situation . . ." *New York Times,* Apr. 30, 2004.

215 "The December 1975 issue of *Playboy* magazine reported . . ." *Playboy,* Dec. 1975, 92.

Sources and References

The starting point for this project was the collection of personal papers that James Henry Harper, my father, gathered from 1959 to 1961 and kept until his death forty years later. In addition to newspaper clippings, he retained copies of letters, memoranda, and contemporaneously prepared summaries of the most important events described in this book. Another primary source, the Sam Romer Papers at the Minnesota Historical Society in St. Paul, provided key information about that newsman's ongoing communications with and connections to Hoffa, Conklin, and the International Teamsters leadership.

A primary published source of information about the relationships among Conklin, Romer, and Hoffa was Clark Mollenhoff's 1965 book *Tentacles of Power: The Story of Jimmy Hoffa* (Cleveland, OH: New World Publishing Company, 1965). Walter Sheridan's book *The Fall and Rise of Jimmy Hoffa* (New York: Saturday Review Press/Doubleday, 1972) is an extensive account of Hoffa's legal difficulties from 1959 to 1967, although it does not discuss in detail the various people and events in Minneapolis Local 544 that mattered most to my father. Nevertheless, because of its precise chronological presentation, Sheridan's book allowed me to learn exactly what was happening in Hoffa's life at critical times during my father's struggle.

The principal nondocumentary sources for this book were conversations with my father and mother that occurred throughout my life, starting from an early age. I also drew upon discussions with my brother and sisters. I will never forget the colorful conversations I had with Marvin Masteller about my father's career as a Werner driver.

Other sources and a short description of each are listed below.

NEWSPAPERS AND PERIODICALS

The *Detroit News* (Nov. 1953) reported on the earliest congressional hearings into Hoffa's activities.

International Teamster (Washington, DC: International Brotherhood of Teamsters, various issues 1956–61 and 1989) helped me understand how the union was presenting to its membership the various investigations and reports concerning Teamsters corruption.

Life (Chicago: Time Inc., Aug. 18, 1958 and May 18, May 25, and June 1, 1959) was one of my father's favorite periodicals; it helped me to understand what he was reading in the press about Hoffa and the Teamsters.

The *Minneapolis Morning Tribune* and *Minneapolis Star* (1953–61) chronicled many of the events related to Local 544 depicted in this book.

Playboy (Chicago: Playboy, Nov. 1963, Dec. 1975) published one Hoffa interview at the height of his power and another that ocurred shortly before his disappearance on July 30, 1975.

The *St. Paul Dispatch* and *St. Paul Pioneer Press* (Apr. 27 and 28, 1961, Aug. 23, 1967) covered the Local 544 insurgency far less extensively than the *Minneapolis Morning Tribune* and its afternoon counterpart, the *Minneapolis Star.*

Time (Chicago: Time Inc., Sept. 9, 1957, Aug. 31, 1959) was a magazine that my dad did not read regularly, but it provided me with insights into the media's coverage of Hoffa.

BOOKS, WEBSITES, AND OTHER REFERENCES

Daniel Bergner, *God of the Rodeo: The Quest for Redemption in Louisiana's Angola Prison* (New York: Ballantine, 1998), discusses the Louisiana State Penitentiary at Angola.

Craig Brandon, *The Electric Chair: An Unnatural American History* (Jefferson, NC: McFarland & Company, Inc., 1999), provides information about the use of the electric chair in Louisiana and throughout the United States.

Charles Brandt, *"I Heard You Paint Houses": Frank "The Irishman" Sheeran and the Inside Story of the Mafia, the Teamsters, and the Last Ride of Jimmy Hoffa* (Hanover, NH: Steerforth Press, 2004), is based upon Brandt's interviews with Frank Sheeran, a longtime Hoffa colleague who claimed to have fired the shots killing Hoffa after he and two others picked him up in front of a Detroit restaurant on July 30, 1975. It consists of the "hit man's" dictated autobiographical statements to Brandt (who was also Sheeran's lawyer) over a ten-year period, interspersed with occasional paragraphs of historical context.

Steven Brill, *The Teamsters* (New York: Simon and Schuster, 1978), was written shortly after Hoffa's disappearance; it attempts to relate the personal stories of nine prominent Teamsters "who represent all that is good and bad about the Teamsters."

Anne Butler and C. Murray Henderson, *Angola—The Louisiana State Penitentiary: A Half Century of Rage and Reform* (Lafayette: University of Southwestern Louisiana's Center for Louisiana Studies, 1990),

includes descriptions and photographs depicting conditions at Angola during the 1940s and 1950s.

Burk Foster, Wilbert Rideau, and Douglas Dennis, eds., *The Wall Is Strong: Corrections in Louisiana,* 3rd ed. (Lafayette: University of Southwestern Louisiana's Center for Louisiana Studies, 1995), includes articles and photographs depicting conditions at Angola during the 1940s and 1950s.

Robert Gabrick, *Autocar Trucks: 1950-1987 Photo Archive* (Hudson, WI: Iconografix, 2002), provides interior photographs of the Autocar that my father drove along the Great Mississippi River Road.

James R. Hoffa, *Hoffa: The Real Story* (New York: Stein and Day, 1976), came out shortly after Hoffa's disappearance and sets forth his thoughts about his life, what he described as Robert Kennedy's vindictive efforts to prosecute him, and what he believed to be Frank Fitzsimmons's betrayal.

Ralph James and Estelle James, *Hoffa and the Teamsters: A Study of Union Power* (Princeton, NJ: D. Van Nostrand & Co., Inc., 1965), is a purely academic treatment of Hoffa and was published at the height of his power. It provides a detailed economic analysis of Hoffa's impact and some historical information.

Robert F. Kennedy, *The Enemy Within: The McClellan Committee's Crusade Against Jimmy Hoffa and Corrupt Labor Unions* (New York: Harper & Row, 1960), is Kennedy's firsthand account of events surrounding his efforts to put Hoffa in jail—starting with Clark Mollenhoff's successful effort to persuade Kennedy to become chief counsel for the Senate committee investigating the ties between the Teamsters and organized crime.

Philip A. Korth, *The Minneapolis Teamsters Strike of 1934* (East Lansing: Michigan State University Press, 1995), chronicles the events surrounding the famous strikes in which Fred Snyder claimed to have participated with his brother.

Dan E. Moldea, *The Hoffa Wars: Teamsters, Rebels, Politicians, and the Mob* (New York: Paddington Press, 1978), was written shortly after Hoffa's 1975 disappearance and focuses on conspiracy theories relating to his presumed death.

Sister Helen Prejean, *Dead Man Walking: An Eyewitness Account of the Death Penalty in the United States* (New York: Random House, 1993), is a recent account of the conditions at the Angola prison.

Wilbert Rideau and Ron Wikberg, *Life Sentences: Rage and Survival Behind Bars* (New York: Three Rivers Press/Random House, 1992), describes Angola from its inmates' perspectives.

Sam Romer, *The International Brotherhood of Teamsters: Its Government and Structure* (New York: John Wiley and Sons, Inc., 1962), is a monograph on the administrative workings of the Teamsters union in 1960. The Teamsters' executive leadership, including Hoffa, helped Romer write this book at the precise time that the reporter was pretending to befriend my father. Romer's contemporaneous notes and correspondence became a primary historical source for this book.

Thaddeus Russell, *Out of the Jungle: Jimmy Hoffa and the Remaking of the American Working Class* (New York: Alfred A. Knopf, 2001), discusses Hoffa's relationship to the broader labor movement generally and focuses on his early life.

Arthur A. Sloane, *Hoffa* (Cambridge, MA: MIT Press, 1992), is the definitive biography of Hoffa. As a graduate student, Sloane traveled with Hoffa in 1962 while writing his doctoral thesis on "Union-Employer Relations in the Over-the-Road Trucking Industry." He eventually followed up with this book. It is the most complete biography of Hoffa written to date.

Statistical Abstract of Louisiana (1967) was used to obtain information about population and electrocutions in the United States during the 1950s.

U.S. Department of Justice, Bureau of Justice Statistics, *Correctional Populations in the United States, 1997* (Washington, DC: U.S. Department of Justice, 2000), was another source of information about electrocutions in Louisiana.

The U.S. government's official website for congressional biographies, *The Biographical Directory of the United States Congress,* http://bioguide.congress.gov/, provided summary biographical information about many of the public office holders mentioned in this book. The U.S. government's official website for federal judicial biographies is the Federal Judicial Center, http://air.fjc.gov/.

Published court decisions in *Cunningham v. English* describe the proceedings that led to the creation of the Board of Monitors and its aftermath. Numerous published decisions in *United States v. Provenzano* and *People of the State of New York v. Provenzano* describe the proceedings relating to the convictions of that New Jersey Teamsters leader.

Acknowledgments

Without the help and encouragement I received from many people along the way, this book would not have been written or published. First and foremost among those is my wife, Kit, who suffered through my periodic immersions as I worked on the manuscript, carefully reviewed my first, intermediate, and final drafts, and then bore the brunt of my defensive reactions to her entirely appropriate comments. Eventually, every single one of her earliest suggestions found its way into the final manuscript. I will be less stubborn next time. My sister Linda urged me to continue as my research and writing began, and she remained committed to the project through its completion. So did my mother, Mary Harper, my sister Sue, and my brother, Mike. My daughter, Emma, was an excellent sounding board and occasional editor. My sons, Ben and Pete, likewise inspired and supported my effort.

I owe a debt I can never repay to my friend Scott Turow and his wife, Annette. Both gave selflessly of their time in reviewing the manuscript as it evolved. Scott in particular has been like the older brother I never had, offering continued enthusiasm for my effort to tell my father's story. His advice at several critical stages ultimately brought the book to a publisher willing to give it a home. Others provided helpful insight, advice, and support: Susan Sheehy, William Contardi, Dr. William Schnaper, Owen Schnaper, Seth Weinberger, and Barbara Goodman, and Seth Traxler. Many people at the Minnesota Historical Society Press/Borealis Books, especially director Greg Britton, assistant director and marketing director Alison Vandenberg, and design and production manager Will Powers, were vital in giving this book life and then its best chance for success. Copy editor Mindy Keskinen put brilliant finishing touches on the manuscript. My publicist, Jennifer Prost, has offered excellent insights that I know will result in the story's broadest possible exposure to the many who, I hope, will read and enjoy it.

But it was my editor, Shannon M. Pennefeather of the Minnesota

Historical Society Press/Borealis Books, whose careful and repeated scrutiny of my work resulted in the final transformations that made this book what it was always supposed to be. Her willingness to become engaged in my father's story has assured that it will now have a new audience and that it will endure. Dad would have liked her.